THE COMMON MARKET
AND AMERICAN BUSINESS

THE

COMMON
MARKET

AND AMERICAN BUSINESS

By **MAX J. WASSERMAN**
Visiting Professor of International Economics
University of Kentucky

CHARLES W. HULTMAN
Assistant Professor of Economics
University of Kentucky

and

RUSSELL F. MOORE
Member of the New York Bar

SIMMONS-BOARDMAN PUBLISHING CORPORATION

New York

Copyright 1964 by
SIMMONS-BOARDMAN PUBLISHING CORPORATION

Library of Congress Catalog Card Number: 64-16951
Manufactured in the United States of America

TO
ROSE AND IRENE

Publisher's Foreword

The formation and continuing development of the European Economic Community (Common Market) represent an event of major historical significance. Economic forces are being created, the ultimate direction and magnitude of which can be predicted only in approximate terms. If the Community expands, if Great Britain in spite of the 1963 setback eventually is admitted, if Austria and the other nations presently seeking membership or association are received into the Market, an integrated economic unit second only to that represented by America will come into being. To trade with this Market, to export goods necessary to meet the growing demand of the people in this vast trading area, outside nations will be forced to reduce their own tariffs and world trade will be increased.

Herein lies a major opportunity for the free world—in its search for survival in a world divided into free nations and Communist nations—to bring about the increase in production and higher standards of living which will again prove the superiority of free men and free institutions over the regimentation inherent in the communistic system.

In achieving the economic and political cooperation essential to the success of the ideal so favorably launched, the path will be strewn with problems and hardships. Outside nations will have to change their trade policies just as have the Common Market nations. Machinery for the settlement of international disputes must be created or perfected. But the free world, if it is to survive, must and will overcome these obstacles and affect the necessary readjustments.

The Common Market and American Business has been published to make readily available—in a single place—concise information on the nature, characteristics, functioning and business opportunities of the Common Market.

There are approximately 200,000 American manufacturers, including the smallest. Only about 4 per cent of these export goods abroad. Even allowing for the firms producing goods which are not adapted for export, at least 25,000—three times the number presently exporting—could enter foreign trade profitably.

Perhaps wider dispersal of information concerning opportunities for profit and increased export business will encourage these firms to do so.

In addition to basic background information concerning the Common Market contained in *The Common Market and American Business,* the authors have sought to develop the practical aspects of engaging in trade with these nations. The businessman will accordingly find practical information relating to forming a company within the EEC; patent laws; antitrust and other regulatory legislation; and essential data on commercial policies, transportation, business and investment practices, and agricultural policies, among others.

Preface

A close student of the European Economic Community is reported to have said that, although some businessmen might not like the Common Market, they cannot afford to ignore it. There may be an element of exaggeration in this statement, because many businessmen will be able to ignore the Common Market without ill effects. However, all of them cannot overlook it and many will find it worthwhile to examine its potential more closely. The Marshall Plan and the Common Market have been two of the most important developments in Europe in the post-World War II economic scene.

Some of the works dealing with the European Economic Community are addressed to an audience of professional economists; others were written primarily to meet the needs of statesmen and officials. Few books have been designed specifically for the businessman. This volume has been written particularly with the interests of American businessmen in mind, especially those who are not yet doing business within the Community. Since many of the works written for the economic profession and statesmen have stressed the macroeconomic aspects of the Common Market, this work is directed toward the somewhat neglected microeconomic aspects of the institution and its impact on individual business units.

However, the authors have not lost sight of other readers. It is their hope that this work will add to the large and growing literature on the subject and will prove useful to those interested in enlarging their fund of information on the Common Market. Statesmen and government officials charged with the responsibility of providing a framework in which business operations take place, may find the work helpful in indicating the impact of the EEC on business units. Military officers responsible for policies, plans and operations within the territory of the Common Market and its associates may be interested in the description and the analysis which the work provides as a backdrop for their thinking. And finally, university and college courses in economics, especially the international aspects of the discipline, may find the work of interest as supplementary reading and for reference purposes.

The authors are deeply indebted to a number of people for competent and courteous assistance in the preparation of this monograph. Mrs. Alma R. Dauman, Information Specialist and Mrs. Ella Krucoff, Assistant Information Specialist, of the Washington Information Office of the European Community, were especially helpful in providing advice and in making the library of the Washington Office available to the authors.

Heinz W. Gottwald, Vice President, Chemical Bank New York Trust Company, and August Maffry, Vice President, Irving Trust Company, were of assistance by giving information and helpful advice. Ted Walser of the Chemical Bank New York Trust Company indicated new sources of information which improved the text. Bernard F. Combemale, President, Monmouth-Lee Corporation, made suggestions which were especially useful in conjunction with the preparation of the chapters on investment. Harold J. Heck of the United States Department of Commerce furnished statistics on the trade of the United States with the Community.

James Greene, Regional Vice President of Business International of New York, furnished data which were not available elsewhere. Miss Elizabeth S. Beleny, Research Librarian, Business International, was helpful in making the library and several pertinent publications of this firm available to the authors.

Mrs. Irene Hultman edited and reviewed the manuscript. Lynn W. Coe, Charles T. Easterly, Christine B. Guimarães and Alice C. Kinkead, graduate students at the William Andrew Patterson School of Diplomacy and International Commerce, University of Kentucky, assisted in the research involved in the preparation of this volume. Miss Ellen Minihan, Secretary, Patterson Shcool, graciously typed most of the manuscript.

Deans M. M. White of the College of Arts and Sciences and C. C. Carpenter of the College of Commerce together with A. Vandenbosch, Director of the Patterson School of Diplomacy and International Commerce, University of Kentucky, encouraged the authors to pursue the project and provided convenient teaching schedules for the prosecution of the work. Dean A. D. Kirwan, Graduate School, and other members of the University Research Fund Committee made a grant available to the authors which enabled them to do much of the necessary research for this volume.

The authors gratefully acknowledge this helpful assistance but assume sole responsibility for all of the material presented in this book.

M. J. W.
C. W. H.
R. F. M.

University of Kentucky
Lexington, Kentucky
February 1964

Table of Contents

THE EUROPEAN ECONOMIC COMMUNITY AND THE
EUROPEAN FREE TRADE ASSOCIATION

EUROPEAN ECONOMIC COMMUNITY
ASSOCIATED AFRICAN TERRITORIES AND COUNTRIES

1

The Nature of the Common Market

FREE TRADE AREAS, CUSTOMS UNIONS, COMMON MARKETS—
ECONOMIC FEATURES OF THE COMMON MARKET—SOCIAL AND
DEVELOPMENT FEATURES OF THE COMMON MARKET—THE
GOVERNMENT OF THE COMMON MARKET—THE EUROPEAN
FREE TRADE ASSOCIATION

The European Economic Community (EEC), Common Market, the Six or Inner Six, as this institution is variously termed, emulates the United States economy in many particulars. America is, and has been ever since the adoption of the Constitution, a common market and much of its economic success can be attributed to this fact.

Free Trade Areas, Customs Unions, Common Markets

Economic unions take various forms, and it is customary to distinguish three principal types: free trade areas, customs unions and common markets. A *free trade area*, defined in simple terms, consists of an agreement between two or more states under which the parties agree to eliminate tariffs, together with other barriers to trade, among them while each member maintains its own tariffs and barriers against states which are not parties to the agreement.

Free trade areas give rise to an important complication. Assume that in a given free trade area, no member state makes shoes. If country A maintains a 25 per cent ad valorem duty on the importation of men's shoes while all other members have tariffs of 50 per cent against this product, country A will be the sole importer of shoes into the area, and it can re-export these shoes to the others at no additional tariff charge. The relatively high tariffs of the other members will be effectively nullified by the low tariff of country A. To avoid problems of this type, some tariff or tax adjustments based on the origin of re-exports in the free trade area will have to be made to equalize the effects of the varying external duties applied by the several members. To equalize the tariffs in the case cited, all other member states might apply a tax of 25 per cent on the import of men's shoes from country A.

In a *customs union* the internal tariff and other barriers to trade on articles imported from member states are eliminated, and the participants apply a common external tariff (CXT) to all goods imported from non-members; there is but a single tariff schedule applied by all members to imports from outside countries. If the common external tariff of the customs union on men's shoes amounts to 25 per cent, it will make no difference, as far as tariffs are concerned, which member brings them in and re-exports them to the others.

Although customs unions contribute substantially toward higher levels of foreign trade, they do not completely integrate the economies of the participants and do not yield all the beneficial results which broader economic unions hold. Therefore, economic communities, or *common markets* may provide, in addition to a customs union, additional elements of economic integration such as common commercial policies; uniform regulations to preserve competition; common policies concerning money, credit, fiscal and balance of payments matters; a single agricultural policy and community-wide investment funds, among others.

Economic Features of the Common Market

In the case of the European Economic Community (EEC), the arrangement includes a customs union whereby the internal tariff among the participants will be reduced to zero for most goods over a maximum period of twelve to fifteen years. During the same period, the EEC provides for the adoption of a common external tariff based upon an arithmetic average of the duty rates of the members. There are a number of exceptions to these tariff adjustments for certain products listed on special schedules which are to be adjusted in the future. The twelve- to fifteen-year tariff time-table has already been advanced and, as things now stand, the common external and internal tariffs should go into full effect between 1967 and 1970. In addition to these customs union features, the Common Market includes:

1. Relatively free movement of labor and capital among the members.

2. "Freedom of establishment," or the right of business firms to organize branches and subsidiaries and do business within the confines of any other member state.

3. Common commercial and agricultural polices.

4. Common anti-trust legislation.

5. Common patent, copyright, trade-mark and industrial property legislation.

6. Common transport policies.

7. Harmonization of the economic policies of the members particularly as they apply to monetary, fiscal, price, full employment and balance of payments questions.

8. Harmonization of social security and other social legislation.

9. Creation of a Social Fund for assistance in retraining and resettling labor.

10. Creation of a European Investment Bank to provide funds for the development of those sectors of the member nations which may require it.

11. Creation of an Overseas Investment Fund to supply the finance needed for the development of certain overseas associated countries and territories.

12. Provision for membership by other European states and for association by other European states and certain overseas countries and territories (especially the former French African territories).

13. Establishment of an Agricultural Stabilization Fund designed to assist in the implementation of the Market's agricultural policies and to stabilize farm prices.

Although the features listed above constitute a long stride toward economic union, they fall short of the more complete integration of the United States. There is as yet no common currency or central fiscal system, no federal government as understood in the United States. The national policies of the members are usually to be aligned or harmonized, but they need not always be identical. The alignment of the individual policies of the member states is frequently left to each country. The central authority ordinarily cannot enforce uniform policies and practices by the legislative process, administrative regulation and executive orders or by taxation as the United States federal government does in many cases. The process of alignment usually is based upon voluntary agreement rather than upon authority.

The Treaty of Rome, which created the Common Market (ratified in 1957), establishes the customs union feature and the time-table of tariff changes with some precision. Many of its other provisions, however, are cast in rather general terms. There are loopholes which enable a member to escape some provisions by alleging dangers to national health or security or by holding that the question is already adequately handled by existing legislation. Many of the details of the Treaty remain to be worked out in the future.

The rationale of the customs union. When the Constitution

of the United States, which includes a customs union feature, was ratified, the size of the market was not a matter of great concern.[1] Much of the industry was of the hand labor type where the principal elements of cost consisted of labor and raw materials. There was little tendency for the costs of production to decline as volume of output increased. The typical cost curve for such an industry or operation is presented on Chart I.1, which shows the selling and delivery costs for the dairies in one of America's large milk-sheds.

CHART I. 1
RELATIVELY CONSTANT COSTS
SELLING AND DELIVERY COSTS PER QUART OF MILK
IN A LARGE METROPOLITAN AREA

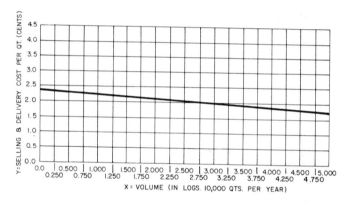

The selling and delivery costs per quart of milk fell slightly over the entire volume of sales and, as a practical matter, they may be said to be constant. A theoretically perfect constant costs curve would be horizontal over its entire length and there would be no cost differential over varying volumes. Such theoretical curves, however, are seldom encountered in practice and this curve, prepared from actual data obtained from the books of account of the dairies, approximates the theoretical ideal about as closely as possible. Where constant costs prevail, there is but little advantage in a large volume of output and sales as compared with smaller ones.

Source: Max J. Wasserman. "Costs and Volume in the Milk Pasteurizing Industry." *The Accounting Review,* XXI, No. 4 (October 1946), p. 428.

The selling and delivery costs per quart of milk fell slightly over the entire volume of sales and, as a practical matter, they may be said to be relatively constant. A theoretically perfect constant cost curve would be flat over its entire length and there would be no cost differential under varying volumes. Such theoretical curves are seldom encountered in practice and this curve, prepared from actual data obtained from the books of account of the dairies of the area, approximates the theoretical ideal closely. Where constant costs prevail, there is but little cost advantage in a large volume of output and sales as compared with smaller ones.

The type of operation illustrated by this chart is that of *constant cost* where the costs of production remain relatively the same over the entire output schedule. Of course, if a businessman can make a profit on each unit produced, he would be interested in a wider market which holds promise of greater sales and consequently larger profits. He would, however, have but little advantage cost-wise in increasing the size of the market.

The cost structure of many industries was modified by the Industrial Revolution which started in England in the last quarter of the eighteenth century. Briefly stated, this Revolution consisted of the use of machinery to perform the work formerly done by hand, the use of machine tools to replace hand tools and application of power to drive the machinery. It was destined to change the character of a large segment of the productive process. Starting in textiles, it spread to other industries in England, from England to the continent of Europe and to the United States.

The use of machinery and power in industry required a relatively large capital investment entailing heavy fixed costs, which had to be amortized as a charge to the product output of the firm. Assume that a manufacturer operated with a fixed capital investment which entailed overhead costs of a million dollars a year. If he produced one unit of goods a year his overhead costs for that unit would amount to $1 million. At an output of 100 units a year, his overhead would drop to $10,000 per unit; at an output of 10,000 units, $1,000; at 100,000 units, $10.00 and at one million units, $1.00.

The owner of such a plant would have a very strong interest in increasing the size of his output, because his costs would fall as his sales increased. A firm, or industry, which operates under such conditions is said to be one of *decreasing costs*. The cost curve for an industry of this type is shown on Chart I.2 which represents the processing costs for the same dairies shown on Chart I. 1.[2]

CHART I. 2
DECREASING COSTS
PROCESSING COSTS PER QUART OF MILK IN A LARGE METROPOLITAN AREA

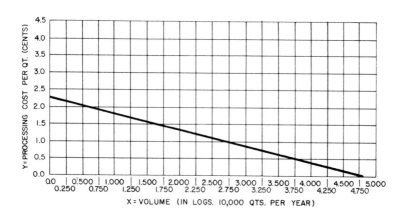

The processing costs per quart of milk decline over the entire volume of output shown on the chart. This curve indicates some of the advantages of scale in the pasteurizing and bottling of milk. The larger the volume of output, the lower these costs. The data used in the preparation of this curve are actual figures derived from the dairies' books of account.

Source: Max J. Wasserman, "Costs and Volume in the Milk Pasteurizing Industry." *The Accounting Review*, XXI, No. 4 (October 1946), p. 427.

This chart indicates some of the advantages of scale in the pasteurizing and bottling of milk. The processing costs per quart of milk decline over the entire volume of output shown on the chart. The larger the output, the lower these costs.

The type of cost curve illustrated on Chart I.2 is typical of a large number of industries in the United States, the Common Market and other highly industrialized countries. For such firms a large market is essential. As the capital investment of the firms increases, it is important that the market potential available to each company grows at least proportionally and preferably to a greater extent. The United States now offers such a market to its industries.

The principal industrial nations of Western Europe have also grown in population. As Table 1.1 indicates, the population of these nations varies from 300,000 in the case of Luxembourg, to 52.5 million for the Federal Republic of Germany. No single nation approaches the population of the United States and none of them possesses the domestic market available to the American manufacturer. Separated as they are by national boundaries, trade among them has been inhibited by tariffs, import quotas, exchange controls, regulations and customs administrative procedures. Under these circumstances, industries of a scale comparable to those of the United States generally have not developed.

The desire to attain a wider market has doubtless been one of the underlying motives behind the customs union feature of the Common Market. The total population of the Six composing the Common Market—Belgium, France, West Germany, Italy, Luxembourg and the Netherlands—is approximately 170 million. Were Britain to join this institution, an additional 50.4 million would be added bringing the total to about 220 million. If all of the nations of the Outer Seven, or European Free Trade Association, joined the Common Market, its population would approximate 255 million.

The importance or potential of a market, however, cannot be measured solely by a count of its inhabitants. Markets possess another dimension, depth, measured by their income. The national income of the Common Market totaled $155.3 billion

TABLE 1.1
POPULATION AND AREA OF SELECTED EUROPEAN COUNTRIES[1]
(Compared with the United States and the Soviet Union)

Country	Population in Millions	Area in 1,000 Square Miles
Austria	7.1	32.4
Belgium	9.1	11.8
Denmark	4.5	16.6
Federal Republic of Germany	52.5	137.6
France	45.3	212.7
Great Britain	50.4	94.2
Italy	50.0	116.4
Luxembourg	0.3	1.0
The Netherlands	11.3	12.9
Norway	3.2	125.1
Portugal	8.4	35.5
Sweden	7.0	173.6
Switzerland	4.7	15.9
The United States	187.0	3,624.0
The Soviet Union	209.0	8,646.0

[1] Belgium, the Federal Republic of Germany, France, Italy, Luxembourg and the Netherlands are included in the European Economic Community; Austria, Denmark, Great Britain, Norway, Portugal, Sweden and Switzerland comprise the European Free Trade Association.

Source: Information Services of the European Economic Community and the European Free Trade Association.

in 1961; that of the Free Trade Association $98.7 billion and the United States, $444 billion. It is evident that markets of these two institutions lack the depth of those of the United States.

The firm desire of the Common Market is to increase the national income of its members so as to provide a market which will permit its industries to move to lower cost levels on their decreasing cost curves. This proposed feature may perhaps develop into one of its more outstanding attributes. Should the managers of the EEC succeed in their efforts the business attraction of the institution would increase, and it would come to resemble more closely the common market of the United States.

The growth rate of the members of the EEC has advanced rapidly since its foundation. There has been some debate as to whether this substantial rate was the result of the Common Market economic integration or whether the members' independent growth was the prime cause of the Market's early success. The rate of growth of the American economy has not kept pace with that of the Six (see chapter 11).[3]

In addition to lacking the depth of the United States markets, those of the Six show a different pattern of wealth and income distribution. Largely for historical reasons—going back to the division of society into a few small wealthy classes and large poorer classes—there is a greater inequality in the distribution of wealth and income in Europe than in the United States. Such a social structure makes for a narrow market and contributes to its lack of depth. European farm programs and increasing wages are narrowing the gap which separates large from small income earners. Although Europe does not have the large and opulent middle class of the United States, it is now creating one.

Trade diversion and trade creation. Two features of the Common Market, or of any customs union, are of considerable importance to world trade. These are *trade diversion* on the one hand and *trade creation* or *expansion* on the other. A customs union may reduce world trade by diverting commerce from the more to the less efficient producers, or it may create and expand world trade by moving business from the less to the more efficient producing units.

These principles may be illustrated by examples. Assume that manufacturers of fractional horsepower electric motors in the United States can turn out the product at a cost of $4.00 per unit, West German plants at a cost of $4.25 and a French producer at $5.25. France applies a specific tariff duty to them of $1.00 per unit. If the motors are of uniform specifications and quality, France will import most of its requirements for them from the United States at a cost of $5.00 each including the duty. Assume that the duty between France and West Germany is abolished, while the external tariff, applied alike by France and West Germany, is set at 50 cents per motor. France will then import these motors from West Germany at a total cost, including the duty, of $4.25 each and the United States will be likely to sell but few motors to these countries.

Under these conditions, trade will have been *diverted* from the low cost American producers to the higher cost West German manufacturers. From the point of view of low cost world trade and of giving free play to the principle of comparative advantage, it would have been better to have abolished the external as well as the internal tariff on these motors. If this were done, France would have been able to obtain them from the United States at a cost of $4.00 each.

Assume now that the cost of these motors is $4.75 in France, $4.25 in the United States, $4.00 in West Germany and that there is no customs union. The French tariff carries a specific duty of $1.00 per motor. In this case, no motors will be imported by France and its domestic industry will supply the requirements of the country at a cost of $4.75 per unit. A customs union between France and West Germany takes effect, the duty between these two nations is abolished while the external tariff of the union is set at 50 cents per unit. In this case, France will buy the motors from West Germany at a cost of $4.00 per unit.

This shift in the international trade in electric motors would have been trade creating or expanding, for France could purchase these articles from a lower, rather than a higher, cost producer. The new tariff arrangements would give play to the principle of comparative advantage and the level of world trade would be improved by the shift in suppliers.

In the first case when the customs union was established, American manufacturers would have been largely shut out of the trade in the specific product. The tariff structure would have *discriminated* against American electric motors. In the second example, no discrimination against American electric motor production was involved, since United States producers would have been on the high cost side as compared with manufacturers in West Germany.

The Common Market is likely to embody many cases of both trade diversion and expansion. Its success as a trade developing institution will, in part, depend upon the amount of trade creation or expansion, as against trade diversion, which it engenders. In its trade diversion aspects, it is likely to discriminate against some producers in the United States.

The rationale of factor mobility. The architects of the Common Market, unlike those of the European Free Trade Association, felt that a customs union was insufficient and that the organization should seek the benefits which more complete economic integration offered. In making this decision, they had the United States and its highly integrated economy as an example. To be effective, integration should provide for factor mobility, certain common economic policies, joint programs of improvement, development and welfare.

Factor mobility is to be obtained by providing for the free movement of labor and capital among the Six and the right of business firms to set up establishments and carry out transactions in any of the countries of the Market. This mobility should operate to equalize the productivity, and consequently the earnings, of labor, capital and enterprise. Its first effects might well be to lower the productivity and returns in sectors where they are high and to raise them where they are low. In the longer run, factor mobility should make for greater productivity and earnings in the entire Market.

Factor mobility will contribute to changes in the comparative advantages and disadvantages the members of the Common Market may have vis-à-vis one another. The substitution of Common Market comparative advantage for that of each of the members is likely to bring about shifts in trade in the years ahead. American industries which had a comparative advantage in trading with specific countries of the Six may or may not retain this advantage after economic integration has moved ahead. Conversely, some American firms which were at a comparative disadvantage with some of the members of the Market may possibly find that they will enjoy a comparative advantage with the Common Market considered as a unit.

Rationale of increasing competition. One aspect of the economic integration of the Six is likely to hold certain advantages for United States business. Instead of having six different commercial policies to face in trade and investment with these countries, American businessmen ultimately will meet but a single, relatively unified commercial policy. This, of course, does not imply that the new policy of the Six will make trade and investment of easier access; it may be stricter and more discriminatory than the previous policy of any of the individual member states—this remains to be seen.

The elimination of the internal tariffs and other barriers to trade probably will result in intensified competition among the industries of the Common Market, and this is one of the principal objectives which the creators of the Market hoped to attain. Although the internal tariff has not yet been reduced to zero and some quantitative barriers to trade still remain, a marked increase in competition in the organization is already manifest. Some smaller, marginal and sub-marginal firms have given way to larger and more efficient units. This increase in size may mean that the surviving firms will have larger outputs and, since many of them operate under conditions of decreasing costs, their per-unit costs of production may decline. There have already been a number of mergers of business firms and a tendency on the part of some, often by arrangement with their competitors in other member countries, to drop certain lines and to concentrate their production on goods for which they apparently possess advantages. The increased competitiveness of Common Market industry will be enforced and reinforced by the provisions of the Treaty for a common anti-trust policy, which is outlined in chapter 9.

Rationale of the harmonization of economic policies. The statesmen who drew up the Treaty of Rome realized that economic integration might not be achieved as long as each member continued to employ its individual internal and external economic policies. Article 104 of this Treaty requires each member to maintain equilibrium in its balance of payments, a sound currency and stable price level. In addition, it holds that the economic policies of any one of the Six are a matter of concern to the others and that each is expected to consult with the members and with the Common Market Commission in the determination of its economic policies. The Commission will assist the members in the task of coordinating their policies and, by unanimous vote, make policy recommendations whenever it feels that a given national policy runs counter to the Market objectives.

As trade restrictions are relaxed, the participants are to liberalize their payments regulations. The Treaty recognizes that rates of exchange are matters of mutual interest, and members are authorized to take retaliatory measures if any participant devalues its currency unilaterally or for competitive reasons.

The balance of payments problems of any member are likewise a matter of concern to the others, which agree to come to the aid of the country in difficulties. This assistance may be in the nature of credits or trade liberalization. The members also will lend their support to requests for drawings or stand-by credits which any one of them may make of the International Monetary Fund. In addition, a member experiencing balance of payments difficulties may, under certain conditions, take appropriate protective steps such as revoking some of its trade concessions.

The Common Market is also committed to the development of policies looking toward the promotion of economic growth and stability and the avoidance of recessions. It has projected a gross national product growth rate of between 4 and 5 per cent a year for the members.

The rationale of uniform agricultural policies. In most industrialized nations, agriculture presents an important economic problem. Industries in these nations generally operate under conditions of decreasing cost and utilize relatively large amounts of capital equipment. The products which they manufacture are not often standardized and each firm, through product differentiation, has a quasi-monopoly over the particular articles which it makes. Many of these firms do not work under conditions of free competition but under what the economists term imperfect or monopolistic competition. Under these conditions, management is able, within limits, to control either the prices of the goods which it makes or to regulate the volume of output.

Agriculture, on the other hand, is usually composed of a large number of small producing units. Relative to industry, agriculture, in industrialized nations, employs small amounts of capital, although more and more heavy equipment is being utilized on the more progressive farms. The cost curve for many small farms is either of the constant or increasing variety where costs remain relatively the same or increase over the output schedule.

The prices at which farm products sell, in the absence of government controls, approach closely the ideal of pure, free competitive conditions, especially where these commodities are sold on large exchanges. No single farm unit is able to exercise any important degree of control over the prices of the products which it sells. Often when a farmer feels that he is not making sufficient income due to low prices, he increases his output. If many farmers were to do this, the entire crop might be sold at lower prices. The total farm income received could be smaller, because the demand for many farm commodities is price inelastic; total revenues received from their sale decline as output increases.

While industry attempts to tailor its production schedules and pricing policies to specific market and economic conditions, farmers acting alone and without government controls have been unable to do so. The results of these divergent practices were particularly manifest in the United States during the 1920's and the depression years. The incomes of farmers lagged behind those of the other sectors of the economy. The Agricultural Adjustment Act of 1933 and successor farm legislation were largely the result of this experience.[4]

In addition to the economic factors, there are a number of social and political questions involved in maintaining the level of the agricultural sector of an economy on a par with that of the industrial. In addition to being a business and an occupation, farming is a way of life for many people. Politically, the agrarian element of the population constitutes a factor making for political stability. These considerations loom large in the thinking of statesmen charged with governing a nation.

The depressed state of agriculture in the United States found its counterpart, and much for the same reasons, in the farm situation of other developed industrial nations. All of the Common Market countries had, at the time of the ratification of the Treaty of Rome, various kinds of agricultural programs. To obtain the integration of the economies of the Six, the diverse agricultural adjustment legislation of the members required alignment. By the end of the Common Market transition period, a single agricultural program is to be put in force. The details of this program are presented in chapter 10.

Given the changes in the structure of agriculture among the Six, which the adoption of a common agricultural policy might entail, some financial assistance is likely to be required by the agricultural sector. The European Fund for Structural Improvement in Agriculture was proposed in 1960 to provide this aid.

The proposed farm program holds certain dangers for American agriculture. The Common Market countries have traditionally been a large export market for many United States farm products. There is a possibility that the Common Market agricultural program will be inward-looking; that it may operate to the advantage of the agricultural sectors of the member nations to the detriment of those of other nations. Continued farm product access to the markets of the Six is likely to require protracted reciprocal trade agreement negotiations.

Rationale of the common transport policy. The European transportation companies are largely state-owned monopolies. At the outset, the Common Market's transportation policy is to be limited to rail, highway and water transportation and will not include air and pipelines. The transport policy has two major objectives: the elimination of discriminatory rates based on nationality and the coordination of the several national systems to provide the unity needed to handle the expanding business of the Community.

The unification of the transportation system presents many thorny problems and has already met with several setbacks. The principal difficulties which the Commission has faced in obtaining the adoption of its recommendations have been those concerned with the disclosure of rates to assist in the policing of discriminatory practices. Not satisfied with the unification of the existing systems, the Commission has also been devoting study to innovations and improvements involving the linking of waterways by means of canals, the integration of trucking with rail and other facilities.[5]

Social and Development Features of the Common Market

Labor policies and Social Fund. The social policies of the Common Market are aimed at both the equalization and improvement of working conditions. Toward this end, the Commission fosters cooperation among the members on working conditions, employment policies, safety, industrial diseases and hygiene, collective bargaining and employment policies. The details of these programs are presented in chapter 7.

Development of associated countries and territories. The Common Market is particularly interested in the development of countries and territories, formerly the dependencies of certain members, which were given the privilege of association with the institution. By providing for Community assistance, the dependence of these areas upon any one member will be lessened and recognition given to the joint responsibility for their development.

The associated countries and territories have the right to export to the Six under preferential tariff and trade barrier terms. In exchange, they extend to all of the Six the preferences which they granted to their former mother countries.

Since these areas are in a lesser developed economic state than the members of the Market, the Treaty allows them to impose tariffs for revenue or to foster the development of their infant industries. The Treaty also affirms the right of individuals and firms of all members of the Common Market to do business and to incorporate in any of the associated countries and territories without discrimination.

The Common Market has established an Overseas Development Fund to aid in the economic growth of these and other areas. This Fund may be used for both developmental and infrastructure projects such as schools, hospitals and libraries.

A large number of these dependent areas won their independence since the Treaty of Rome was signed. Although the Treaty does not contain any clauses regarding the change in status of these areas, many of them have already elected to associate with the Common Market. By granting rights and concessions to these associates the Common Market extends the trade diversion and discriminatory features of the Market to a specific group of newly-emerging countries.

The European Investment Bank. Title IV of the Treaty of Rome establishes the European Investment Bank and charges it with the tasks of assisting underdeveloped regions lying within the geographical confines of the Six in the conversion and modernization of their industry; aiding in the development of new industries in Common Market areas where old ones have disappeared as a result of the Market's activities; and, supplying the funds needed for projects of interest to two or more members.

The capital of the Bank is $1 billion; France and West Germany each contributed 30.0 per cent, Italy 24.0, Belgium 8.65, the Netherlands 7.15 and Luxembourg 0.2 per cent. The first 25 per cent of each subscription is to be paid in installments and the remaining 75 will be available on call if and when needed.

The Bank has the power to raise funds and to guarantee loans to both private and governmental enterprises up to a total of $2.5 billion. Since the Overseas Development Fund makes loans to areas outside the territorial confines of the Common Market, financing by the Investment Bank is restricted to projects lying within the Market territory—although consideration will be given in exceptional circumstances to loans outside. Contrary to the loans of the Export-Import Bank of Washington, those of the European Investment Bank are not tied, that is, the funds need not be expended within the Community itself.

Expansion in membership of the Common Market. Until the French veto of the British bid for membership in the Common Market, a fundamental tenet of this institution held that membership was open to other *European* states which were willing to accept the obligations of the Treaty. For those nations which were unwilling to accept the full obligations of membership, a form of association with the Common Market was provided by Article 238 of the Treaty. The failure of the United Kingdom to attain membership in 1963 has cast some doubts concerning the ease of accession to membership of other nations.

Association with the Common Market appears easier to attain than full membership. Greece and Turkey have been admitted to association and applications from Tunisia and the Netherlands Antilles, among others, are under consideration. Each application for membership or association is apparently the object of extensive individual negotiations.

The Government of the Common Market

The government of the EEC occupies a unique place in the annals of political organization. Strictly speaking, the political institutions of the Market may not form a government as this term is commonly understood. The political organization can be described as an *economic confederation with limited supra-national powers.* From the point of view of political science, it occupies a place somewhere between an alliance and a confederation and resembles in some respects the American Articles of Confederation of 1777. The Treaty of Rome, perhaps for public relations considerations, does not refer to the government of the Common Market, but only to its institutions and provides for them in its concluding sections.

At present the Common Market is less a political than an economic entity. Its organization resembles in many ways that of a European non-profit corporation with the Assembly as the stockholders, the Council the directors, the Commission the officers. The Treaty is more in the nature of an association charter than a political constitution. Many of the officials of the institution envisage political union of the members as its ultimate goal, however.

Although the EEC possesses certain attributes of sovereignty, some essentials are lacking and it cannot be termed strictly a sovereign state. It cannot levy taxes, although some revenues from the common customs tariff accrue to the Market and it has the power to require contributions from the member states, draw up and administer a budget and disburse funds. It is a legal person under international law, but it is not empowered to raise and maintain an army or police force. It possesses few police powers to protect the health, welfare and morals of the people within its confines.

The officers and representatives of the Common Market are either appointed by the member governments or elected by their parliaments. At the present time, no provision has been made for the choice of Assembly or European Parliament representatives by popular vote, but many EEC officials envisage popular elections as a distinct possibility in the future. The capacity of the Market to enforce its policies and regulations—the Treaty does not call them laws or legislation—rests upon sanctions which it is empowered to take and upon retaliatory action on the part of the member states. The power to enforce the Market's sanctions is not spelled out and ultimately rests upon the good faith of the participating countries. The regulations and decisions of the Common Market resemble in certain respects the laws voted by the United States Congress under the provisions of the interstate commerce clause of the Constitution.

Under the Treaty, the members are required to unify, harmonize or approximate their laws where this is necessary for the creation or functioning of the Common Market.

Unification involves making a given law the same for all the members. It means the substitution of the Common Market proposed law for each of its member's existing law. Thus if the Common Market proposals for a uniform law of sales and a uniform law of agency become effective, they will replace those of the individual members and the legislation of all will be identical for sales and agency.

Harmonization does not involve the substitution of a single uniform statute for the several laws applied by the members, but the removal of the major points of divergence within each national system. The test for harmonization is usually the impact of the provisions of a member's law upon the way the Common Market functions as a whole. Laws may be harmonized but still have differing provisions.

Approximation of laws—as the term is used in the Treaty—means more than harmonization, but less than unification. Under this concept the several laws in question of the members need not be unified, but they must be approximately the same in the case of each member nation.

The major political institutions of the Common Market are the Assembly or European Parliament, the Council of Ministers, the Court of Justice and the Commission. Chart I.3 presents a simplified picture of EEC's organizational structure.

The Assembly or European Parliament. The Treaty of Rome establishes an Assembly, but this body now designates itself as the European Parliament. Although it resembles a parliament in certain aspects, its functions appear closer to those of a meeting of a European non-profit association. Its principal enforcement powers are negative—largely those of censure. Because it has limited ability to enforce its decisions, it must rely upon public opinion and persuasion.

CHART I.3
ORGANIZATION CHART OF THE EUROPEAN ECONOMIC COMMUNITY

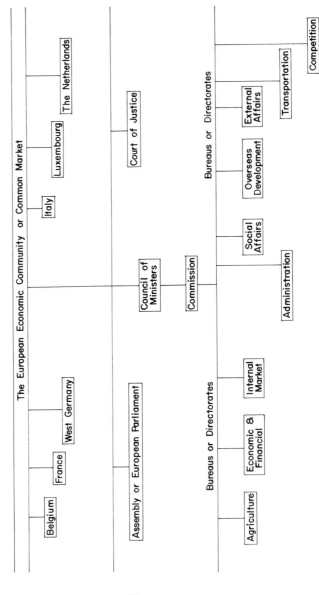

Since 1958, the European Parliament has gained stature. It operates as a quasi-legislative body for the European Economic Community, the European Coal and Steel Community (ECSC) and the Atomic Energy Community (EURATOM). Parliament meets each spring in Strasbourg and is composed of 142 members; 36 each from France, Italy and West Germany, 14 each from the Netherlands and Belgium and 6 from Luxembourg. The members, who are now appointed by their national legislatures, are seated and vote in groups by political party rather than by nationality. When, and if, the Parliament is elected by direct vote, it may be granted additional powers in the formulation of the policies of the Community.

The Council of Ministers. Each member of the Common Market has the right to send one representative to the Common Market Council of Ministers to represent it directly. This body is the highest policy-making institution of the Market but, in certain cases, it can only act on the basis of recommendations transmitted by the Commission. It may accept or reject these recommendations, but it can modify them only by unanimous vote. The advice of the Monetary Committee, the Assembly and the Economic and Social Committee must be sought, in some cases, before the Council can act. The Council has considerable authority over the budget, which it must approve before it becomes effective.

The Council now acts by vote of what the Treaty calls a "qualified majority" under which France, West Germany and Italy have four votes each, Belgium and the Netherlands two each and Luxembourg one. Many decisions can be made on the basis of a majority vote. The Council of Ministers has wide authority over tariff and quota changes, discrimination, competition and other basic policy matters.

The Court of Justice. According to the Treaty, the Court of Justice was established to "ensure observance of law and justice in the interpretation and application of this Treaty."[6] The Court consists of seven judges appointed by agreement among the members and two or more Advocates General. The Advocates General are charged with the duty of publicly presenting reasoned conclusions concerning cases submitted to the Court to assist this body in the discharge of its duties. This Court is the jurisdiction of both first instance and last appeal and has the functions usually associated with the highest judiciary or a constitutional court.

The Court receives cases instituted by member states, business firms, individuals, agencies of the Common Market, and cases referred to it by the Commission. The field of responsibility of the Court is not clearly defined in the Treaty and the body of law which it is to follow is not specified. Presumably it will follow international law or make its own law where needed. Among its more important functions are: the interpretation of the Treaty and of statutes enacted or actions taken by bodies established under the Treaty; the determination of the obligations of members of the Community; the settlement of disputes between members; the validity of the acts of the institutions of the Community; the adjudication of actions arising from claims for compensation for damages; the settlement of cases arising between the Market and its employees and the arbitration of Market contracts under both private and public law.

The Court of Justice has wide judiciary powers, but the means available to enforce its decisions and its relations with the legal codes and jurisprudence of the members are not spelled out. In spite of these apparent limitations, it may well be destined to play a decisive role in the life of the Common Market and to create its own body of law and jurisprudence.

The Commission. The Commission is the principal administrative body of the Common Market as well as its activating agency. It consists of nine members, appointed by agreement, no three of whom may come from a single member state. Its major functions consist in the implementation of the provisions of the Treaty, deciding issues arising from the application of the Treaty, making basic policy recommendations to the Council and the exercise of those duties assigned to it by the Council. Its decisions are taken by majority vote.

The Commission acts in the interests of the Community

as a whole rather than in that of any of the member states and speaks for the Market both in reference to the members and outside states. Much of its power arises from the fact that it originates as well as administers policy.

The Commission is destined to exercise considerable authority in the negotiation of the level of the Market's external tariff under the auspices of the General Agreement on Tariffs and Trade (GATT), the maintenance of competition, the creation of the Community's agricultural and social policies, the implementation of the EEC's general economic policies, the development of investment programs including those of the European Investment Bank and Overseas Investment Fund. The Commission has already done important work in conducting negotiations on applications for membership in the Common Market, especially in the case of the United Kingdom.

In order better to carry out its responsibilities, the Commission has established a number of *Directorates* under its jurisdiction, each charged with one or more of the Commission's principal functions. The more important of these Directorates are those concerned with the internal market, competition, social affairs, agriculture, transport, overseas areas, external relations, economic and financial affairs and administration.

These Directorates resemble somewhat the ministries of European governments or the departments and agencies of the United States and are staffed with officials and employees. The Commission is located in Brussels, although the Common Market has not as yet decided upon its definite center. The Council has evinced considerable interest in the establishment of a type of "federal district," somewhat on the order of the District of Columbia, for the seat of the organization. The Commission has already established close working relations with the EURATOM Commission and the High Authority of the Coal and Steel Community.

The advisory committees. Several advisory committees have been established to service the needs of the agencies of the Common Market, especially the Council and the Commission. The most important of these are the Monetary Committee and the Economic and Social Committee.

The Monetary Committee consists of fourteen members. Two members are appointed by the Commission and two by each member government. Like many consultative bodies, the importance of this Committee depends upon its ability to make its influence effective, especially in the decisions of the Commission and the Council. Due largely to the caliber of its members, it has already played an · important role in the determination of the monetary, fiscal and balance of payments policies and operations of the member states.

This Committee carries out a continuing examination of the financial and monetary operations of the members and provides a forum for the exchange of views and information in these fields. It also furnishes advice on matters under its jurisdiction to the members and assists in the coordination of the policies of the participants.

The Economic and Social Committee consists of 101 members; West Germany, France and Italy are represented by 24 members each, Belgium and the Netherlands by 12 each and Luxembourg by 5. Its powers are spelled out in the Treaty and provision is made for the establishment of specialized sections of the Committee corresponding to its main fields of activity. The Committee has been frequently consulted on matters of agricultural policy; regulations for the Social Fund; transportation, commercial, economic and fiscal policy.

Among the other committees created by the Treaty, attention should be drawn to the Committee on Tariff Negotiations, established to aid the Commission in GATT tariff negotiations with outside countries. This Committee appears destined to play an especially important role and should prove of special interest to American exporters and investors.

The European Free Trade Association

During the negotiations leading to the elaboration of the Treaty of Rome, as well as those which followed its ratification, some members of the Organization for European Economic

Cooperation (OEEC) showed considerable interest in the formation of a free trade association which would be joined to the European Economic Community. For a variety of reasons, now largely of historical interest, these proposals were not accepted.[7]

After the ultimate breakdown of these negotiations, a group of nations outside the Six and led by the United Kingdom undertook the formation of a free trade association which went into effect under the name of the European Free Trade Association (EFTA) in 1959. Its membership included the United Kingdom, Sweden, Norway, Denmark, Austria and Switzerland. The organization was also joined by Portugal and is often termed the *Outer Seven* or the *Seven* in contrast to the *Inner Six,* which it partially surrounds geographically.

The Convention of Stockholm which established the EFTA is, in contrast to the Treaty of Rome, a relatively simple document. Its major features provide for the gradual elimination of internal tariffs and import quotas among the Seven; escape clauses; a rules of origin system to prevent goods imported into low external tariff members from being freely re-exported to others with higher external tariffs; a body of principles designed to prevent both public and private trade restrictions as well as discrimination together with a small organization to administer the Association.

The EFTA provides for the gradual elimination of the internal tariff among the members by 1970 at the latest. Each member retains its own external tariff, and duty rate differentials among the members are equalized by a rules of origin arrangement. It is neither an economic union (common market) nor a customs union.

Such an organization, at the outset, apparently suited the desiderata of the Seven better than a common market. It permitted the United Kingdom to maintain its Imperial Preference System, which doubtless would have been seriously modified under a common market or customs union arrangement. Since it did not entail an economic, as a possible prelude to a political, union with the West, it suited the neutral nations, Austria,

Switzerland and Sweden. Portugal found this loose type of institution well adapted to its status as a relatively underdeveloped nation. Although a substantially weaker type of organization than the EEC, it does serve to strengthen the hands of the Outer Seven nations in dealing with the Inner Six as well as with countries outside both institutions.

The principal administrative organ of the EFTA is a Council with representation from all of the members. In most instances the Council can only act by unanimous decision, although provision has been made for certain actions to be taken by majority vote. In the first instance, EFTA relies upon publicity to enforce its decisions. If such measures are not effective, then, upon approval by a majority vote of the Council, the other members of the organization may be relieved of some of their obligations to the offending member.

Certain exceptions were made to the elimination of the common internal tariff of the EFTA, principally with respect to agricultural and fishery products. The EFTA welcomes the accession of additional members, and there is apparently no intention to make it an exclusive institution. It appears that the EFTA membership remains hopeful of some form of attachment with the EEC.

From an exporter's point of view, the EFTA both resembles and differs from the EEC. With an ultimate zero internal tariff on most goods, it is likely to practice similar trade discrimination and diversion as the Six. Since each member has its own external tariff, exports enter the organization under the different rates of tariff duty applied by the importing country. The rules of origin provisions equalize, on internal EFTA trade covering re-exports, the external duties of the participants. From the point of view of imports from the EFTA, the provisions of the Convention of Stockholm involve no important direct changes, although the resultant improved efficiency of the members may work indirectly toward lower-cost sources of supply.

Direct investment enterprises inside the EFTA in the form of branches and subsidiaries will enjoy the same benefits as any other national resident firm of the area, and in this respect the advantages of incorporation in one of the member states of the organization are similar to those of the Common Market. Due to its relatively lower degree of economic integration, competition and efficiency, the growth of national incomes and products is likely to be less important than that in the EEC.[8] Some businesses are likely to find a more agreeable economic climate in the Common Market than in the EFTA; for others the reverse may be true.

Although the Common Market is laying down many new rules of business policy and conduct, American firms will still need to import from, export to, or invest in, a specific member country. Doing business in the Common Market involves familiarity with the organization of the Market and also with the business climate in the particular member state or states concerned.

❧

NOTES

[1] Article I, Section 9, Paragraph 5 of the Constitution of the United States stipulates: "No Tax or Duty shall be laid on Articles exported from any State."

[2] In addition to constant and decreasing costs industries, economists recognize a third category, increasing costs. Industries of increasing costs show an upward rising cost curve indicating that as output is increased, the per unit costs of production rise. Some authors believe that many American firms are now operating on the increasing segments of their costs of production curves. Cf. George L. Bach. *Economics: An Introduction to Analysis and Policy*. Englewood Cliffs, N.J.: Prentice-Hall, Inc., 1960, pp. 514-515.

[3] Cf. Emile Benoit. *Europe at Sixes and Sevens: The Common Market, The Free Trade Association, and the United States*. New York: Columbia University Press, 1961, pp. 160-170.

[4] Cf. Mordecai Ezekiel and Louis Bean. *Economic Bases for the Agricultural Adjustment Act*. A publication of the United States Department of Agriculture. Washington, D.C.: U.S. GPO, 1933.

[5] Cf. Emile Benoit, *op. cit.*, pp. 52-55.

[6] Treaty, Article 164.

[7] An account of these negotiations is given in Isaiah Frank. *The European Common Market: An Analysis of Commercial Policy*. New York: Frederick A. Praeger, 1961, pp. 7-91, 202-240.

[8] Regionalism is proving to be contagious. A number of other arrangements are examined in chapter 12.

2

The Changing Business Climate of the Six

THE EUROPEAN PRODUCT — BUSINESS MANAGEMENT — COMPETITION — PRICE POLICIES — THE EUROPEAN DISTRIBUTION SYSTEM — LAISSEZ FAIRE AND DIRIGISME — EUROPEAN LEGAL SYSTEMS — TAX SYSTEMS — MONEY MARKETS — INDUSTRIAL DIVERSIFICATION, INSTALLMENT SALES AND CONSUMER'S CREDIT — EUROPEAN NATIONAL INCOME AND PRODUCT

If the Common Market continues on its present path it will ultimately come to resemble more closely the United States economic organization, because it is based upon some of the principles which give this economy its essential characteristics. This growing resemblance is not accidental. The American economy is an open one and publishes more facts about itself than any other. These facts speak for themselves; overseas observers have long noted its strong and weak features.

Although the economies of the Common Market may create institutions which resemble those found in the United States, many important differences between the two will probably remain. European institutions in part are the offspring of custom and tradition which change but slowly.

This chapter outlines some of the features of the European economy which differentiate it from the American and indicates some of the changes which the Community is likely to bring in its wake. The picture which it presents is drawn in general terms and ignores many important details as well as exceptions to the characteristics described. It is designed primarily to serve as an introduction to the business climate of the Six.

The European Product

With the exception of standardized and uniform commodities which are sold on the world exchanges, products often bear the hallmarks of the civilization which created them. Although based on universal science, they are made under varying technical procedures and embody differing cultural concepts. A product is not merely the processing and assemblage of raw materials by labor and capital equipment; it frequently represents the essence of the culture in which it is made. Archeologists and anthropologists have long been aware of this fact. Many of the inferences which they draw concerning the nature of bygone civilizations are based on a study of the artifacts or the products of the culture under study.

American consumer's goods are produced for a public which enjoys a higher income level than that which prevails in Europe. The European consumer has only recently started to purchase in substantial quantities many of the durable goods which American consumers have been using for the past two or three decades. The original consumer's durable, introduced on the American market twenty or thirty years ago, has been often "upgraded." The original electric refrigerator of six cubic feet capacity is now a thirteen cubic foot model with separate freezing and refrigeration compartments and doors, automatic defrosting devices, magnetic door locks, modernistic design and "decorator" colors. Such a modern appliance is beyond the purchasing power of many European consumers who are in the market for the older and simpler six cubic foot model at a relatively low price. Many American manufacturers of these products have fallen into the error of assuming that the European can buy the same type of goods that he has been selling recently to his American customers. American consumer's goods, to be saleable in quantities on the European markets, must be designed and priced to fit European tastes and pocketbooks.

Consumers judge products on the basis of the ability of the item to satisfy specific wants according to their notions of the characteristics which the product should possess. The

European consumer has, in the past, felt comfortable in the presence of goods which possess European or national traits and dubious concerning products which are less familiar. This traditional attitude is undergoing change, and American goods are coming to enjoy a certain prestige and saleability on the markets of the old world.

It is impossible to generalize this tendency to include all American consumer goods. Some of them may prove more welcome than formerly; others no more saleable and still others less. A market study or survey is needed in the case of some products. Others can best be introduced on a limited or pilot project basis to ascertain their acceptability to European consumers and to discover what changes, if any, will be required to insure their sale.

Tools, machinery, equipment and producer's components are apt to be judged by other standards. A manufacturer is not likely to be greatly influenced by traditional and accustomed styles and is prone to judge the items used in his productive process by their efficiency, adaptability to his procedures, cost, durability, quality, cost-reducing capacity, speed, availability of replacement parts, maintenance and service.

Business Management

Perhaps the greatest single difference between business methods in Europe and the United States is the role which tradition and custom play in the methods of the former. Each succeeding period in business life bears the imprint of the methods of earlier systems, and European business practices of today have their roots far back in the aristocrat-dominated civilizations of the Middle Ages.

European business has been more of a family affair than in the United States. One of the aims of the man of affairs in these countries has been to establish a solid and secure enterprise, if not a large and expanding one, which would remain a substantial piece of family property for generations to come. Management was often recruited from the family rather than from the market place or by promotion from the subaltern echelons of the firm. Employees could sometimes work their way up — up to a point, that is — but the top positions were usually reserved for the family. European business management has suffered from these practices and the science of management has not progressed as rapidly under the rule of nepotism as might be desirable.

The art and science of business management has been the topic of intensive study in the United States for many decades by business, management associations, research groups and university colleges of commerce. Under the impact of this examination, an important body of principles and techniques has been developed and widely disseminated in the business management community. As one result, the practice of management has been improved in the United States, where it has made far greater progress than elsewhere.

Although it may be inaccurate to refer to business managers in the United States as a class in the generally accepted sense of this term, there is a fairly definite community or group of business executives who have made management a career and are both trained and experienced in this type of work. Members of this group are frequently recruited from the graduates of colleges and universities. Since they are "in charge" of the operation of the American economy, they play a key role in the life of this country.

Under the impact of the Marshall Plan, the use of modern, "Made in U.S.A.," production techniques was accelerated in Europe. The Organization for European Economic Cooperation (OEEC) fostered the organization of a Productivity Council. Under the auspices of this Council and aided by Marshall Plan financing, representatives of the OEEC industries and distributive firms undertook the study of means of increasing the productivity of their economies. Study teams were organized which visited the United States and investigated the organization of the more important industries and distributive channels. Their findings were published upon the team's return home and circulated throughout the OEEC area.

Industry in other lands is already noting the improved

productivity of factories and competitiveness of Europe's plants. The business integration, specialization and increase in size which are taking place in the Common Market will require still further improvements in the art of management. Although there remain many family firms in Europe, their number appears destined to decrease. Only the more effectively managed firms are likely to survive the forthcoming competitive struggle.

The late American economist, Sumner Slichter, informed one of the visiting European productivity teams that United States businessmen not only enjoyed making money, they also liked business as a way of life, as a challenge, as a combination vocation-avocation and felt that the larger and more complex business became, the greater the enjoyment it offered. European businessmen are frequently satisfied to manage small or medium-sized firms and to concentrate their efforts on stability, security and freedom from worry rather than to seek wider spheres of activity with the dangers that expansion often holds. This attitude, too, may change as the Common Market economy moves into "high gear."

Competition

An American businessman reported his experiences in attempting to buy some silk in a European city a few years after the close of World War II. He visited several mills in that city in an effort to obtain quotations and terms on a certain type of silk fabric. He was quoted identical prices and terms by all of the mills. The next day he received a visit at his hotel from a representative of a silk association who icily informed him that it was useless to seek better prices and terms from the mills of the city and indicated that his efforts to do so met with the industry's disapproval. The American silk importer left and purchased his silk in another country. This incident took place during the days of the dollar shortage when the country in question was sorely in need of dollar exports to assist in balancing its international accounts.

This story illustrates one aspect of European competition as it stood before the advent of the Common Market. It was characterized by a spirit of live and let live and there was little tendency to expand at the expense of one's competitors. Prices were often set at a point so that the least efficient firms could survive. Both tacit and formal agreements — cartels — often allocated the market among the several producers. When not cartelized, manufacturers sometimes banded together in trade associations which wielded considerable power. Intensive competition was not generally promoted by these organizations.

Prior to the EEC, tariffs, exchange controls, customs administration, taxes, legislation and regulations sometimes operated to reduce competition from without and, in combination with monetary areas, served to reserve the trade of the colonies for the firms of the mother country. Direct investment by foreign firms was not prevented, but it was frequently discouraged by laws, regulations and administrative procedures.

This comfortable business situation met with increasing government disapproval after World War II and many governments became desirous of introducing more competition into their economies. Some of the provisions of the Treaty of Rome furnish the means of rendering business more competitive, especially the tariff-reducing and the anti-trust clauses. At first many businessmen on the Continent opposed the Treaty, but later they accepted its principles, and it is now receiving the general support of the business community.

There is little doubt that competition will become more severe as the Common Market presses forward with its program of economic integration. Some enterprises are unlikely to survive when the competitive struggle gets under way; those that survive will be the stronger, more efficient and larger firms.

Price Policies

One of the principal differences in pricing policy between some American and European industries is that the former tend to price on the mass and the latter on the unit. In other words, many American manufacturers endeavor to obtain a profit on total sales, on the mass of revenue, while the European often desires to make a profit on each unit of goods sold.

Prices in Europe tend to be higher, *relative to costs,* than those which prevail in the United States and the volume sold smaller. The industries of Europe do not always reap the full advantage of the economies of scale or of decreasing costs (see chapter 1, chart I.2.). As noted in chapter 1, the ability of the industries of the Six to enjoy these advantages has been hampered by the size of each national market. This fact may have contributed to the use of the unit rather than the mass pricing method. It is difficult to determine whether or not European industry would have made larger or smaller profits under the mass method, given the other handicaps to scale. It is certain, however, that the unit pricing method does not redound to the advantage of the consumer and does not make for high income economies.

The cost structure underlying the pricing process in Europe is also different. European industry, relative to American, is based on low labor costs. Since labor is relatively cheap, there has been a tendency for European industry to use larger proportions of labor and smaller of capital than their American counterparts. Such a cost structure is not conducive to steep decreasing cost curves and is more characteristic of the constant cost type of industry (see chapter 1, chart I. 1).

The relatively low earnings of labor operate to restrain further the development of mass markets by holding down the level of purchasing power available for the acquisition of the products of industry. In one sense, the economies of the Six prior to the advent of the Common Market moved in a vicious circle. The industries themselves did not promote the development of mass markets and they, in turn, were held in check by markets where low purchasing power prevailed.

The Common Market holds promise of breaking this circle by providing a wider market of growing income, eliminating marginal firms, creating larger and fewer business units utilizing more capital. Unless other factors operate to maintain or to raise prices, new pricing policies should develop on the order of those employed in the United States. The implications of these changes for Americans who trade with, and invest in, the EEC nations are obvious.

The European Distribution System

In advanced industrial nations, the technology of distribution has lagged behind that of production, and the lag has been greater in Europe than in the United States. Since the areas of the European nations are smaller, one might think that distribution in these countries would present fewer problems than in the United States. The contrary, however, is the case.

European distribution has been characterized by the proliferation of a large number of small wholesale and retail outlets. But few of these units handle a sufficiently large volume to benefit from the economies of size. By American standards, mark-ups at both the retail and wholesale levels are substantial. In spite of the large number of firms, prices remain relatively high, for the outlets tend to serve neighborhood and regional customers and are not as competitive as their number might lead one to think. In addition, the European transportation system is not, as it now stands, as well adapted to the swift and economical movement of goods from factory to user as it might be.

Important changes in the distributive system are likely to result from the integration of the economies in the Common Market and the improvements in the transportation systems of the Six which are being programmed. Reports from the Continent indicate that changes are being made in distributive methods to make them more efficient.

Laissez Faire and Dirigisme

Businessmen the world over are vitally interested in the freedom which they have to conduct their operations and the restraint which their governments exercise over their activities. Absolute freedom, or pure laissez faire, exists no place today and never has existed. On the other hand relatively complete dirigisme or state control over economic life exists only in the Communist Bloc countries.

As a general proposition, European nations lean more heavily to the side of dirigisme than the United States. They have had long historical experience with government regulation which came to its full flower under the Mercantile system. A younger nation, lacking some of this historical experience, the United States has tended more to favor regimes of laissez faire. The American businessman, trading or investing in Europe for the first time, is apt to be struck by this difference.

There are great differences among the European nations in regard to the extent of state control which prevails. France, Italy, Portugal and the Scandinavian countries are relatively strongly controlled; Germany, Switzerland and Belgium are less so, while the United Kingdom, Austria and the Netherlands occupy a middle position.

The principal difference between government regulation in Europe and the United States lies in the fact that the Europeans generally place less confidence in the ability of economic laws, the price and market systems, to manage the economy than their American counterparts. European statesmen apparently feel that the free market does not operate precisely as some models represent it and even were it to perform according to model, the results might not accord entirely with their concepts of the public interest. As a result of the prevalence of dirigisme, the European bureaucracy plays a much more important role in the economic life of Europe than in the United States. American public officials and legislators believe that laissez faire is effective, and they are inclined to allow it to operate as long as the results are satisfactory in terms of public welfare and no serious abuses result.

Business life in America is characterized by less paper work; fewer required licenses, permits and authorizations; less delay in consummating certain transactions and more liberty of individual action. Freedom of enterprise contributes to the dignity of businessmen, and the important place which they occupy in American life is due, in part, to this liberty.

The advent of the Common Market is not likely to reduce appreciably the extent of government controls. In all probability, it will call for more regulation, for the dirigisme of the EEC will probably be added to that of the member nations. In those cases where the regulations of the Market supersede those of the member nations, there is no guarantee that they will be any softer or easier to handle. In this respect the development of the Common Market is not likely to bring the European economy to resemble more closely the American.

European Legal Systems

There is a fundamental difference between the legal systems which prevail in Europe, with the exception of the United Kingdom, and that which is found in the United States. The European systems are based on Roman law; that in America upon British common law. Although the two types of legal systems have much in common, there are some important differences in fundamentals and many in detail. In spite of their common origin, there is no single legal system which applies to all European countries, but there is more similarity between the laws of those countries than between those of the United States and the Continental nations.

Jurisprudence and the doctrine of *stare decisis* are less important in Europe than in America, and the European courts "make" less law than their American counterparts. Judicial procedures and the rules of evidence also differ widely between the United States and the Continent. The power of the European official to make law or quasi-law by means of decrees and decisions is larger than the rights enjoyed by the American executive branch.

Although a European invention, the doctrine of the tri-partite division of government powers finds a wider application in the governmental organization of the United States than in Europe. The ability of the courts to find laws unconstitutional appears more restricted in Europe than in the United States, and European businessmen do not possess as wide powers to challenge the constitutionality of laws and decrees as their American colleagues. In addition, the authority of government officials to perform acts and make decisions is less frequently questioned in European courts than in the American.

The Common Market will undoubtedly bring changes in the laws and regulations affecting European businessmen and will probably create a greater degree of uniformity among some of them. American businessmen trading and investing in the Common Market countries will be well advised not to assume that the laws which apply there are identical to those in the United States. On all questions where points of law arise, or which may give rise to litigation, the American businesman will do well to consult a competent European attorney before proceeding very far with his transactions.

Tax Systems

In general, the tax systems of Europe rely more heavily on indirect taxes (imposed on things and acts) than on direct taxation (levies on persons). Various forms of the sales tax (such as the transactions or turnover levies) are widely employed, and the effective rates are often several times as high as in the United States. The net income tax is universally utilized, but its rates and relative yields are low by American standards. The gross income or receipts tax, which does not provide for many deductions representing expenses, is applied to a large number of business enterprises.

There are also fewer tax jurisdictions in Europe than in the United States for, with certain exceptions, these countries do not have a federal political organization. European governments commonly collect a number of excise taxes on goods and services and many fees and stamp taxes on acts and documents. Due to the large number of taxes (the burden of each is often small), the total tax bill may be large.

There is a tendency for the principal incidence of European taxes to fall more heavily on consumers than on business, and the American investor in the Continent may be pleasantly surprised in this respect. The pleasant surprise may prove to be of short duration, however, because heavy taxes on consumption reduce purchasing power and tend to make for more shallow markets and reduced revenues from sales.

There is a tendency for some turnover taxes to have a cumulative or *cascade* effect. Assume that a given turnover tax of 10 per cent is levied on all sales by the manufacturer, wholesaler and retailer. The manufacturer's price of the product in question is $5.00. After the 10 per cent turnover tax has been paid, the price to the wholesaler is $5.50 per item. The wholesaler adds a 20 per cent mark-up and prices his goods at $6.60. A 10 per cent turnover tax is added to his sale to the retailer, bringing the cost of the item now to $7.26. The retailer adds a 50 per cent mark-up bringing the price to $10.89. When the ultimate consumer has paid a 10 per cent turnover tax on the product, the amount he pays is $11.98.

Some countries, notably France, have endeavored to reduce the cumulative or cascade effect of turnover taxes by calculating them on the basis of the *value added* principal. Under this plan, the seller, whether manufacturer or dealer, only pays the transactions tax on the value which he added to the product or his mark-up. In addition, he is given certain rebates on the turnover tax which he paid to his supplier. Some other nations avoid a part of the cascade effect by utilizing a single stage turnover tax on either the manufacturer's, wholesaler's or retailer's sales.

The relatively lower taxes on business incomes tend to promote business initiative and efficiency by allowing businessmen to retain or reinvest a larger proportion of profits than the American tax system does. Thus under the European system business finds it easier to retain, reinvest or distribute profits. The simplicity of indirect taxes as compared with income taxes makes for fewer loopholes and opportunities for tax avoidance, and the European businessman does not require the services of tax consultants as urgently as his American colleagues.

Payroll taxes, both as a substitute for income taxes levied on workers and as a means of raising revenue for extensive social security systems, are common among the EEC and EFTA nations and are levied at rates which are far higher than those applied in the United States. The social security taxes in one

European country amount to more than 50 per cent of the cash or take-home wages paid workers and generally finance a broader range of benefits than those which prevail in the United States. These taxes add considerably to the employer's wage bill and often render international comparisons of wage costs difficult.

Many European governments refund some or a part of certain direct taxes paid, or do not collect specified direct taxes, on goods when they are exported. Income taxes, however, under GATT rules, are not refundable on export sales. This gives a price advantage to some European exports over the competing American shipments. Although certain American excises are not levied on exported items, since they apply only to sales made in the United States, taxpayers here shoulder a heavy burden of income taxation which is recouped, where possible, in the prices of goods sold on both the domestic and foreign markets. As a general proposition, American exporters are handicapped tax-wise with reference to their European competitors. American businessmen contemplating direct investments in Europe would do well to consult competent tax lawyers and accountants in the countries in question before embarking on the project.

Although the Treaty of Rome does not give the EEC any direct tax powers, it does provide this body with some authority over the tax systems of members which affect the Community and the other members as well as over fiscal policy. Within the broad limits of the Treaty provisions, member states are free to establish such taxes as they deem appropriate. As matters now stand, and pending political integration, the Common Market nations will probably continue to employ tax systems similar to those now in effect.

Money Markets

European money markets are of interest to United States direct investors who have, or propose to establish, branches and subsidiaries in the countries of the region and who desire to raise capital there. The banking systems of Europe differ in many particulars from that found in the United States. They are older and are more tradition-bound. The rates of interest, with the possible exception of Switzerland and Portugal, are higher than those which prevail in the United States. The banks of Europe are often established along functional lines, specializing in certain types of transactions or providing credit for specific lines of industry and trade.

Branch banking is highly developed in most of these countries and there is perhaps less competition than the businessman is accustomed to find in the United States. Checks are not generally used, but the domestic bill of exchange and the deposit account overdraft have general acceptance. The regulation of banking by national authority is extensive and there is a strong tendency to use the banking system to attain national objectives.

The large amount of borrowing by European firms in United States markets bears witness to the fact that interest rates are lower in this country and the markets are wider and more highly developed. The United States Secretary of the Treasury has reminded Europeans on several occasions that larger and more flexible money markets would reduce their dependence upon American sources of capital.

Although many European sources of both short- and long-term financing are available, they are not always easily accessible, especially for foreign-owned firms. Working capital is usually supplied for short periods only, but in many cases the loans are renewable. United States branches and subsidiaries must be prepared to furnish excellent financial and earnings records and a high credit standing to obtain financial accommodation in Europe. For longer loans, collateral is often required together with the guarantee of the parent company.

As a general proposition, the European stock exchanges are not as large or as well developed as those found in New York. The markets for long-term security capital are narrower; raising funds through public issues as well as the purchase and sale of securities is a more difficult process than in the United States. In addition, some governments require official authorization and approval before securities can be floated publicly. Some stock exchanges are closed to foreign issues. Although there are some specialized investment banks, investment banking is generally carried out by the more important commercial banks.

The European banking systems and money markets are under study by both the OECD and the EEC. Restrictions on capital markets are being gradually lifted and the spirit of financial interdependence is gaining in the EEC. In addition, the demands for financial accommodation of the increasingly large business units of the EEC and the EFTA may well exert a salutary influence upon bankers and stock exchanges to organize to meet the new requirements.

Industrial Diversification, Installment Sales and Consumer's Credit

Diversification. Long practiced by insurance companies the world over, diversification is being more widely utilized by American industrial firms to counter the several aspects of economic rhythm: the business cycle, seasonal and irregular variations, and other business uncertainties. Since the larger enterprises embody a heavy capital structure, many businessmen are increasingly unwilling to risk the entire investment in one or a group of closely related types of activity. The result has been that these companies have invested a part of their funds in a variety of unrelated types of business.

Economic rhythm has been of less importance in Europe than in the United States, especially the amplitude of the swings of the business cycle. Their growth rate in the last few years, however, has been greater, their business units of smaller size and the amount of capital risked in a given venture less important. The urge toward diversification has consequently not been as powerful in Europe as it has in the United States. Although there are many business firms with far-flung interests in a wide variety of activities, the American businessman is likely to find many firms which, like the proverbial shoemaker, "stick to their lasts." Under the impact of the economic integration of the Common Market, and the resulting changes in the size and character of the business firms, it is not improbable that those which survive the competitive struggle will find it advisable to diversify their operations.

Installment sales. Installment sales are no novelty to Europe, which utilized them some time before the United States did. This type of selling, however, has not assumed the dimensions in Europe that it has in America and is viewed with a jaundiced eye by some governments. It is difficult to predict the future of this kind of merchandising in Europe. Many social factors, which are difficult to forecast, are involved.

Consumer's credit. Consumer's credit, especially that provided by credit unions, is also older in Europe than in the United States. However, it has greatly expanded in the last few decades in this country. Like installment sales, it has not been encouraged by all European governments. The American businessman exporting to Europe is likely to find that more consumer sales of his product are made on a cash basis than in the United States. Again, since many unpredictable social factors are involved, the future of this type of credit is not readily predictable.

European National Income and Product

Industrially, labor is more important relative to capital in Europe than in the United States and the earnings of labor are lower and those of capital higher. The existing institutions of Europe have a long history and bear the marks of a past which divided society into classes and maintained a substantial gap between the wealthy and the poor.

Property rights are firmly ingrained in both Europe and the United States, but they have had a longer history in the former than in the latter. In spite of a relaxation in the rights of property in favor of those of persons, which has gone on apace in both Europe and the United States in recent years, the rights of capital to relatively high rewards seems to be more widely admitted in the former countries than in the latter. For one thing, the earnings of labor and capital are not as well publicized in Europe as they are in the United States and the public is not as fully informed of the situation.

During the depression of the 1930's measures were taken by the United States government to improve the operation of the economy, to eliminate abuses and to increase the worker's and the farmer's shares of the national income. Some of these measures were reinforced and others added during the World War II years and those immediately following. These steps were not entirely new; they served primarily to reinforce the continuing trend in reform programs which were initiated by the Interstate Commerce Commission Act of 1887 and the Sherman Anti-trust Act of 1890. Their impact on the American economy has been large. Coupled with the initiative, ability and imagination of American businessmen, they have created a new form of capitalism in this country.

The gap which separated the highest from the lowest income earners in the United States has been narrowed since the 1930's. The incomes of both groups have increased, but those of the less well-off have grown at a higher rate than the better-off groups. The earnings of unskilled workers have increased more rapidly than those of the semi-skilled which, in turn, have grown more rapidly than those of the skilled. The gains attributable to personal effort on the part of workers, professional people and businessmen climbed relative to those having their source in property rights such as interest, rents and royalties.[1]

These developments have created a large and relatively high income middle class in the United States which means that its markets have depth, provide outlets for a wide variety and a large volume of goods. Table 2.1, showing the per capita consumption expenditures of the EEC and the EFTA countries together with those of the United States, sheds some light on the relative standards of living of these areas. In Table 2.2, certain consumers' "status symbols" are shown which indicate the extent to which some of the amenities of life are enjoyed in Europe and the United States. Their use is increasing rapidly in Europe at the present time.

TABLE 2.1

CONSUMPTION EXPENDITURES PER PERSON IN THE EEC, EFTA
COUNTRIES AND THE UNITED STATES, 1953 AND 1960

U.S. Dollar Equivalents at 1960 Prices

E E C	1953	Increase 1953-1960	1960
Belgium*	$ 780	12.6%	$ 878
Luxembourg*	688	18.9%	818
France	639	29.2%	826
West Germany	490	36.7%	670
Netherlands	435	25.5%	546
Italy	318	28.9%	410
Greece (assoc.)*	194	40.7%	273
E F T A			
Switzerland*	$ 803**	16.9%	$ 939
Sweden	805	18.1%	951
United Kingdom	730	21.2%	885
Denmark	708	22.0%	864
Norway	631	16.3%	734
Austria	330	50.0%	495
Portugal	154	25.3%	193
Finland (assoc.)	419**	39.1%	583
U.S.A.	$1,589	13.5%	$1,804

* 1953-59 at 1959 prices.
** estimate

Source: Morgan Guaranty Trust Company of New York, *Market Europe.*
1961, p. 88.

TABLE 2.2

SELECTED CONSUMER DURABLES IN USE, 1960
(per 1000 persons)

	Phones	Autos	Radios	TV Sets
Austria	98	56	278	27
Denmark	233	82	331	117
Finland	134	40	274	20
Norway	201	70	283	13
Portugal	43	18	92	5
Sweden	351	153	365	137
Switzerland	305	93	266	23
United Kingdom	155	107	283	206
EFTA	166	92	274	138
Belgium-Luxembourg	125	82	266	65
France	95	117	240	41
West Germany	111	80	306	86
Italy	73	40	161	42
Netherlands	139	45	270	69
EEC	98	77	241	59
USA	407	337	932	294

Source: United Nations, *Statistical Yearbook, 1961.*

One of the cardinal features of the Treaty of Rome is to establish growing economies with high standards of public welfare. In the words of the Preamble of the Treaty:

✿   ✿   ✿

DECIDED to ensure the economic and social progress of their countries by common action in eliminating the barriers which divide Europe.

DIRECTING their efforts to the essential purpose of constantly improving the living and working conditions of their peoples.

✿   ✿   ✿

ANXIOUS to strengthen the unity of their economies and to ensure their harmonious development by reducing the differences existing between the various regions and by mitigating the backwardness of the less favored.

❃   ❃   ❃

The specific steps which the nations of the Common Market are taking to improve their economies are set forth in the body of the Treaty and were sketched in chapter 1. Table 2.1, showing the increase in per capita consumption of the EEC and EFTA nations, and Tables 2.3 and 2.4, presenting the increase in their per capita incomes and gross national products, indicate some of the success which these two institutions have already had in creating greater economic welfare.

TABLE 2.3

NATIONAL INCOME IN SELECTED EUROPEAN COUNTRIES AND IN THE UNITED STATES, 1957 AND 1961

(In millions of U. S. dollars)

Country	1957		1961	
	Total	Per Capita (a)	Total	Per Capita (a)
Austria	3,930	567	5,229	739
Belgium	8,251	969	9,517	1,035
Denmark	3,854	166	5,302	1,156
Germany (West)	40,099	754	60,160	1,114
France	38,199	892	47,387	1,018
Italy	20,025	424	27,757	550
Luxembourg	337	1,162	366	1,166
Netherlands	7,649	795	10,061	1,045
Norway	3,153	962	3,733	1,139
Portugal	1,750	207	2,944	330
Sweden	9,391	1,334	12,073	1,611
Switzerland	6,321	1,322	8,225	1,515
United Kingdom	49,635	988	61,214	1,162
United States	366,900	2,425	444,000	2,476

(a) Estimated on basis of population for nearest year.

Source: Computed from IMF *International Financial Statistics*, Vol. XVI, No. 7, July 1963, and U. N. *Demographic Yearbooks*.

TABLE 2.4

GROSS NATIONAL PRODUCT, 1957 AND 1961,
SELECTED EUROPEAN COUNTRIES AND THE UNITED STATES

	GNP(a)	
	1957	1961
Austria	5,021	6,807
Belgium	11,068	12,233 (c)
Denmark	4,746	6,553
Germany (West) (b)	50,832	77,676
France	50,154	63,081
Italy	25,591	35,307
Luxembourg	437	487 (c)
Netherlands	9,306	12,327
Norway	3,965	4,826
Portugal	2,000	3,422
Sweden	10,193	13,359
Switzerland	7,281	9,453
United Kingdom	61,629	75,085
United States	442,800	538,600

(a) In millions of U. S. dollars. (b) Including West Berlin. (c) 1960.

Source: Computed from IMF *International Financial Statistics,* Vol. XVI,
No. 7, July, 1963.

Even before the inauguration of these two institutions, European labor unions had started to improve their collective bargaining techniques, and the growing strength of the post-World War II economies made it possible for them to negotiate more effectively. In the United Kingdom, wages in 1960 rose by 8 per cent over 1959, in 1961 by 6.5 per cent over 1960 and in 1962 by 3.5 per cent over 1961. The gains in wages in 1962 over 1960 were: Belgium 7.0 per cent, Denmark 10.5, France 8.5, West Germany 8.5, Italy 11.0, the Netherlands 10.0, Sweden 7.5 and Switzerland 6.0 per cent.[2]

The hourly cash wages of several European nations have been increasing in the past few years at a greater rate than in the United States. In 1960 the hourly cash wages paid labor, in terms of percentage of those which prevailed in the United States, stood at 50 in Sweden, 28 in West Germany, 18 in France and 16 in Italy. By 1962 these percentages had risen to 55, 33, 21 and 18, respectively.[3]

Although still far below America rates, the rise has disturbed European manufacturers who fear that increased costs may price them out of their domestic and export markets. Businesses in Europe are consequently resisting the efforts of labor to obtain higher wages, and some of their governments have come to their aid to avoid wage-cost-push type of inflation and to maintain exports at a high level. Similar opposition to rising wages is also prevalent in the United States.

The points at issue in this struggle between the unions on the one hand and business and government on the other is of considerable importance to the future of the EEC. If European wages are held level while the gross national product and national income increase, a large sector of the economy will not receive much benefit from any progress made. Such a situation is likely to be a de-stabilizing factor and may turn the political climate toward the left in the direction of socialism.

Perhaps more important is the possible braking effect which low wages will have on economic growth, the development of markets well supplied with purchasing power and the emergence of a more modern capitalistic economic organization. If wages are held at low levels, the economy of the EEC is not likely to approach that of the United States, and some of the hopes expressed in the Preamble to the Treaty of Rome are likely to be frustrated.

Although it is impossible to predict the outcome of this conflict, there appear to be some decided advantages on the side of labor. For one thing, the Common Market appears to be dedicated to the improvement of agriculture and to the raising of farm standards of living (see chapter 10). If the lot of farmers is improved, it would prove politically difficult to refuse similar improvements to labor. Since the growth of the Common Market is likely to benefit certain businessmen, labor may not wait long before demanding similar benefits. With the increase in the size and specialization of business units more capital will probably be used, thus contributing to a reduction in the marginal productivity of capital (interest) and the increase in that of labor (wages). As matters now stand, it is possible that the pattern of income distribution among the factor shares—wages, interest, rents and profits—will come to resemble more closely that which prevails in the United States.

Changes in the income and production of the EEC nations are probably the most important of all the potential economic developments ahead. They may serve to create two important economic blocs in the Western world, increase the power of the free nations and the attraction of the capitalist system for the yet uncommitted nations.

NOTES

[1] Cf. Simon Kuznets. *Shares of Upper Income Groups in Income and Savings.* (Occasional Paper 35.) New York: National Bureau of Economic Research, Inc., 1950.

[2] Dan Cordtz. "Europe Pay Spiral," *The Wall Street Journal.* June 12, 1963, pp. 1, 8.

[3] Dan Cordtz, *op. cit.*, p. 1.

3

Importing From
the Common Market

COMMON MARKET INTEGRATION AND UNITED STATES IMPORTS
—THE UNITED STATES TARIFF AND THE COMMON MARKET—
IMPACT OF IMPORTS FROM THE COMMON MARKET ON UNITED
STATES DOMESTIC INDUSTRY

The integration of the economies of the Common Market is certain to have a number of consequences for American importers. Some of the more important results are likely to develop from the following potential changes:

1. A decrease in the number of Community manufacturers
2. An increase in the size of the producing units which survive integration
3. Greater industrial specialization
4. Changes in the nature of Common Market competition
5. Changes in the cost structure of EEC industry
6. Greater factor efficiency due to the freer movement of labor and capital as well as the improved right of establishment
7. Growth of the EEC gross national product
8. The progress of innovation
9. Changes in price levels

The ability of the United States to import from the Community, however, is not solely a function of developments which take place within this institution. Businessmen and economists know that the capacity of the United States to import is partly a function of its national income. The movement of the American national product, the ability of United States industry to supply the wants of its economy, and price elasticities of American demand for Common Market goods also serve to determine both the volume and character of imports from EEC sources.

Common Market Integration and United States Imports

Like many other institutions, the European Economic Community provides a framework in which economic laws function and the operations of private businessmen take place. Since the adoption of the Treaty of Rome in 1957, several short-run results are already manifest. The intermediate and longer-run results must be forecast from the facts at hand as well as from past experience with other forms of economic integration.

Increased size, specialization and smaller number of EEC manufacturers. Shortly after the inauguration of the institution, a number of EEC businessmen took the first steps toward meeting the challenge which it posed. Several of the smaller EEC firms have merged with larger ones. Some enterprises have entered into agreements with their competitors by which they consented to specialize in the production of certain lines and types of goods and left the production of different kinds to the other parties.

This specialization makes for shifts in the nature, volume, and prices of goods which American importers will find available on the markets of the Six. As firms integrate and adapt their output to wider markets, there may be at first a smaller choice of different kinds of products available for import, since the larger remaining firms will probably concentrate on the production of greater quantities of a narrower range of goods. However, the variety of products made in the future probably will be extended.

As the firms grow in size and utilize more capital equipment, the hand-made, individually-styled type of goods tends to give way to the machine-made, uniform product. Although these products are likely to retain some of the European design features, they may be less individual and come to resemble more closely the goods made in the United States. Some of the American market demand for these products should decline as a result of these changes and they will come to compete more directly with American-made articles.

Changes in competition. Increasing size, greater specialization and smaller number of firms are certain to bring about changes in the nature and extent of competition prevailing on the Common Market. It does not appear likely that the smaller number of surviving concerns will result in much lessened competition, at least at first. Competition will be less atomized but may well be equally or more severe. If the movement toward combination continues, the nature of competition may change in the future. The Community nations could move closer to systems of imperfect or monopolistic competition. The extent to which industrial combination and concentration can continue without running afoul of the Community's anti-trust policies and regulations, as well as those of the members, is problematical (see chapter 9).

Costs and innovation. During the first six years of the life on the Community, the fruits of increased productivity have gone principally to labor in the form of higher wages and benefits. The continuation of this tendency will depend upon a number of factors. If management is content to pass wage increases on to the consumer, the Common Market may fail to meet one of its objectives: substantially increased standards of living for the inhabitants. During the early years of the Community, wage raises often were passed forward in the form of higher prices and resulted in a cost-push type of inflation.

Although there have been many instances of inflation in the United States, the drive of labor unions for increased wages, especially since the passage of the Wagner or National Labor Relations Act of 1935, has sometimes served, in the opinion of some businessmen, to increase the efficiency of American industry. In these cases increased wages have been followed by industrial economies which have permitted enterprises to absorb the increased cost without proportionately raising prices.

The extent to which this American experience will be emulated by the industries of the EEC is difficult to forecast. Much will depend upon the nature of competition which will come to prevail in the area. One way of promoting increased competition in the Common Market would be for the institution to reduce its external tariffs and permit the entry of competitive goods in greater quantities.

The EEC nations have suffered from markets constricted both in area and depth. When combined with stable prices, higher earnings of labor, together with increased farm income resulting from agricultural programs, could conceivably serve to create more important markets and result in a wider distribution of purchasing power.

Although the industries of the Six do not, at the present time, spend as much money on research and development as their American counterparts, they are lacking neither in technical ability nor imagination. Innovation is likely to be stimulated by the EEC integration process, and it would not be surprising for American importers to find attractive products in the future which offer good sales possibilities on the United States markets.

The free movement of labor, capital and the right of establishment. The increased factor mobility, including enterprise, in the EEC may well promote industrial efficiency. Capital is far more mobile than labor, and the increased facilities for its movement which the Treaty provides should stimulate its migration among the industries of the Six. Differences in risk, lack of information and the fear of strange and unfamiliar surroundings have served in the past to impede its movement. In addition, the capital markets of the Common Market are not as well organized as those of the United States, and European interest rates are generally higher.

Common Market capital can be presumed to take advantage of the provisions of the Treaty to move from country to country. It will doubtless seek its most productive outlets, thereby bringing about an increase in its marginal efficiency and creating a tendency toward the equalization of the varying Market interest rates.

The freedom of establishment provided by the Treaty of Rome has a broader significance than that usually associated with this term. It refers to the right of business firms, service organizations as well as certain trades and professions to move freely from country to country, to engage in operations any place in the area with a minimum of formalities and restraint. Common Market firms will be able to enjoy the advantages of location — such as proximity to natural resources, supplies, labor, markets and transportation facilities. These advantages should increase the efficiency of the firms of the area, make for lower costs and increase competition as a first result.

The American importer will be faced by changed sources of supply in the Community. Suppliers may move from one member to another. The character and the available amounts of the products which he is able to purchase may also change due to shifts in labor and capital.

Changes in supply elasticities. The concept of supply elasticity refers to the response of amounts of goods offered for sale to changes in price. If the amounts supplied rise or fall substantially as prices offered increase or decrease, supply is said to be elastic; if the amounts offered do not respond substantially to changes in price, supply is inelastic. The element of time is important in analyzing supply elasticities. In connection with the availability of goods for import from the Six, at least two periods can be distinguished: (1) a short-run period with already produced supplies ready for the market; and (2) a longer-run period where goods must be produced and where differing conditions of cost come into play (see chapter 1).

In the short-run it is doubtful that the EEC will produce many important changes in the supply elasticities of the goods which American importers purchase there. In the longer-run, industrial economic integration is probably destined to create changes in cost patterns. Industries of the decreasing cost type are likely to find themselves operating under more sharply declining cost curves; those having constant costs may turn to mass production methods and move to the decreasing cost type; some agricultural and mining enterprises which work under conditions of increasing costs may find that increased output is only available at higher levels of cost.

In the long-run, the supply is likely to prove more elastic

for the decreasing cost type industries and more inelastic for those increasing costs. American importers may find supplies of many products available on the markets of the Six highly responsive to changes in price. Such a situation is likely to promote competition among the industries of the EEC which will redound to the advantage of American importers.[1]

The gross national product of the Six. According to a recent report prepared for the EEC Commission, the gross national product of the Six is expected to increase, in terms of 1960 prices, by 27 per cent during the period 1960-65, 25 per cent during 1965-70 and 59.1 per cent for the years 1960-1970. The rate of increase is 4.75 per cent a year for the period 1960-1970.[2]

The increasing productivity of Common Market members is further illustrated by the figures in Table 3.1 presenting general indexes of production of the EEC countries and the United States. The rate of growth in productivity of the Six has outstripped that of the United States, especially since 1958, the year after the Treaty of Rome went into effect. The productivity of the member nations has increased by 40 per cent since that year while that of the United States grew by about 33 per cent.

As outlets for increased production the internal EEC market will prove attractive to the industries of the Six, because the tariff on trade among the members and associates is being reduced and will eventually be eliminated on many products made in the area, while the import tariffs applicable to third countries will remain except as reduced by GATT negotiations. These considerations could well reinforce the traditional European preference for continental and former colonial markets to the difficult and expensive, albeit profitable, American market. United States importers may find themselves relegated to a secondary position in the marketing plans of the EEC industries.

Table 3.2, presenting indexes of EEC exports to selected destinations, shows the tendency for the exports of the EEC members to one another and to the associated overseas countries and territories to grow at a greater rate than those to the United States. The inter-EEC trade increased from 67 per cent in 1958

TABLE 3.1

GENERAL INDEXES OF INDUSTRIAL PRODUCTION: EEC AND THE UNITED STATES, 1954-1963

(1958 = 100)

	EEC	United States
1954	75	92
1955	85	105
1956	92	108
1957	97	109
1958	100	100
1959	108	114
1960	121	118
1961	129	118
1962	137	128
1963(a)	140	133

(a) 1963: 2nd quarter

Source: EEC, *General Statistical Bulletin*, No. 6, 1963, p. 21.

to 132 per cent in 1962, while the exports of these countries to the United States amounted to 74 and 109 per cent respectively for these years. Compared with other third countries, however, the United States appeared to be holding its own as far as imports from the Six are concerned.

Prices of goods imported from the EEC. The EEC demand for goods has been increasing steadily since the formation of this institution, as suggested by the figures in Table 2.1, page 47, showing the movement of national income (1957-1961) of member countries. Production costs have also risen bringing about a slight inflation. Although there has been considerable merging of firms, greater plant specialization and increasing size of business entities, competition has grown and monopolistic and imperfectly competitive pricing policies have not yet shown much development.

TABLE 3.2

INDEXES OF EEC EXPORTS TO SELECTED DESTINATIONS,
1958-1962
(1960 = 100)

Destination	1958	1959	1960	1961	1962
World	77	85	100	109	115
Inter-EEC	67	80	100	116	132
Overseas Departments	90	87	100	84	58(a)
Associated Overseas Countries and Territories	116	97	100	112	118
All Third Countries	81	88	100	106	109
United States	74	105	100	99	109

(a) The decline in exports to the Overseas Deparmtents is due largely to the fact that France's large Overseas Department, Algeria, gained independence in 1962.

Source: EEC, *Foreign Trade Statistics*, 1962, p. 31.

As a *net* result, prices have risen in the Common Market countries. Table 11.3 shows the movement of the prices of consumer's goods in the EEC countries and the United States, 1954-1963, and Table 11.4 that of general wholesale prices, 1960-1963 (see chapter 11). The prices of consumer's goods rose substantially and the movement was strong in France and Italy. The changes in the average values of EEC and United States exports and imports, 1960-1963, are presented in Table 3.3. They indicate that the prices of the exports of both the EEC and the United States recently rose more rapidly than those of imports during these years, with the prices of United States exports increasing to a greater extent than those of the EEC. A list of the principal imports figuring in United States trade with the Common Market is given in Appendix A.

For the immediate future, and perhaps until 1965, it appears likely that the prices of goods available for import into the United States will continue to rise, but at a somewhat slower rate than in the past. In the longer-run, the pricing policies likely to be employed will be those of monopolistic competition.

TABLE 3.3

INDEXES OF THE AVERAGE VALUE OF EXPORTS AND IMPORTS, EEC AND THE UNITED STATES, 1960-1963

	1960	1961	1962	1963(a)
Exports: EEC	98	99	100	101
Exports: U.S.	102	105	n.a.	n.a.
Imports: EEC	96	95	95	n.a.
Imports: U.S.	100	99	97	n.a.

(a) February 1963.
n.a. Not available.

Source: EEC, *General Statistical Bulletin*, No. 6, 1963, p. 71.

These policies do not necessarily mean higher prices; they tend to make for stable prices.

These forecasts are based on a number of assumptions: that economic integration will proceed as planned; that there will be but little inflation and that manufacturers will absorb rising labor costs by recourse to greater efficiency rather than to increases in price. In addition, they imply certain changes in the pricing policies of the Community industrialists. European manufacturers, when faced by a recession and a decline in sales, have usually reduced their prices in an effort to rid themselves of excessively high inventories. American manufacturers preferred to maintain their prices and to reduce the output of their factories to meet a similar situation.

The United States Tariff and the Common Market

Because membership in the EEC is reserved for European countries, the United States cannot join the institution to avoid its discriminatory tariff structure. Even if membership were possible, it is doubtful that either the legislative or the executive branches of the United States government would sanction participation, with its accompanying surrender of so many attributes of sovereignty. Some other means of avoiding the disadvantages of tariff discrimination had to be found. The solution proposed lies in the extension and broadening of the

Reciprocal Trade Agreements Acts, the first of which became law in 1934. The new version of these Acts, the Trade Expansion Act of 1962, went into effect on July 1, 1962.

Table 3.4 shows the movement of United States average duty rates, 1926-1960. The duties, 1926-1930, reflect the high rates of the Fordney-McCumber Tariff of 1922, while the substantial increase in rates during 1931-1935 shows the impact of the Hawley-Smoot Tariff of 1930, the highest in the history of this country. The results of the Reciprocal Trade Agreement Acts are shown in the decreasing duty rates which characterized the period 1936-1957. In the years following 1957, the duties showed a slight tendency to rise, largely because of

TABLE 3.4

UNITED STATES AVERAGE RATES OF DUTY ON DUTIABLE
IMPORTS, 1926-1960
(In per cent of total duty applicable to dutiable imports)

1926-1930	40.1
1931-1935	50.1
1936-1940	37.9
1941-1945	32.1
1946	25.6
1947	19.3
1948	13.9
1949	13.5
1950	13.1
1951	12.3
1952	12.7
1953	12.0
1954	11.6
1955	11.9
1956	11.3
1957	10.8
1958	11.2
1959	11.5
1960	12.2

Source: U. S. Department of Commerce, *World Trade Information Service*, Part 3, No. 61-43, 1961.

escape clause actions. The tariff is, of course, but one aspect of restrictive foreign trade policies; freer multilateral trade would require the elimination or reduction of other barriers as well.

To implement American policy of freer multilateral trade, an expanded and broadened type of Reciprocal Trade Agreement Act was required. The limitations of the peril point and escape clause features of these Acts, together with product-by-product tariff negotiation procedures, rendered further *substantial* reductions in the United States tariff virtually impossible.

Principal features of the Trade Expansion Act of 1962. As a general proposition, the President, under the Trade Expansion Act of 1962, is empowered to reduce, on a reciprocal basis, some existing tariffs by 50 per cent. It is anticipated that most negotiations will take place on this basis in the 1964 GATT sessions. In negotiations with the EEC, the President may reduce tariffs to zero on products for which the external trade of the United States and the EEC accounts for 80 per cent or more of world exports as measured in a representative period. Duty reductions or eliminations may be made on certain agricultural products which do not meet this 80 per cent dominant supplier rule if the President finds that such action will expand or maintain the exports of these products. In addition, the President is authorized to negotiate agreements on broad categories of goods instead of product-by-product, as was the case in previous Trade Agreements.

Provided that the EEC takes similar action, the President is authorized to eliminate or reduce tariffs on tropical agricultural or forestry products if the commodity is not produced in significant quantities in the United States. The President can also eliminate tariffs on products which are presently dutiable at 5 per cent or less.

The Act sets up certain procedural steps which the President is required to take in connection with reciprocal trade negotiations. He is obliged to furnish the Tariff Commission with a list of products on which he proposes to negotiate, and the Tariff Commission must inform him of the economic effects of the proposed reductions.

The President is further required to withhold from trade agreement negotiations all products subject to an escape clause or national security action taken under this or prior Trade Agreement Acts. He must give public notice of his intention to enter into tariff negotiations and give interested parties an opportunity to present their views on the question. As in prior Trade Agreement Acts, the U.S.S.R. and nations dominated by communism cannot be accorded any concessions.

The national security provisions of previous Acts are repeated in the Trade Expansion Act of 1962. Under these clauses, the President is required to restrict imports when he finds that a product is being imported in such quantities that it threatens national security. The escape clause provisions of preceding Acts are substantially modified in the new legislation. Past escape clause actions will continue, but those which went into effect more than three years prior to July 1, 1962, terminated on June 30, 1963 unless extended by the President. The Act continues the most-favored-nation principle embodied in earlier Acts, and the President is authorized to suspend concessions granted to any nation which discriminates against United States foreign trade.

Generally, tariff reductions take effect in five equal installments, but provision is made for unequal installments if the total of all installments at any one time does not exceed that which would have occurred under the five equal installments principle. This principle does not apply to tariff reductions of 25 per cent or less, to reductions on tropical products or to the elimination of duties of less than 5 per cent.

In the post-World War II trade agreements, and prior to the Trade Expansion Act of 1962, the national approach to the problem of increased imports was that of avoidance of injury to American industry. This was accomplished by the use of the peril point and escape clause features of the Acts. Under the peril point amendment, the President was obliged to submit to the Tariff Commission a list of the imports on which he desired to grant tariff concessions. If the President wished to reduce tariffs below the peril points recommended by the Commission, he was obliged to transmit his reasons for doing so to Congress.

The escape clause amendment required the Tariff Commission, whenever it found that increased imports were injuring, or held the possibility of injuring, United States industry, to report that fact to the President with its recommendations concerning modifications of the concessions required to eliminate the injury.

The avoidance of injury approach has been abandoned in the Trade Expansion Act of 1962 in favor of the absorption of increased imports principle. Under this principle, recognition is given to the fact that some injury might be occasioned domestic producers as a result of tariff reductions made in the *national interest,* but that the imports should not be impeded; injury to domestic industry should be parried by government assurance measures.[3] Both the peril point and escape clause provisions of previous Acts have been considerably softened in the new Act. The Tariff Commission no longer advises the President concerning specific minimum rates (peril points) but gives him its opinion concerning the domestic repercussions of proposed concessions. Escape clause actions will only be taken after the Commission has determined that widespread injury will occur throughout the industry, that the industry concerned has made a reasonable attempt to meet the situation and that adjustment assistance from the federal government does not provide adequate relief.

To alleviate injury resulting from tariff concessions, adjustment assistance to industry is provided in the form of loans, technical assistance and tax relief. This aid is temporary in nature and is designed to promote *adjustment* to increased import competition rather than to *compensate* for injury. Benefits are also extended to injured workers in the form of unemployment compensation, provisions for retraining for other types of employment and relocation allowances to aid in moving to areas where employment is available.

Price and revenue effects of tariff reductions on importers. An example will illustrate the potential benefits which tariff reductions hold for importers. Assume that an American importer purchases watches from a Swiss manufacturer and that their cost is $10.00 each laid down in New York. The specific duties on these watches, before the first tariff negotiations under the Trade Expansion Act of 1962, are assumed to amount to $5.00 per watch. The total cost of the watches, including the tariff, is $15.00 each. If the importer adds a 20 per cent mark-up, the watches will be priced wholesale at $18.00 each.

Now assume that as a result of tariff negotiations, the duty on these watches is reduced by 50 per cent and now amounts to $2.50 per watch, bringing their total cost, including duty, to $12.50. Adding a 20 per cent mark-up, the wholesale price to the retail trade will be $15.00. These figures are presented in Table 3.5.

TABLE 3.5

EFFECT OF A 50 PER CENT TARIFF REDUCTION ON WHOLESALE PRICES OF IMPORTED WATCHES

Original Tariff 50%		Reduced Tariff 25%
$10.00	Laid Down Cost of Watch	$10.00
5.00	Tariff Duty	2.50
15.00	Total Cost	12.50
3.00	20% Mark-Up	2.50
18.00	Wholesale Price	15.00

The demand for these imported watches is assumed to be price elastic, i.e., the total revenue derived from sales increases as the price is lowered. Table 3.6 gives data showing the total number of watches sold at different prices, the total revenue which the importer derives from sales, and the gross profit earned both under the original tariff of $5.00 per watch and under the reduced duty of $2.50 each.

At a price of $18.00 (original duty of $5.00 each), the importer sells 75,000 watches to the retail jewelry trade. He realizes a sales revenue of $1,350,000 and a gross profit of $225,000 from the transactions. Under the price of $15.00 (reduced duty of $2.50 per watch), the importer sells 160,000 watches for a total revenue of $2,400,000 and a gross profit of

$400,000. The reduction in price from $18.00 to $15.00 enabled the importer to realize sales of an additional 85,000 units, an increased revenue from sales of $1,050,000 and an additional gross profit of $175,000.

Now assume that the demand for the watches is price inelastic with the total revenue from sales declining under lowered prices as indicated on Table 3.7.

TABLE 3.6

TOTAL SALES, REVENUE FROM SALES AND GROSS PROFIT FOR WATCH IMPORTS UNDER ORIGINAL AND REDUCED TARIFF
(Price Elastic Demand)

Wholesale Price (each)	Total No. Watches Sold (thousands)	Revenue from Sales (thousands)	Original Tariff Gross Profit @ $3.00 Mark-Up (thousands)	Reduced Tariff Gross Profit @ $2.50 Mark-Up (thousands)
$20	50	$1000	$150	$125
19	60	1140	180	150
18	75	1350	225	175
17	100	1700	300	250
16	130	2080	390	325
15	160	2400	480	400
14	200	2800	600	500

TABLE 3.7

TOTAL SALES, REVENUE FROM SALES AND GROSS PROFIT FOR WATCH IMPORTS UNDER ORIGINAL AND REDUCED TARIFF
(Price Inelastic Demand)

Wholesale Price (each)	Total No. Watches Sold (thousands)	Revenue from Sales (thousands)	Original Tariff Gross Profit @ $3.00 Mark-Up (thousands)	Reduced Tariff Gross Profit @ $2.50 Mark-Up (thousands)
$20	50.0	$1000.0	$150.0	$125.00
19	52.0	988.0	156.0	130.00
18	52.5	945.0	157.5	131.25
17	52.6	894.2	157.8	131.50
16	52.7	843.2	158.1	131.75
15	52.8	792.0	158.4	132.00
14	53.0	743.0	159.0	132.50

Under these conditions and before the tariff reduction, the watch importer will have sold 52,500 watches at $18.00 each for a total revenue of $945,000 and a gross profit of $154,500. With the reduced tariff of $2.50 per watch, he will have sold 52,800 units at $15.00 each for a total revenue of $792,000 and a gross profit of $132,000. Under price inelastic demand, the importer's gross profit will have been smaller than with elastic demand.

However, it is doubtful that a sophisticated importer, aware of his sales potentials at different prices, would have followed the pricing policy indicated in the previous paragraph. *If market conditions and competition permitted,* he would doubtless have maintained his original price of $18.00 per watch and pocketed the tariff reduction of $2.50 per unit for a profit on each watch sold of $5.00 ($2.50 mark-up plus $2.50 reduced tariff). Under these circumstances, with sales of 52,500 units, his gross profit would have amounted to $262,500.

These examples present highly simplified illustrations of a few of the many possible effects of tariff reductions under the Trade Expansion Act of 1962 on American importers. They take cognizance neither of the reactions of domestic American manufacturers of competing or substitute products nor of the impact of similar or substitute products from other sources. The examples presented deal exclusively with *gross profits;* many other factors must be taken into account in the determination of *net profits.* The principles which they embody, or similar ones, however, can be applied to other and differing types of transactions.

Impact of Imports from the Common Market on United States Domestic Industry

The Common Market has already proved of value to the American importer and consumer. This conclusion is reinforced by the fact that the United States has been obtaining a substantial and increasing fraction of its total imports from EEC country sources as Table 3.8 shows. In 1957, this country received 11.9 per cent of its total imports from these sources. By 1960, the percentage had increased to 15.4.

If the Common Market will prove a boon to United States

importers, the same cannot be said of its impact on American domestic industry, in the short-run at least. The adverse affects of its competition arise directly from the growing strength of its industries and indirectly from the impetus which the EEC will give to substantial future reductions in the United States tariff.

Degree of protection afforded by the tariff. Two American studies published within the past decade, the one by Beatrice N. Vaccara and the other by Howard S. Piquet, deal with the problem of the effectiveness of the tariff as a protective device. As far as it is known, no comparable studies have been made of these effects in other countries.[4]

The evidence adduced by Beatrice Vaccara's study leads to the inference that the ratio of imports to output is higher for firms of declining than for firms of increasing importance. The rate of industrial growth is apparently but little related to the degree of tariff protection. The decline in the output of certain industries is more a function of decreasing demand than of increasing competitive imports. In addition, her study indicates that the highly protected industries are more labor-

TABLE 3.8

UNITED STATES MERCHANDISE TRADE WITH THE
EEC NATIONS, SELECTED YEARS, 1926-1960
(Millions of dollars)

	Total Imports	EEC Per Cent of U.S. Total Imports
1926-30 Average	617	15.3
1936-40 Average	244	9.8
1946-50 Average	333	5.0
1957	1,547	11.9
1958	1,682	13.1
1959	2,402	15.8
1960	2,263	15.4

Source: U. S. Department of Commerce. *Statistical Reports: Trade of the United States with the European Economic Community and the United Kingdom,* 1956-1960. WTIS, Part 3, No. 62-8, p. 2.

intensive than those which enjoy less tariff protection and that they tend to pay lower wages.

Using 1951 data, Howard Piquet estimates that, *if all tariff duties were suspended,* imports would have increased between 8 per cent as a minimum and 17 per cent as a maximum. The minimum increase in imports would have amounted to $845 million and the maximum $1,825 million in 1951.[5] There is considerable variation in Piquet's findings among the imports of different categories of goods. The greatest increase in imports, from 37 to 74 per cent, would have occurred in textile fibers and manufactures; followed by machinery and vehicles, 33 to 67 per cent; and inedible animal products, 20 to 42 per cent. The smallest increase in imports would have been found in wood and paper products, 4 to 7 per cent.[6]

Piquet's study further indicates that more than 40 per cent of the dutiable commodities would not be greatly affected by this tariff elimination.[7] He also notes that the products most injured by total tariff suspension would be: a group, including such items as coarse linen toweling, hemmed linen handkerchiefs, cotton hosiery, woolens and worsteds, apparel wool and linoleum; the machinery and vehicle group including knitting machines, bicycles, and sewing machines; the miscellaneous group which includes clocks, optical instruments, toys and dolls. Those commodity groups which would show the smallest increase in imports as a result of tariff elimination include wood and paper products, vegetable food products, beverages, metals and metal manufactures.[8]

Piquet points out that the increase in the proportion of the total market supplied by imports would be relatively small under tariff elimination. The area of maximum import competition would be even smaller, and the list of domestic products completely displaced by imports would be almost infinitesimal. He further states that many of the products involved in the tariff suspension are either not produced in the United States at all or those for which imports would probably not be increased appreciably. About 63 per cent of the imports subject to duty which he analyzed are not highly competitive with domestic production. A host of considerations is involved in the determination of injury to United States manufacturers arising from imports, and the tariff is but one factor in a complex situation.[9]

Although the findings of Beatrice Vaccara and Howard Piquet confirm the opinion that the United States tariff is protective, they point to the inference that it is less protective than is often assumed. They lead to the conclusion that the United States tariff could be substantially reduced or even eliminated without any great increase in imports or over-all injury to American enterprise. The effects on American industry of tariff reductions under the Trade Expansion Act of 1962 are thus likely to be small.[10]

The competition which will be felt as a result of the economic integration of the industries of the EEC, together with the leverage which this competition may exert when combined with tariff reductions, is not likely to make itself seriously manifest for a number of years.

Counter-measures against imports from the EEC. The well-known and highly successful head of an American automobile manufacturing company is reported to have stated that he preferred to meet competition on the market place rather than in the legislative halls. In other words, he would rather meet competitive threats by his own initiative than by tariff protection. American businessmen may find the adoption of this philosophy useful in meeting the competitive threat of EEC industry.

The steps which American business can take against additional imports from the EEC should be familiar to many. They are similar to those needed to meet the continuing impact of technological change. As Table 3.4 indicates, the rates of duty on dutiable products have been reduced from an average of 37.9 per cent for the period 1936-1940, to 12.2 per cent in 1960. In other words, the duties today are about one-third of what they were when this Act was first passed. American business has been successful in competing with the additional imports resulting from these tariff reductions without much help from its government.

A principal effect of duty reduction is to lower the price of imported goods laid down in the United States and cleared through customs. American industrialists have long had to face similar situations when competing domestic concerns reduced their price. The problem of price competition from foreign concerns is complicated in the United States by the constant pressure of rising costs often due to increased wages and fringe benefits. However, the American industrialist is not alone here; his European competitors are also subject to increasing costs. In general, given the relatively low wages prevailing in the Community and the growing interest of some European labor leaders in business unionism, it appears that the United States manufacturer will have the advantage over his Common Market competitor as far as the future cost-push type of inflation is concerned.

The classic method of meeting price competition, domestic or foreign, is to reduce prices by cutting costs. American industrialists have usually sought lower costs by employing larger amounts and more efficient types of capital, and the answer of many American producers to EEC competition will doubtless take this form.

In addition to cost-cutting methods, reduction of the expenses of distribution offers another possibility to the industrialist harassed by low-cost foreign merchandise. Although improved distribution techniques have received considerable attention in recent years, they have lagged behind factory economies and offer a fruitful field to exploit in meeting foreign price competition.

Marketing and sales promotion are other activities in which Americans have long excelled and which can be employed to advantage to counter the sale of lower-priced foreign goods. The redesigning of products, including both greater adaptability to end-use and increased sales appeal, also presents opportunities to check the influx of imports.

If it is not possible to meet foreign price competition on the domestic markets successfully, American manufacturers can turn to overseas markets as yet unexploited, or unsuccessfully exploited, by his foreign competitors. It appears likely that the manufacturers of the Six will be heavily occupied in meeting the demands of the Common Market itself, as well as those of the associated overseas countries and territories, before they are able to supply fully the demands of markets in other areas. The conquest of these third area markets could compensate, in part, for the loss of sales on the domestic market.

Manufacturers who make a variety of related products can abandon the production of those goods which face the strongest competition from the Six and concentrate on the production of the remaining items. If competition is strong for the entire line of products, an industrialist might abandon the line and take up the manufacture of products which use similar machinery, equipment and labor skills, but where the foreign competition is less severe.

Innovation in the form of discovery, development and design of new products which require similar types of machinery and labor skills has often been employed by progressive industries to meet domestic competition. These devices may also be employed against foreign competition.

Since many foreign products are made by the smaller and less efficient EEC manufacturers, American industry as a whole has little to fear from them. As a general proposition, the American industries which are the most vulnerable are those which employ relatively large proportions of hand labor. By American standards, hand labor is not very productive, but it must be paid high wages because of the competition of factories which employ larger amounts of labor-saving machinery and in which the wage rates are high because the productivity of labor is greater. Firms using much hand labor have more to gain by taking steps to improve their efficiency than by relying on tariffs for protection.

Already the most highly competitive in the world, the United States market appears destined to become more so by reason of EEC competition and reduced tariffs. The challenge to American enterprises is obvious. Less obvious is the fact that thousands of American industrialists manage not only to make good livings in spite of market difficulties, but to enjoy the experience of solving thorny problems successfully. The challenge increases as Common Market industries move into "high gear" but the profits and rewards will be even greater.

NOTES

[1] For a fuller development of the concept of supply elasticities, especially with reference to international transactions, see: Max J. Wasserman, Charles W. Hultman, and Laszlo Zsoldos. *International Finance*. New York: Simmons-Boardman Publishing Corp., 1963, pp. 222-227.

[2] Cf. Communanté Economique Européenne—Commission, *Les Perspectives de Développement Economique dans la CEE de 1960-à-1970* (the Uri Report). Brussels: Services des Publications des Communantés Européennes, 1962, pp. 48-63.

[3] Howard S. Piquet. *Aid, Trade and the Tariff*. New York: Thomas Y. Crowell Co., 1953, p. 50-59.

[4] Cf. Beatrice N. Vaccara. *Employment and Output in Protected Manufacturing Industries*. Washington: The Brookings Institution, 1960; Piquet, *op. cit.* For an appraisal of the effects of tariff reduction on employment, see: Walter S. Salant and Beatrice N. Vaccara. *Import Liberalization and Employment: The Effects of Unilateral Reductions in United States Import Barriers*. Washington: Brookings Institution, 1961.

[5] It should be noted that the tariff was higher in 1951 than it is today, and it is possible that the increase in imports due to tariff suspension would be relatively smaller today.

[6] For further details concerning other groups of products see Howard S. Piquet, *op. cit.*, pp. 27-49, especially Table 4, p. 37 and Chart III, pp. 38-41. In the commodity digests, pp. 79-346, Piquet shows the effects of tariff suspension for a long list of products.

[7] See Piquet, *op cit.*, pp. 36-37.

[8] *Ibid.*, pp. 36-37.

[9] *Ibid.*, pp. 35-37.

[10] This conclusion is supported by the findings of Walter S. Salant and Beatrice N. Vaccara. "Primary Effects on Employment of Shifts in Demand from Domestic to Foreign Products." *Review of Economics and Statistics*. Vol. 40, No. 1 (February 1958), pp. 91-103. Salant and Vaccara estimate that an increase in United States imports of $1 million would have, as its primary effect on employment, a mean loss of 117 jobs and a median loss of 115 for the 72 industries which they studied. Cf. also *The Relationship Between Imports and Employment*. U.S. Department of Labor, Bureau of Labor Statistics. Washington, D.C.: U.S. GPO, 1962; "Employment in Relation to U.S. Imports, 1960" (mimeographed). U.S. Department of Labor, Bureau of Labor Statistics. Washington, D.C.: U.S. GPO, n.d.

4

Exporting to the Common Market

GENERAL CONSIDERATIONS — THE COMPETITIVENESS OF
AMERICAN INDUSTRY — FEATURES OF THE COMMON MARKET
CXT — THE IMPACT OF THE CXT ON AMERICAN EXPORTS

One of the challenges which the European Economic Community poses for the American export trade stems from the tariff structure of the organization. With the exception of certain specified groups of products, the internal tariff, or that which prevails among the members themselves, will be reduced to zero in three stages by not later than 1972. The EEC will erect a new external tariff, common to, and employed by, all the members during the same three stages. This common external tariff (CXT) will consist of the simple, unweighted arithmetic average of the tariffs of the six members as they stood on January 1, 1957.

Chart IV.1 illustrates the movement of this tariff structure during the three periods. The decline in the internal tariff will be generally larger for Italy and France than for Germany and the Benelux countries. The CXT will represent a rise for most goods in the cases of Germany and the Benelux nations and a decline for those of Italy and France over their pre-CXT duties.

American business will be faced by Common Market competitors who will be able to sell on their internal market under the favorable circumstances of no tariff for many products. This privilege will also be enjoyed in certain cases, by the industries, including agriculture, of the associated overseas countries and territories. Although these overseas associates may maintain

75

certain tariffs against imports from the Six, the industry of the Common Market will enjoy a tariff structure, within the territories of these associates, more favorable than that accorded third countries.

CHART IV.1

CHANGES IN THE COMMON MARKET INTERNAL AND EXTERNAL TARIFFS

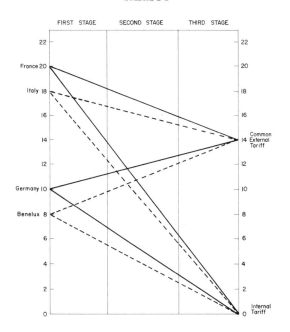

The Common Market external tariff (CXT) will move to the simple arithmetic average of the tariffs of the members in three stages. The internal tariff applicable to the members moves to zero, with the exception of certain specified groups of commodities, during the same three stages. Assume that the tariff on a given commodity on January 1, 1957 was 20 per cent in France, 18 in Italy, 10 in Germany and 8 in the Benelux countries. The CXT on it is established at 14 per cent. By the end of the third period, France will have to reduce its external tariff from 20 to 14 per cent and Italy from 18 to 14. Germany will have to raise its external tariff from 10 to 14 per cent and Benelux from 8 to 14. The internal tariff by the end of the third stage will be zero for all members. To simplify the illustration, it was assumed that the common external tariff on this commodity was not changed by GATT negotiations.

The Common Market external tariff (CXT) will move to the simple arithmetic average of the tariffs of the members in three stages. The first stage adjustments were made in 1960. The second stage was concluded in 1963, and the third will terminate not later than 1972 and perhaps as early as 1969. The internal tariff applicable to the members moves to zero, with the exception of certain specified groups of commodities, during the same three stages. Assume that the tariff on a given commodity on January 1, 1957 was 20 per cent in France, 18 in Italy, 10 in Germany and 8 in the Benelux countries. The CXT on it is established at 14 per cent. By the end of the third period, France will have to reduce its external tariff from 20 to 14 per cent and Italy from 18 to 14. Germany will have to raise its external tariff from 10 to 14 per cent and Benelux from 8 to 14. The internal tariff by the end of the third stage will be zero for all the members. To simplify the illustration, it is assumed that the common external tariff on this commodity was not changed by GATT negotiations.

By the end of the first stage, the Community's internal tariff had been reduced by 50 per cent of the basic duties for industrial products. On July 1, 1963, these duties were reduced by an additional 10 per cent, leaving a 40 per cent reduction to be attained by the end of the third stage.

At the same time, imports into the Common Market customs territory from third countries such as the United States will be subject to the applicable duties of the CXT. This tariff structure discriminates in favor of the members and associates against third countries. In addition to the tariff discrimination, the members of the EEC may continue to maintain, for a time at least, quantitative restrictions against specified imports from abroad as well as a type of "invisible tariff" consisting of taxes, laws and administrative procedures which operate to discourage imports from third countries.

Attention has already been drawn to the possibility that this tariff structure may operate to create trade diversion, whereby imports into the Common Market will be shifted from low-cost industries in countries outside the institution to those which operate at higher costs inside it. It may also result in some trade creation by moving imports from higher cost industries outside its boundaries to lower cost industries within them.

General Considerations

The CXT will be, in principle, neither higher nor lower *on the average* than were the tariffs of the member nations before the inauguration of the EEC. Some industries, however, will enjoy more protection than they had before; others will have less. This is a matter of interest to businessmen who, if they have been exporting to France and Italy, may find the duties lowered; if they have been exporting to Germany and the Benelux countries, they may find them raised. Once the CXT tariff has been paid on imported goods, they can then move to any of the countries of the Six without further duties.

The tariff as a protective device. The tariff is but one of a number of devices which may be employed to protect domestic industry. Import and exchange controls, quantitative restrictions on imports, domestic tax systems, tied loans and grants, customs administration, monetary areas, colonial administrations, among others, are either protective in essence or have strong protectionist characteristics. Many of these devices protect *absolutely;* the tariff only protects *relatively* and its trade-restricting effects frequently can be parried by alert businessmen.

The degree of protection afforded by a tariff cannot always be inferred from its level. To the extent that imports survive protection, the tariff produces revenue rather than protection. Domestic industry may be so import-competitive that the tariff is surplus rather than protective.

Once established, the tariff remains fixed until altered. During the time that it is in effect, dynamic economic societies change and a once-protective tariff may become less or more so under the impact of these changes. Many industries manufacture more than one type of product. If a tariff is levied upon one, or upon a group of products, the domestic industry may concentrate its output on the protected items and reduce or abandon the production of those which are not. Should the

CXT of the Common Market display such "loopholes," adversely affected American industries could respond by exporting products which do not enjoy protection. In such cases, *individual products* may be protected, while the *industry as a whole* is not.

Price is but one factor among many which determines the ability of a domestic industry to compete with imported goods. Style, quality, adaptability to end-use or consumer tastes, availability of supply, service facilities including the ready availability of replacement parts, credit terms, merchandising and promotional methods, durability, product prestige, the manufacturer's reputation, the inclination to use traditional sources of supply, among others, determine a product's competitive potential. The mere fact that an import sells at a lower price than a comparable domestic product does not necessarily mean that the domestic producer will be outsold by the imported item.

The price effects of some protective tariffs may be offset or increased through changes in the terms of trade. If the international price of a commodity moves down, the protection afforded by an ad valorem tariff remains proportional to the price movement while that of a specific duty increases; if the international price rises, an ad valorem duty provides proportionally the same, and a specific duty less, protection.

The effects of a tariff depend in part upon the price elasticity of the demand for the protected good and the cost conditions (constant, decreasing or increasing) underlying its production. In the case of products for which the price is highly elastic, the imposition of a tariff duty may serve to restrain the quantity imported to a greater extent than the new price (laid down cost plus tariff) might seem to warrant. The reduction or the elimination of a tariff duty may raise the quantity imported by a larger amount than the tariff change would apparently indicate. In the case of goods for which the demand is price inelastic, an increase (or decrease) in the price of imports resulting from shifts in the rate of duty will not greatly alter the amount of imports.

If a firm's exports to the *protected country* constitute a substantial fraction of its total output, the cost effects of a new, increased, reduced or eliminated tariff will depend in part upon the nature of its cost curve. If its cost curve is of the constant type, the change in sales to the export market resulting from tariff shifts will probably not make a great deal of difference in the per-unit costs of the exporting firm. If the curve is of the decreasing type, a decline in sales due to higher duties may bring about an increase in its per unit costs and an increase in sales from reduced or eliminated tariffs, a decline.

For enterprises of the increasing cost type, the lowered sales on the export market due to increased duties may serve to reduce costs of production and increased sales from tariff reduction, increase them. In the case of industries with outputs beyond the point of maximum efficiency, a reduction in output due to lowered exports may serve to reduce the costs of production and increased output arising from greater exports, increase these costs still further.

To have the protective effects which the authors of a tariff project, prices in both the exporting and importing countries must remain stable. If a tariff is levied or increased and the prices in the importing country should rise while those in the exporting country remain stable, some of the protective effects may be lost. Were prices to fall in the exporting country while those in the importing nation remained stable, the protective effects of the tariff will be likewise diminished. Should the prices in the exporting country rise, the protective effect of the tariff will be reinforced, provided prices in the importing nation rise less or remain stable.

The phase of the business cycle will also affect the amount of protection afforded by a tariff. If the importing nation moves into an ascending phase of the cycle, its propensity to purchase goods from abroad will be increased and the protective character of the tariff will decline. On the other hand, should the importing nation move into a declining phase of the cycle the protective effects of the tariff will be increased.

There are many variables which enter into the determination of the protection afforded by a given tariff, and it is often difficult to determine in advance just what they will turn out to be. For this reason the tariff is a hit-or-miss proposition; it may have the desired protective effects or it may not. The common external tariff of the EEC is no exception; it may or may not incorporate the protection which the architects of the Treaty of Rome hoped to attain. The amount of protection is likely to vary substantially over time as well as from product to product.

Miscellaneous objectives of the tariff. Tariffs are applied for a variety of reasons and to attain different objectives. Some nations use them to obtain revenue. Countries experiencing balance of payments problems employ them to assist in attaining equilibrium or surplus. They often form a part of national economic planning programs. Sometimes tariffs are used by nations which desire to direct imports into channels held to be beneficial, and away from those of less direct utility to the economy. The tariff also constitutes a means of retaliation against the restrictive trade policies of other nations and a bargaining weapon in international negotiations.

Developing countries use the tariff to protect their infant industries in an effort to attain a more highly diversified economy. The tariff is often also thought to be of use to nations engaged in long-range programs of military preparedness in that it assists in attaining a higher degree of self-sufficiency. Customs duties may also form a part of programs designed to reduce unemployment, maintain or increase wage levels.[1]

The protectiveness of the CXT. In chapter 3, evidence was presented indicating that the United States tariff was less protective than it is often held to be. Since the United States tariff is about as high as the CXT and does not afford its estimated protection, the question immediately arises: how protective will the CXT prove to be? Since protective tariffs operate in much the same fashion in all advanced industrial countries, it might not be too far amiss to conclude that the CXT will also afford the Common Market less protection than some apparently assume. If this inference proves to be correct, American exporters may be at a relatively small disadvantage vis-à-vis their EEC competitors.

A contrary view is expressed in a study prepared by Walter Salant and a group of associates. These authors find that the United States exports to this area may be reduced by as much as $650 million in 1968. In addition, they estimate the loss of United States exports to third countries through tariff preferences granted the associated overseas countries and territories at $100 million.[2]

The Salant Study estimates United States merchandise exports to Western Europe at $8.85 billion in 1968 (projected at 1968 real incomes and 1961 relative prices).[3] Taking five categories of manufactures producing 61 different products, it shows that the Common Market CXT will be raised over the pre-EEC tariffs in the case of 46 of these products, lowered for 10 and will remain the same for 5.[4]

Since many of the low cost producers are found in Germany, the inter-EEC trade (carried out ultimately under a zero tariff) will pass from the high cost producers, presumably in France and Italy, to Germany. Under the higher protection of the CXT, Germany, which was able to compete under its relatively low pre-EEC external tariff, will find itself over-protected. The Salant Study apparently holds that the proposed CXT reductions expected to be obtained by tariff negotiations are not likely to overcome this surplus protection.[5]

There seems to be but little doubt that the CXT will afford some protection and in some cases more than the affected industry really needs. It also seems clear that some United States exporters will be placed at a disadvantage as a result. However, the CXT does not appear to constitute an insurmountable barrier. It would not be surprising if it proved to be less protective than its authors hope, and American businessmen fear, it will be. The somewhat disappointing United States manufactured goods export performance, 1953-1962, was more the result of the lack of competitiveness of American industry than of export tariff barriers.

The Competitiveness of American Industry

The protectiveness of the CXT, or of any tariff for that

matter, depends, among other factors, upon its nature and height, the competitiveness of the industries within and without its walls as well as changes which occur in industrial technology, capital structure and innovation. By and large, EEC industry has grown increasingly competitive since 1953. *America's ability to "buck" the CXT will depend in no small measure upon substantial improvements in its competitive position.*

The decline in the United States share in external markets, 1953-1961. The international competitive position of a country is often reflected by a comparison of its exports of manufactured goods with those of other industrial nations.[6] In 1957, the United States accounted for 25.5 per cent of the total exports of twelve leading industrial countries. By 1962, this percentage had declined to 19.9. Germany's exports constituted 17.6 per cent of this total in 1957 and 20.1 in 1962. The share of France rose from 8.0 in 1957 to 9.2 per cent in 1962, while Italy's proportion increased from 3.8 to 6.1 per cent during the same period.[7]

In comparison with the like exports of the EEC and EFTA countries, Japan and Canada, 1953-1959, the United States had a declining share of world markets in machinery, transportation equipment and chemicals.[8]

American manufacturers not only did less well in terms of certain industrial exports than these countries, they also lost ground on their own domestic markets. In 1953, the share of the American market obtained by European manufacturers amounted to 2.2 per cent of all non-food consumption goods. By 1959 this percentage had risen to 3.7.[9]

According to the findings of Harold J. Heck of the U. S. Department of Commerce, in 1958 the Common Market countries supplied 29.1 per cent of their individual import needs. By 1961, this percentage had risen to 36.4. The EEC trade between member countries increased by 15.8 per cent in 1961 as compared with 1960, but their imports from the United States rose by only 6.2 per cent during this period.[10]

Heck studied the EEC import patterns for 181 standard international trade classification (SITC) product groups for 1960 and 1961 and discovered that United States exports to the organization increased in 86 groups, decreased in 79 and remained the same in 12 (no exports were recorded for four groups by the United States in 1960 and 1961).[11]

In another study ". . . undertaken to review the experience of the United States in its export trade with the Common Market in 1961 . . ." Heck among other findings, concluded that:

1. The total share of the EEC market supplied by the United States declined slightly between 1960 and 1961.

2. During the decade 1950-1960, United States exports to the EEC just about held their own while the Common Market members supplied an increasingly large proportion of their own market.[12]

Factors in the decline of the United States competitive position. Two groups of factors contributed to the decline in the competitive position of the United States, 1953-1961, relative to certain other industrial countries: price, and non-price, or qualitative, factors.

United States export prices of manufactured goods increased, 1953-1959, by about 14 to 16 per cent. In Germany they rose 5 per cent. They declined, in terms of dollars, in France and rose 10 per cent in the United Kingdom. During the same period, United States import prices remained approximately level, but the volume of American imports rose by 135 per cent while that of its non-military exports increased by but 9 per cent.[13]

United States internal prices rose, 1953-1959, more than the European export prices for a number of industrial products. These include fabricated metals, machinery, chemicals, apparel, furniture and fixtures. Steel prices were approximately the same in Europe in 1953 as in the United States, but the European prices of these products had dropped by 1959 by 15 to 30 per cent of those of the American on the Continent. Similar price movements are shown in the cases of aluminum, a number of other basic industrial commodities, as well as producers' equipment.[14]

Indirect evidence that European industry has become more competitive than American is afforded by the uses to which countries put the loans of the International Bank for Reconstruction and Development. In 1953-54, about half of the proceeds of these loans were used to buy United States equipment; by 1958-1959 this proportion had declined to about 30 per cent.[15]

Among the non-price or qualitative competitive factors, availability of supply plays an important role. In the immediate post-World War II years, Europe's diminished industrial potential made the United States the principal source of readily available goods. With the recovery of Europe, following the Marshall Plan, its industrial capacity increased and the United States lost to a certain extent the advantages which earlier supply availability had conferred on it.

Some students of the subject feel that the quality of American products has declined relative to that of EEC goods. Although the United States has probably made more progress in the development of the principles of quality control, the findings of workers in this field have not received the application which might be desired.

During the years immediately following World War II, American industry had a definite leadership in the field of innovation. It was spending more money on research and development than its overseas rivals, with the result that the attractiveness of its products was superior. With the recovery of Europe, the "innovation gap" between the industries of the two areas was substantially reduced. In addition, the time lag between the introduction of new products, features and technology by the industrial nations has been reduced.[16]

Since United States export markets are relatively small as compared with domestic, some American firms which do not need to rely heavily upon foreign markets tend to concentrate their attention on United States buyers and to regard foreign markets as accessory or surplus outlets for sales. The overseas markets have, therefore, not received the first or best attention of American producers. Exports are much more important to EEC manufacturers, and many of them devote their strongest efforts to sales abroad.

Costs have risen relatively more in the EEC nations than in the United States, and the decrease in American competitiveness

cannot be ascribed to this factor alone. Basically, it appears that
the decline should be ascribed to a drop in industrial productivity
in the United States. From 1953 to 1959 the increase in United
States output per manhour was 13 per cent; in Germany 44,
France 48, Italy 46, Belgium 38 and the Netherlands 27 per cent.
It was also substantially higher in all of the EFTA countries for
which data are available. In addition, the cost of materials required by American industry appears to have risen more in recent
years than those utilized by the industries of the EEC.[17]

As chapter 11 shows, the rate of growth of the United States
economy lagged behind that of the EEC nations during the 1950's.
Many economists are of the opinion that the lag in the American
growth rate accounts, in part, for the deteriorating performance
of its industries in the international economy.

Features of the Common Market CXT

Shortly before the Treaty of Rome was signed, some of the
prospective EEC members lowered their tariffs. All of these
changes were not included in computing the average tariff which
is, therefore, slightly higher than it might have been had the
actual tariffs in effect on January 1, 1957 been used as a base.

Computing the CXT. The use of an average external tariff
was dictated, in part, by the General Agreement on Tariffs and
Trade which provides that customs union tariffs should be no
higher on the average than those which the members applied
before the union went into force. The arrangements made by the
Common Market are generally believed to respect this principle.

Exceptions to this general averaging rule were made in the
case of certain commodities carried on specified lists. List A includes a number of chemicals, plastics, paper products and some
machinery items. The French duties on List A goods are to be
applied on the basis of certain rates which were slightly higher
than those which prevailed in that country on January 1, 1957.
List B consists of a group of relatively unimportant raw materials
for which the average duty on each is not to exceed 3 per cent.

The products included on List C consist of a number of semi-
finished goods comprising stone products, oils, newsprint, yarn,

leather products, glass, building materials and certain non-ferrous metals. The average tariff duty for products on this list may not exceed 10 per cent. A small number of inorganic chemicals are included on List D and the duty on these products is not to exceed 15 per cent. List E comprises some organic chemicals with a maximum tariff set at 25 per cent. List F includes farm products, chemicals and textiles on which the duty has been fixed by mutual agreement.

List G is an important one in terms of United States exports and includes a number of products which are not included in the general average rule. The separate negotiations required to establish these duties were completed, with some exceptions, in 1960 and the rates as of this year are shown in Table 4.1.

Stages in attaining the CXT. In advance of the tariff negotiations under GATT which were held in 1960-61 in Geneva (the Dillon round of tariff negotiations), the Common Market reduced the CXT on a number of goods by about 20 per cent. This step was taken as an act of good will to establish the EEC as an "outward-looking" organization. The first stage negotiations, therefore, represented an adjustment by approximately 30 per cent of the difference between those in effect on January 1, 1957 and the final CXT rates as reduced under the Dillon round. The second stage, completed on July 1, 1963, reduced the duties by another 30 per cent of the modified CXT average. The third stage reductions will doubtless be made toward the new CXT levels established under the Kennedy round of negotiations, scheduled for 1964, and any others which may take place before this stage is concluded, between 1969 and 1972.

These complex adjustments may be made clearer by specific examples. The CXT on electric washing machines of a certain type was originally established at 19 per cent to be attained by the end of the third stage. Under the 1960-1961 GATT negotiations, the CXT was reduced to 15 per cent.

In Germany, the tariff on this product on January 1, 1957 was 10 per cent. The first stage saw an increase in the German duty of 1.5 per cent which was 30 per cent of the difference between the prevailing German duty of 10 per cent and the

TABLE 4.1
SELECTED "G" LIST ITEMS AND EEC FINAL EXTERNAL TARIFFS*

Brussels Nomenclature	Description of Item	Tariff
15.07	fixed vegetable oils, fluid or solid, crude, refined or purified	0-20%
15.12	animal or vegetable fats and oils, hydrogenated, whether or not refined, but not further prepared	17 and 20%
18.03	cocoa paste	25%
18.04	cocoa butter (fat or oil)	22%
18.05	cocoa powder (unsweetened)	27%
18.06	chocolate and other food preparations containing cocoa (depending upon degree of sugar content)	30 and 80%
21.02	extracts, essences or concentrates of coffee, tea or mace; preparations with a basis of those extracts, essences or concentrates	30%
40.02	synthetic rubbers, including synthetic latex, whether or not stabilized	0
	except for factice derived from oils	10%
45.01-02	natural cork in different forms	5-12%
47.01	pulp derived by mechanical or chemical means from any fibrous vegetable material	0 and 6%
50.02-05	silk in different forms	0-12%
62.03	woven jute sacks and bags for packaging, used	11%

* Many of the G list items—in total or in part—are subjects of special protocols altering duties; classification headings appearing above to which such protocols apply follow:
45.02 (cork); 47.01 (pulp); 50.02, 04, 05 (silk); 73.02 (ferro-alloys); 76.01 (aluminum waste); 77.01 (magnesium); 84.06 (engines for flying machines, some vessel engines); 84.08 (other engines); 88.02 (flying machines); 88.03 (parts of flying machines).

TABLE 4.1 (Continued)

Brussels Nomenclature	Description of Item	Tariff
73.02	ferro alloys (other than carburated ferro-manganese)	6-10%
76.01	unwrought aluminum	10%
	aluminum waste	5%
	aluminum scrap	0
77.01	unwrought magnesium	10%
	magnesium waste	5%
	magnesium scrap	0
71.01	tungsten (wolfram) unwrought, in powder	6%
81.02	molybdenum, unwrought	6%
81.03	tantalum, unwrought	4%
81.04	other metals, unwrought	
	bismuth	0
	cadmium	5%
	cobalt	0
	chrome	6%
	germanium	6%
	hafnium (celtium)	4%
	manganese	7%
	niobium (colombium)	6%
	antimony	8%
	titanium	6%
	vanadium	4%
	zirconium	6%
	rhenium	6%
	gallium, indium, thallium	4%
84.06	engines for motor vehicles, flying machines and vessels, and parts	
	engines for motor vehicles	19 and 22%
	engines for flying machines	10 and 15%
	engines for vessels	13-18%
	parts for all above engines	12-19%
84.08	other engines, propellers and parts	12 and 15%

TABLE 4.1 (Continued)

Brussels Nomenclature	Description of Item	Tariff
84.45	metal-working machine tools (excluding those falling under headings 84.49 and 84.50) (1)	4-12%
84.48	accessories and parts suitable for use solely or principally with the machines falling under headings 84.45-47, (2) including work and tool holders, self-opening die-heads, dividing heads and other appliances for machine tools; tool holders for the mechanical hand tools of headings 82.04, 84.49 and 85.05 (3)	8%
84.63	transmission gear for engines of motor vehicles	13-19%
87.06	parts and accessories of motor vehicles falling under headings 87.01-03 (4)	19%
88.02	flying machines, gliders and kites; rotochutes	12-18%
88.03	parts for items under headings 88.01 (5) and 88.02	12%

Footnotes explain references to tariff classifications not under List G.

1. 84.49—hand tools, pneumatic parts
   84.50—welding machines
2. 84.46—mechanical tools for working stone, ceramics, cement, etc.
   84.47—woodworking machine tools
3. 82.04—soldering, welding equipment, glass cutters, etc.
   84.49—hand tools, pneumatic, parts
   85.05—electrically-operated hand saws
4. 87.01—track-laying tractors with spark ignition engine
   87.02—assembled and unassembled cars, assembled commercial vehicles
   87.03—special vehicles (fire engines, snow plows, etc.)
5. 88.01—aerostats (airships, balloons, etc.)

Source: Business International, *Europe's Mass Markets: A Guide to EEC and EFTA.* New York: Business International, 1960, p. 50.

GATT 1960-1961 rate of 15 per cent. The German tariff on this product thus was 11.5 per cent at the end of the first stage. In the second stage, the German rates were raised by another 1.5 to 13 per cent. Unless modified by future GATT negotiations, the final German tariff will have to be raised by 2 percentage points to attain the prescribed CXT level.

The Benelux tariff on electric washing machines was 8.8 per cent at the end of the first stage. At the end of the second, it was raised to 11.5 per cent. By the end of the third stage it will have been raised by 3.5 per cent to attain the CXT of 15 per cent. At the end of the first stage, the French duty on these products stood at 16 and the Italian at 23.5 per cent. The French duty was reduced to 15 per cent at the end of the second stage and need not be further lowered. The Italian tariff was cut to 18.7 per cent at the end of the second stage and will require a further reduction, to 15 per cent, by the end of the third stage.[18]

In any comparison of EEC tariff rates with those of the United States, the fact that the former are based on c.i.f. valuations and the latter on f.o.b. should be kept in mind. In tariff negotiations between the United States and other countries, it has been the general practice to regard the United States f.o.b. values as about 10 per cent lower than those on the c.i.f. basis.

The Impact of the CXT on American Exports

Although the American exports performance to the Common Market has been disappointing, it holds promise of future improvement. The United States lost ground as a supplier to the Community in certain fields; it gained in others. Table 4.2 showing the leading EEC imports supplied by the United States, is divided into two parts: A, commodity groups for which the United States competitive showing was better than that of the EEC, and B, commodity groups for which the United States competitive showing was inferior to that of the EEC. This table indicates that America has gained ground in certain fields and lost in others. In Part B it shows some of the product groups for which greater United States export effort may be required

TABLE 4.2

LEADING EEC IMPORTS SUPPLIED BY THE UNITED STATES, 1961

A. Groups for which U.S. competitive showing was better than that of EEC:

> Meat, fresh, chilled, or frozen
> Wheat
> Corn
> Hides and skins, undressed
> Oilseeds, oil nuts, and oil kernels
> Iron and steel scrap
> Nonferrous ores and concentrates
> Petroleum products
> Leather
> Paper and paperboard
> Power generating machinery, nonelectric
> Agricultural machinery and implements
> Office machines
> Metalworking machinery
> Machines for special industries
> Other nonelectrical machinery, appliances, and parts
> Electric power machines and switchgear
> Scientific, medical, measuring and controlling instruments
> Special transactions not classified according to kind

B. Groups for which U.S. competitive showing was inferior to that of EEC:

> Cereals, unmilled, other than wheat, rice, barley, and corn
> Fruits, preserved, and fruit preparations
> Feeding-stuff for animals
> Tobacco, unmanufactured
> Rubber (crude, synthetic, and reclaimed)
> Pulp and waste paper
> Cotton
> Nonferrous metal scrap
> Coal, coke, and briquettes
> Animal oils and fats
> Fixed vegetable oils, soft

TABLE 4.2 (Continued)

Organic chemicals
Inorganic chemicals
Medicinal and pharmaceutical products
Plastic materials, regenerated cellulose and artificial resins
Chemical materials and products, n.e.s.
Textile yarn and thread
Iron or steel universals, plates, and sheets
Copper
Aluminum
Textile and leather machinery
Telecommunications apparatus
Other electrical machinery and apparatus
Road motor vehicles
Aircraft

Source: Harold J. Heck, "EEC Imports from the United States, 1961" (mimeographed). Washington: U. S. Department of Commerce, n.d., pp. 8-9.

if it is to improve its trading status with the Community. A list of the more important commodities figuring in the United States export trade with the EEC is given in Appendix B.

The tariff structure of the EEC has not as yet had its full effect on the foreign trade of the United States. Its implications will not be completely apparent until the third stage has been attained, or even until a few years later. American business will thus have some time ahead to make an appropriate adjustment.

Diverting trade from the United States. Some students of the EEC tariff structure fear the effects of its trade diversion features on the United States.[19] Although there will doubtless be some trade diversion, it will probably be of less importance than the tariff structure of the EEC tends to indicate on the surface. Approximately 65 per cent of United States exports to the Common Market consist of basic commodities, many of which are of agricultural origin. Some of these exports, notably corn, coal, raw cotton, rubber, scrap iron and steel, are subject to small or no duties. Seeds, vegetable and animal fats and oils do not compete with EEC products and will be subject to small duties. Some United States exports are conditioned more by technical than price factors, and others are not produced in the EEC.

Emile Benoit estimates that the area of *possible* tariff diversion which will be occasioned by the CXT comprises about one-fourth of all United States exports to the Community. Included in this group are manufactured products such as machinery, petroleum products, chemicals, paints, pigments and varnishes. Many of these products are, however, in a strong position to resist diversion because of their strong comparative cost position. Benoit holds that it is not likely that more than 5 to 10 per cent of all American exports to the area will be seriously affected by trade diversion.[20]

American manufacturers of these products are in a strong position to counter this possible diversion. Some of these products are technically superior to those made by the EEC industries. In other cases, United States industrialists may be able to cut prices and meet the tariff challenge in this manner.

Relative height of the CXT. Even before the inauguration of the Common Market, the tariff of its members could hardly be considered high. The CXT will represent a tariff reduction for France and Italy, both of which are large economic units, and a rise for Benelux and Germany, but one of which is a large economy. Many European manufacturers will have less tariff protection under the CXT than they had previously.[21] The products carried on list G, for which the CXT was determined by negotiation among the Six on May 2, 1960, is an important one for American business. The duty rates on these products, with few exceptions, are relatively low and average about 10 per cent.

The structure of the CXT differs substantially from that of the United States. United States duties have a wide range, varying from low to high rates. The CXT, by contrast, exhibits less variation and most of its duties fall in the moderate class. The EEC external tariff, albeit a distinct problem for American business, does not appear to offer an insurmountable barrier.

EEC growth potential and American exports. The officials of the Community often point out to critics in other countries that, although the CXT may discriminate against them, the growth of the EEC national income will be so great that it will more than counteract the tariff disadvantages. This reasoning is based on the well-established fact that a nation's imports are, in part, a function of its national income. Imports rise as national income increases and decline as it falls.

This point appears to be well taken. In chapter 11, the past increase in the national income of the Community is sketched and the prospects for its future growth outlined. A recent report projects a growth rate of 4.75 per cent a year for the gross national product (GNP) of the institution. It states that the GNP will increase by a total of 59.1 per cent between 1960 and 1970. This growth will mean a substantial rise in EEC national income and its propensity to import from the United States as well as other third countries.[22]

The effects on imports of the Common Market's estimated increase in national income could be seriously altered if prices were to change within the Community or in the United States. If prices rose to higher levels in the EEC than America, United States exports to it would probably increase. If the reverse were true, American exports to the institution could well be smaller. In chapter 11, price movements in the EEC and the United States were projected as relatively the same for the period 1960-1970.

Largely due to the gradual reduction to zero of the internal tariff of the EEC, any increase in United States exports to this area is likely to be smaller than that of the internal trade among the EEC members themselves. This may be disappointing to some American businessmen, but it could hardly be termed disastrous.

Tariff reductions under the Kennedy round of negotiations. The forthcoming GATT sessions give promise of being difficult, protracted and characterized by hard bargaining on both sides. Already, some basic difficulties have been encountered in establishing the procedures to be followed in their conduct. The

United States desired an across-the-board cut in both its own duties and those of the CXT. The EEC negotiators, acting principally under the leadership of France, countered that such a step would not give the members the relief which they desired. The United States tariff, they held, consisted of some high and some low duty rates, while the CXT is composed of a large number of medium duties. Such a reduction, they maintained, would leave less than 1 per cent of the Community's tariffs over 15 per cent, while 20 per cent of the United States tariffs would remain over 20 per cent.

After much debate, a compromise was reached on May 21, 1963 under which the high United States duties will be dealt with under special negotiations, product by product, and the lower rates will be negotiated on a linear or across-the-board basis. In this way, tariffs on large groups of goods will be cut by a fixed percentage and only the peak tariffs will need to be negotiated separately. The negotiators also agreed that farm products will be included in the negotiations, but that they will be handled differently from those of industry.[23]

These negotiations are coming at a time when the full effects of the final CXT are unknown. The negotiators will be bargaining in the dark and without full knowledge of the impact of their work on future trade. More fruitful results are likely to be obtained at later negotiations when the final stage of the CXT has been in effect for a time and its results are apparent. In addition, the CXT may generate some dissension in the Common Market and dissatisfaction with its results. The position of the United States may well be strengthened in future negotiations by such developments. A satisfactory and desirable adjustment of the CXT doubtless lies several years in the future.

The CXT is not the only impediment to exports which the United States faces. There are import quotas, which apply principally to farm products, various internal taxes, customs classifications, valuations and administrative regulations which often discriminate against American exports to the Common Market. Some of these, notably tariff quotas, are gradually being reduced and the reduction or the elimination of others can take place at

GATT negotiations. For the future of American exports to the Community, it is important that they be eliminated.

United States negotiators at the GATT sessions are handicapped, for they do not enter the meetings with entirely clean hands. In 1922, with the Fordney-McCumber tariff and again in 1930 with the Hawley-Smoot tariff, the United States raised its duties against all outsiders. This country still maintains quotas applied against certain agricultural products. The excise taxes, especially those on wines and spirits, discriminate against some foreign products. The classification, valuation and administrative provisions of its customs administration, until the Customs Simplification Acts came into force, operated to restrain imports. In the forthcoming GATT negotiations, the United States will reap the harvest of the dragon's teeth which it has sown in the past.

For reasons such as these, American exporters should not place too much confidence in the forthcoming GATT negotiations to obtain the relief needed for easier access to the markets of the Community. Although any concessions which the American negotiators can obtain will be helpful, increasing United States exports to the Common Market are likely to depend heavily upon the imagination, efficiency and competitiveness of the businessmen of this country.

The measures available to American exporters in scaling the CXT wall and in meeting competition in the Community are similar to those which American industry can take in protecting itself against imports from the area (outlined in chapter 3).

In spite of the EEC tariff structure and other impediments to United States sales to the Community, there is a great deal of profitable export business to be done with the firms of this organization. The CXT will probably not prove any greater handicap to American exports than the United States tariff has to the European. The prospects for an increasingly large volume of exports to the Common Market are good, and they hold promise of improving as time goes on.

NOTES

[1] A brief but excellent exposition of tariff objectives is given by John Parke Young. *The International Economy*. (4th ed.). New York: The Ronald Press Co., 1963, pp. 263-320.

[2] Walter S. Salant, Emile Depres, Lawrence B. Krause, Alice M. Rivlin, William A. Salant and Lorie Tarshis. *The United States Balance of Payments in 1968*. Washington: The Brookings Institution, 1963, pp. 95-118.

[3] Salant Study, p. 57.

[4] *Ibid.*, p. 102. The categories of manufactures are: chemicals, textile products, other manufactured products, machinery and transport.

[5] The projections of the Salant Study are reminiscent of the predictions made in an earlier study of the Common Market to the effect that this institution might lead to the domination of the European economy by Germany. See: E. Strauss. *Common Sense About the Common Market: Germany and Britain in Post-War Europe*. New York: Rinehart and Co., Inc., 1958, pp. 150-157, especially.

[6] See: Emile Benoit. *Europe at Sixes and Sevens: The Common Market, the Free Trade Association and the United States*. New York: Columbia University Press, 1961.

[7] The twelve countries are: United States, United Kingdom, Germany, France, Italy, Japan, Belgium, Luxembourg, Canada, the Netherlands, Sweden and Switzerland. See: Salant Study, p. 65.

[8] Benoit, *op. cit.*, pp. 140-143.

[9] *Ibid.*, p. 143.

[10] Harold J. Heck. "Study of 181 Items Exported to EEC Reveals Little Ground for Complacency." *International Commerce* (a publication of the U.S. Department of Commerce), Vol. 69, No. 8 (February 25, 1963), pp. 2-6.

[11] Heck. *op. cit.*, p. 3.

[12] Harold J. Heck. "EEC Imports from the United States 1961" (mimeographed). Washington: U.S. Department of Commerce, n.d., pp. 1-4.

[13] Emile Benoit, *op. cit.*, pp. 148-149.

[14] *Ibid.*, pp. 149-154.

[15] *Ibid.*, p. 155.

[16] Cf. A. O. Hirschman. "Invitation to Theorizing about the Dollar Glut." *Review of Economics and Statistics*. February 1960.

[17] Emile Benoit, *op. cit.*, pp. 161-164.

[18] Cf. Walter Buchdahl. "Exporters Await Impact of EEC's Tariff Adjustment." *International Commerce* (a publication of the U.S. Department of Commerce), March 11, 1963.

[19] Cf. Salant Study, *op. cit.*, pp. 97-112.

[20] Cf. Benoit, *op. cit.*, pp. 170-175.

[21] *Ibid.*, pp. 23-25.

[22] Cf. Salant Study, *op. cit.*, p. 57.

[23] "GATT Tariff-Cutting Principles Agreed at Geneva." *The European Community* (a publication of the European Community Information Office). No. 63, Washington, June 1963.

5

Investing in the Common Market: General Considerations

Motives for Investing in the EEC—Forms of Direct Investment—The Regulation of International Investment

Greatly improved transportation and communications systems have reduced the effective size of the globe with the result that more and more business firms are expanding their operations overseas. The Common Market, as well as its sister organization, the European Free Trade Association, offers new and challenging opportunities for those businessmen who seek greater profits over a wider geographic area and who like to play the business game on a larger board and with more pieces.

Motives for Investing in the EEC

International economists commonly divide overseas long-term investments into two broad groups: portfolio and direct investment. Portfolio investments refer to the purchase of the securities of firms or governments abroad for the return which they yield, for speculative and long-term capital gains or to cement relations between firms which transact business with one another. The essence of the portfolio investment is that it does not give the investor an important voice in the management of the firm the securities of which have been acquired.

Direct investment consists of the purchase of securities, property, equities and other interests in a foreign concern which gives the investor a voice in the management of the enterprise. The line which separates no voice from a voice in management is not a definite one. The Department of Commerce, as a rule-of-thumb, holds that the ownership of 25 per cent or more of the voting stock of a business confers a voice in management and is a direct investment, although it often takes other facts into account in making this determination.

The discussion in this chapter is devoted entirely to direct investment since this type of capital movement is one of the principal financial attractions of the European Economic Community. A number of motives prompt American enterprises to invest directly abroad and some of them apply with particular force to direct investments in the EEC and, incidentally, to the EFTA nations as well.

Vaulting over barriers to trade. American exporters to the EEC and EFTA are placed at a competitive disadvantage by the tariff structure of these two organizations. In the case of import quotas and exchange controls, the absolute quantities which American firms can export to these countries may be limited. In the case of tariffs, the disadvantage is relative and can be roughly gauged by the amount that the duty adds to the laid down price of the exports.

To avoid this discrimination, some American firms may be able to vault over the trade barriers by manufacturing or assembling their products in one of these nations. If they establish branches or subsidiaries in these countries, their establishments there will be resident firms and enjoy similar treatment to that accorded firms organized by the nationals of the country in question.[1]

Obviously, if an American subsidiary manufactures a product inside the EEC, this product, as it moves in trade within these areas, will pay only the internal tariff, if any, of the Community. The same item, manufactured in the United States, will have to pay the external tariffs applicable to it before it can be sold in any of these countries. The competitive price advantage of manufacturing American goods inside the confines of the EEC can be substantial. Although trade barriers prompt American direct investment in many countries, the tariff structure of the EEC (and EFTA) is one of the leading reasons for this type of investment in these areas.

Proximity to supplies, labor and markets. Proximity to sources of supply, specialized labor and markets is one of the important factors in the determination of plant location in the United States. These considerations apply with equal force to the location of plants abroad. The attraction of these proximities is not peculiar to the Common Market; it applies to location in a number of other foreign countries. Certain features of this new institution, however, may serve to make business location within its area especially attractive to American enterprises.

As competition becomes more severe in the EEC, it will probably be necessary for firms which sell there to price many products more closely. Savings in transportation costs due to location close to supplies and markets, and the advantages of a specialized labor force near at hand, may spell the difference between success and failure in marketing goods in these countries.

The European labor force is well trained and highly skilled. Under the free movement of labor provisions of the Treaty of Rome, location in any of the Common Market nations is likely to provide relatively easy access to a large and versatile body of employees. As indicated in chapter 7, the wage rates paid European labor are substantially lower than those which prevail in the United States. One of the reasons for the wage differentials is the larger amount of capital employed in American industry. If United States subsidiaries in the Common Market can utilize amounts of capital similar to those which are employed at home and still benefit from the low prevailing wage scales, manufacturing costs will be relatively low, and the possibility of wider profit margins will be enhanced.

Tax avoidance. Tax avoidance has long been a prime motive inducing American firms to seek direct investments overseas. An American branch, which is not established as a corporation in a foreign country, is regarded by the United States Internal Revenue Service as a part of the parent firm. Its profits are lumped with those of the parent and are taxed at the rate applicable to the combined profits. There is thus no United States income tax advantage in establishing branches abroad. An American subsidiary, incorporated abroad, is regarded as a foreign resident by the Internal Revenue Service and, with certain exceptions, its profits are not fully taxed in the United States, but are subject to certain credits. Such a foreign-incorporated business must, however, pay all the applicable taxes of the country in which it is incorporated.

Generally speaking, business income taxes of the Common Market nations are lower than those which apply in America, and the taxes which both branches and subsidiaries pay to foreign governments are deductible in part from United States corporate income tax liability. The United States has tax treaties for the prevention of double income taxation in effect with all the Common Market countries except Italy. Although the provisions of these treaties vary, all of them attempt to avoid double income taxation by reserving certain tax sources to the country of incorporation and others to the United States.[2] Incorporation in the EEC generally carries lower total income taxation than would result from the establishment of a foreign branch in the area.

Many European products are exempt from the payment of certain turnover and other taxes when they are exported. The goods made by a United States subsidiary located in the Common Market enjoy the same tax exemptions on exports as those accorded the products of firms owned by nationals.

The future of taxation under the aegis of the Common Market does not lend itself easily to prediction. From all indications, efforts will be made to equalize the burden of business taxes among the members. American subsidiaries incorporated in the EEC will benefit from the tax advantages and will suffer from any disadvantageous tax situations which the regulations and decisions of the Community may bring. Given the dedication of the Common Market authorities to growth and economic expansion, it seems likely that EEC business firms will receive favorable tax consideration.

The subject of taxation is a complex one, especially when the tax systems of several countries are involved. Obviously, American firms contemplating the establishment of branches and subsidiaries in the Common Market should utilize the advice of tax lawyers and accountants well versed in both the American and EEC tax systems before making a final investment decision.

The public relations advantages of foreign subsidiaries. The advent of the Common Market is not likely to bring an end to national prejudice against some imported products and foreign-owned firms. On the contrary, the EEC may add another dimension to this attitude. This institution is developing a "nationalism" of its own. Although it is not likely that it will take a strong official position against imports and foreign enterprises, these products and companies may prove somewhat less welcome than those of the members.

By the use of appropriate public relations methods, American subsidiary enterprises can lessen the harmful economic effect of some of these prejudices. These subsidiaries are residents or nationals of the country in which they are incorporated. Their national or Common Market character can be reinforced if they take names in the language of the country of incorporation; employ a local-type name for their products; hire local labor; include some foreign nationals in management; sell some of their equities to residents of the country in question and thus claim to be part locally-owned; utilize local service agencies in their operations.

National prejudice does not apply equally to all products or companies. In some cases, the foreign quality of the company and its products may be an advantage. Witness the prestige attached to French perfumes and cosmetics and to West German beer. In deciding whether or not it is better to export or to establish a manufacturing subsidiary in the EEC, whether to "nationalize" a subsidiary and its products, the public relations aspects should be surveyed and weighed so that the maximum advantages and minimum disadvantages can be obtained from the type of operation selected.

Profit and growth opportunities in the EEC. In 1960, United States direct investments in Western Europe earned, before taxes (United States share only), approximately 16 per cent on the book value of their invested capital. The figure for 1960 earnings in the United States of domestic firms was about 9.5 per cent.[3] The difference is substantial and illustrates a point made in chapter 2, that the profits of European business, in relation to assets, tend to be higher than in the United States. The higher potential earnings have proved a powerful magnet in recent years to attract increasing amounts of United States direct investment in the Common Market.

If profits in the United States are unsatisfactory, while those for similar industries in the EEC are higher, the average rate of profits for the enterprise as a whole might be improved by the creation of appropriately located subsidiaries. A Common Market subsidiary plant might prove to be a good investment for those firms which are either at or beyond the point of optimum return with present plant capacity and levels of output, and which desire to sell *additional* products abroad. Some manufacturers have reached the point where the American market for their goods is virtually saturated. In such cases, expansion and increased sales may be obtained from either exports or by establishing manufacturing or assembly plants abroad.

Cost considerations. Within the confines of the United States, problems of plant location have often revolved around questions of cost. Generally speaking, Europe has been a low industrial cost area relative to the United States. Like many generalities, however, there are important exceptions to the rule.

Since Europe is less well endowed with raw materials than the United States, some raw materials are generally more costly there. As chapter 7 explains, European wage rates are lower than those found in the United States. Low labor rates, however, do not necessarily mean lower labor costs. The wage rates of automobile workers are much higher in the United States than in Europe, but American automobiles, as far as they can be compared with the European product, are not more costly. The wage rates of coal miners are higher in the

United States than in Europe, yet American coal, including ocean transport, has been delivered to European industrial centers at a lower price than the domestic product.

Through the use of large amounts and more effective types of capital, American industry is able in many cases to pay higher wages and still have lower labor costs per unit of output than European producers. In those cases where American manufacturers can furnish their Common Market factories with equipment similar to that employed in their home country and utilize equally effective technology, they may be able to take advantage of the low labor costs to produce more efficiently than competing industries abroad or at home. On the other hand, the experience of some American manufacturing enterprises located in the Common Market indicates that labor-saving equipment cannot always be as successfully utilized there as in the United States, and that some efforts to take advantage of low wage rates have been disappointing.

The lower Common Market rates of corporate taxation also make for lower costs. Utilities, transportation and business services are generally cheaper there than in the United States. Under the present distribution systems of the EEC, the costs of placing a product in the hands of the ultimate consumer are relatively higher than in the United States. Since each proposal to establish manufacturing plants within the Community presents a different problem, careful comparative cost analyses should be made before embarking on a proposed investment.

Servicing products sold in the EEC. Products differ widely in the amount of servicing which they require after they are in the hands of the final user. For those products which occasion frequent and extensive servicing, the establishment of appropriate facilities is essential to the continued acceptance of the goods. Many Americans hesitate to purchase certain foreign automobiles because of insufficient service facilities for repairs and maintenance.

Service facilities do not necessarily imply the establishment of subsidiary plants abroad. They may only entail the appointment of a number of strategically located distributors or dealers recruited from the local business population. Where the servicing requirements are especially heavy, American firms may find it advisable to establish an organization to supervise service facilities.

Common Market assembly plants. The tariff structure of some countries imposes lower duty rates on components than on finished goods, and transportation charges are sometimes lower on parts than on finished products. Whenever either, or both, of these situations applies, American manufacturers may find it more economical to ship the components or parts of their products to the Common Market and to establish an assembly plant there. In addition to cost advantages, a local assembly firm, because it employs local workers and perhaps some local capital, may enjoy certain public relations advantages.

Assembly plants, since they often involve substantial capital investment and extensive operations, are usually established as subsidiary corporations. In the assembly operation, either all of the components may be manufactured in the United States or some of the parts may be acquired abroad from local manufacturers. The decision to manufacture all of the parts in the United States, or make them abroad, will depend upon considerations of cost, convenience and public relations. Servicing problems are usually more easily solved where an assembly plant is located in reasonable proximity to the consumers.

Where there are lower corporation income taxes in a European country than in the United States, some taxes may be saved by an assembly plant. Generally speaking, if the product were assembled in the United States, the taxes of this country would be applied to the profits realized on the complete product; when assembled in the EEC, the United States taxes would apply to the profits realized on the parts made in this country and the EEC taxes to those derived from the assembly operation.

Forced EEC location. Some types of business have no choice of location; they must locate in a specific area by the nature of their operations. Utilities must be situated in the areas which they serve; retail establishments have no alternative to opening stores in the places where customers are found; extractive industries must set up their operations where the minerals lie. The foreign direct investment decision in these cases is a relatively simple one and involves few alternative plans of action. The decision is generally one of whether or not to go into this type of business in the Common Market.

Non-economic considerations. Before modern psychology became well established, business motives were generally held to be largely economic in character. Businessmen continue to respond to economic stimuli, as indeed everyone does, but non-economic factors are recognized as of considerable importance in business decisions.

Just as farming is a way of life for many farmers, business is a way of life for many businessmen. The larger and more complex the field of operations, the greater the number and the more difficult the decisions, the more important are the psychic rewards of the business game. Foreign establishments, with their many new, and often strange, problems to solve, offer a fascinating field of business endeavor. The dynamism and shifting circumstances of business operations in the EEC make it an exciting center and outlet for the activities of the man for whom business is a way of life.

Forms of Direct Investment

The American businessman who plans to establish an enterprise in the EEC or EFTA has a wide variety of forms, or types, of enterprise at his disposal. The more important forms from which he may select are: branches, foreign incorporated subsidiaries, participation with existing firms in the areas and licensing arrangements.

The foreign branch. The foreign branch is an extension of the home or parent company in a foreign land. It is not a separate corporate entity and is generally a sales office or other facility of the parent firm. Thus an American office equipment company might establish a sales office and service center in Paris to handle sales in the Common Market and to service the equipment. It can rent or purchase office and warehousing space, send over managers and hire such local help as might be required.

This unincorporated branch *is* the parent company in the EEC. It has to conform in all particulars to French and Common Market laws and regulations and is taxable under the applicable French laws. The profits earned by the branch are also taxable under United States law as a part of the earnings of the parent company whether or not they are remitted to the American parent firm, retained or reinvested. The income taxes paid to the French government will, however, serve as an offset to the income taxes due to the United States.

The alternative to the establishment of such a branch is the appointment of a French firm as agent, representative or distributor for the firm's line of office equipment. The decision of whether to establish a branch or to appoint a French representative is dictated by the facts in each individual case and by the policies of the parent firm. In either case, the branch or the French representative will have to pay the EEC common external tariff when the goods shipped from the United States enter its customs territory. The decision involved in the choice of the type of foreign distribution usually turns on the question of the kind of sales representation which will produce the best results for the parent company.

Branches can be established for types of operations other than sales and servicing. It is conceivable that an assembly plant or factory can be set up as a branch. As a general matter, since these operations usually involve large amounts of capital, it is better to handle them by establishing subsidiaries, creating joint participations with already-existing local firms or licensing local concerns to assemble the products.

Foreign incorporated subsidiaries. The foreign incorporated subsidiary has been used by many American companies with substantial operations in both the EEC and EFTA. Such a subsidiary is a person in the eyes of the law of the country in which it is incorporated. In most European nations, authorization to establish a corporate subsidiary of an American (or any foreign) company is necessary and the enterprise has to comply with the incorporation laws of the country in question. Generally speaking, these laws in Europe are more complex than those found in the

American states and it is more difficult and time-consuming to obtain a corporation charter.

Most European countries have several similar types of corporations, quasi-corporations or limited partnerships. In France, for example, the closest approach to the American corporation is the *société anonyme* (United Kingdom, limited company; Germany, *Aktiengesellschaft;* the Netherlands, *naamloze vennootschap*).

Although differing in details, these foreign corporations are essentially similar to those found in the United States. They possess both corporate personality and the perquisites which this characteristic confers. Both have limited liability which means that, in general, liability for the debts of the firm is limited to the amount of the stockholder's subscription.

The *société anonyme,* like its counterparts in other European nations, can usually issue various types of stocks and bonds. European laws governing the public issue of securities are generally more restrictive than those found in America, and as a result the corporations of these nations usually issue fewer different types. The management of these enterprises is generally in the hands of the holders of the voting stock who elect a board of directors *(conseil d'administration)* and the board appoints the officers of the company.

Another type of quasi-corporation or limited partnership is called in France the *société en commandite par actions* (United Kingdom, company limited by shares; Germany, *Kommanditgesellschaft auf Aktien;* the Netherlands, *commanditaire vennootschap*). These firms have two classes of stockholders: one group, called in French law the *associés commandiataires* or *bailleurs de fonds,* is not liable for any debts of the firm above the amount of its subscriptions, but it has no voice in the management of the firm; another group, the *associés solidaires,* is responsible for the debts of the business and is charged with its management. These types of firms have some of the characteristics of both a limited partnership and a corporation.

The *société en commandite simple* (United Kingdom, limited partnership; Germany, *einfache Kommanditgesellschaft;* the

Netherlands, *zuiver commanditaire vennootschap*) is similar to the *société en commandite par actions* except that the financial interests in the business are not represented by shares of stock. There are other types of business organization available to the American direct investor such as the *société à responsibilité limitée* or limited liability company; *société en nom collectif* or partnership; *société* or *association en participation* or special (secret) partnership, among others. Each type of business organization has its own characteristics, advantages and disadvantages and they vary slightly from country to country.

With United States income and corporate taxes at their present levels, tax considerations loom large when direct investment overseas is contemplated. The tax rates in the United States and the Common Market countries applicable to various forms of American branches and subsidiaries located in the latter nations call for analysis before the type of organization is finally decided upon. The principal corporate income and other taxes of the EEC and EFTA countries are presented on Table 5.1.

TABLE 5.1

CORPORATE INCOME AND OTHER TAXES, EEC AND EFTA COUNTRIES

EEC Countries	Income or Profits Taxes	Other Taxes [*]
Belgium	30% to 45% on retained profits; 50% on distributed profits	
France	50% of total profits	
Germany, West	15% on distributed and 51% on undistributed profits	An average 13.75% trade tax based on income
Italy	Income plus local and other taxes, 20% to 51%	0.75% of net worth plus 15% on income in excess of 6% of net worth
Luxembourg	40% of total profits	Trade tax averaging 8%
Netherlands	43% of total profits	
Greece	25% on distributed and 35% on undistributed profits	

TABLE 5.1 (Continued)

EFTA Countries	Income or Profits Taxes	Other Taxes
Austria	28.32% to 51.92% on total profits over $19,000	Local tax of 15% of profits plus taxes on capital and payroll
Denmark	44% nominal tax; with reductions, it averages 35% of total profits	
Norway	National tax of 30% of net income. Local income tax 14% to 18% plus surtax	
Portugal	About 30% on either assessable capital or presumptive gross profits	
Sweden	National tax of 40% of gross income; local 10% to 15%	
Switzerland	Defense tax of 3% to 8% of profits; low cantonal and communal profits taxes	
United Kingdom	Income tax of 38.74% of total profits; profits tax of 15% of total profits	
Finland	Total profits taxed at 40% on undistributed part; 30% on distributed	Local, church and property taxes, 10% to 17%

Source: Morgan Guaranty Trust Company of New York, *Market Europe*, pp. 52-53.

The incorporated foreign subsidiary is a national or resident of the country of incorporation and usually enjoys the same advantages as a firm chartered by the nationals or residents of the nation in question. It can import and export goods to all of the other members of the EEC or EFTA, paying only those tariffs and subject to the same import quotas and exchange controls which prevail for any other resident firm of the area. Such a company imports goods from outside nations at the common external tariff, if it is a resident of the EEC, or the external tariff of the particular EFTA country of which it is a national.

If the EEC grows, the benefits and problems associated with economic growth will effect the American subsidiaries incorporated within its confines. If the national income of the area increases, these subsidiaries will share a deeper market with the locally-owned enterprises. They will also be subjected to the increasing competition which appears to lie ahead within the Community.

The extent of foreign participation in the capital structure and management of American subsidiaries located in the Common Market constitutes a policy decision of some importance. From a public relations point of view, local participation is desirable, as the history of some Canadian-based American subsidiaries bears witness.

Experience with foreign participation in the ownership and management of American subsidiaries overseas shows that participation arrangements have both good and bad points. In addition to the public relations advantages, local management is generally more familiar with domestic business conditions. The salaries paid Common Market executives are generally lower than those earned by Americans. Business managers inside the Common Market usually have wider contacts and business relations in their areas than American executives. The fact that they are national businessmen rather than Americans may help them in their business dealings with those who find compatriots more acceptable than Americans. They also better understand the stimuli to which the people of the EEC respond.

Some American firms have found that, where EEC businessmen held a minority financial interest in their subsidiaries and some executive positions, it was often difficult to retain managerial control over the firm and to enforce home office policies in management. Since the points of view of Common Market owners and executives may differ from those held by the American home company, friction can easily develop in the management of the subsidiaries and in the elaboration of their policies.

These subsidiaries must do business in a climate different from that which prevails in the United States. Laws, institutions, customs and business practices sometimes prevent policies which have been used successfully in the United States from proving effective abroad. One large American manufacturer endeavored to apply his employee benefit and welfare programs to his subsidiary operation in one of the countries of the EEC and met with opposition on the part of his competitors, colleagues and the government there. Although his employment policies produced good results in the United States, he could not put them into effect in his subsidiary. On the other hand, some firms have found that their American policies were well received and produced good results in the Common Market.

Participation with existing EEC firms. Participation with an already well-established Common Market firm is an alternative to the establishment of an American subsidiary based there. As the term participation is used here, it includes the purchase of a relatively large amount of stock or equity rather than the acquisition of a small interest in a foreign firm for the purpose of cementing closer business relations.

As an alternative to establishing a new plant or business unit, a firm already established might be purchased outright. There may be inactive firms which can be acquired as well as active firms which the owners desire to sell. If such companies have established reputations, the advantages of such a purchase are obvious.

Some going concerns may welcome American participation either through the acquisition of a substantial block of stock or through a partnership arrangement. The growing size of business units in the EEC may make the additional capital welcome. If the manufacture of an attractive American line of products is included in the investment arrangement, these new items can help diversify the operations as well as improve the competitive position and earning power of a European firm. The addition of American executives to the management of a company may also serve to strengthen the enterprise. The American investor in an established company is likely to save time in gaining acceptance of his product in the Common Market since his goods will be made and sold by a firm known to the local dealers and public.

The creation of a jointly-owned and managed enterprise poses a number of problems. The policies of the respective firms may differ and it may not be possible to arrive at a satisfactory compromise. The manufacturing standards of the two firms may not correspond. If the product, manufactured by a Common Market firm and sold under an American trademark, were of inferior quality, serious damage might be incurred. Problems concerning the staffing of the EEC firm such as the type and number of American executives to be employed can also occur. Additionally, financial, pricing, labor relations, marketing, re-investment, distribution of profits as well as a host of other problems can arise which may serve to make the arrangement unsatisfactory.

The most satisfactory participation arrangements are likely to be those between firms which have already had considerable business dealings with each other and where the firms are thoroughly familiar with the personnel, policies and standards of one another. Americans contemplating such participation might do well to consult with other firms which have had experience with these types of arrangements. A contract or agreement setting forth the understanding and the undertakings of both parties on all problems which are likely to arise, and which may be foreseen, may avoid future problems and disappointments.

Licensing arrangements. Where an American firm has valuable industrial property in the form of patents, trademarks, copyrights, technology and design, and desires to have its products manufactured in the Common Market, it may designate a local company to manufacture or reproduce the items, employ the trademark, technology and design, under a licensing agreement. Simply stated, a licensing agreement is an arrangement by which the owner of industrial property permits another party to utilize the property under stated conditions in return for the payment of a royalty or other consideration.

Thus if an American pharmaceutical company obtains a patent on a new anti-biotic and a trademark on the name given the product, it may permit an EEC firm to manufacture and sell the new drug in agreed countries under the trademarked name and under specified terms. In return for the use of this industrial property the American company will ordinarily receive royalties.

The licensing agreement is, in certain respects, the simplest form of international direct investment and one that usually involves a minimum of financing. It permits an American firm to have its products sold in the Common Market without the payment of external tariffs or investment in branches, subsidiaries or participation arrangements.

The simplicity and economy of licensing are deceptive. If an American firm has spent a considerable amount of money in the development of a patented process or product and in promoting its sale under a trademarked name, it would not like to see a foreign firm manufacture a shoddy duplicate and thereby lessen the value of the industrial property involved. It would not desire to become involved in expensive and lengthy litigation which the interpretation of the licensing agreement might involve in the hands of an unscrupulous or difficult licensee.

Some aspects of a licensing agreement, such as technology, methods and "know how," may not be protected by the patents, trademarks and copyrights owned by the American investor and their protection can present serious legal problems. In spite of the fact that the EEC nations adhere to the several international conventions for the protection of industrial property, the laws on these matters vary from country to country. Italy, for example, affords no patent protection on certain drug and pharmaceutical inventions. An American licensor may find his license agreement with an EEC firm cancelled; the licensee may continue to manufacture the product, or a slightly different one, and be willing to take his chances in one of his own courts of law or an out-of-court settlement if the licensor decides to sue for infringement.

Some of these difficulties can be avoided by a licensing agreement which takes into account as many forseeable problems as possible and gives the licensor a strong legal position in both the United States and the Common Market.

Licensing arrangements must be carefully considered in the light of United States, other national or EEC anti-trust laws. Assume that an American electronic manufacturer patents a new, efficient and low-cost diode, obtains a trademark for the name he gives it and copyrights the descriptive advertising and instructional literature dealing with the diode. He spends a substantial amount of money in developing the North and South American, the Far and Middle Eastern markets for the new product. He then licenses a French electronic firm to manufacture and sell the diode under the industrial property rights which he has acquired. In view of the sums which he has expended to develop his markets, the licensing agreement provides that the French licensee shall sell *only* on certain specified European and African markets at not less than a stipulated price.

The American licensor, who feels that he is acting solely as a prudent and reasonable businessman, may find with dismay that he has violated the United States, French or EEC anti-trust laws and is liable to prosecution![4]

The gains to the American licensor usually accrue through the payment of royalties by the licensees and a number of different royalty arrangements may be utilized. Royalties can be computed on the basis of the payment of a given amount of money for each item manufactured or sold, a percentage of the gross or net income from sales of the licensed product, or they can be based on a percentage of the total earnings of the licensee. The agreement may provide for fixed payments, it may stipulate certain minimum and maximum royalties or any combination of these arrangements, among others.

Licensing agreements often arrange for the licensor to furnish certain technical help to the licensee and additional payment may be required for this assistance. They frequently permit the licensor to inspect and exercise some supervision over the licensee's manufacturing process, his selling methods and to prevent the sale or exchange of any disapproved finished licensed products. These agreements usually contain stipulations relating to the termination of the license for cause, other specified reasons or at a given date.

Cross-licensing agreements have proved popular between American and Common Market firms where both possess, or expect to acquire, a number of patents and trademarks. Under cross-licensing arrangements, each party licenses the other to use specified patents, trademarks and copyrights.

In spite of many problems, international licensing agreements are popular with many American firms and most of them have proved profitable to both parties to the agreement. Although international licensing has a long history, since the end of World War II (and especially since the inauguration of the Common Market) interest therein has increased. Such licensing provides a simple and inexpensive method of reaping some of the advantages which the EEC holds for American manufacturers.

Critics of the American patent system have raised a number of objections to the monopoly-breeding character of the industrial property system. Some of the criticisms stress the fact that where patent owners refuse to license others to use their patents, the system tends to create monopolies and gives far too exclusive rights to the owners of industrial property. One of the proposed solutions to these alleged abuses of the patent system includes obligatory, or legally forced, licensing of the use of the patents to all who meet specified conditions and terms. International licensing agreements seem to be a step in the direction of divorcing some aspects of monopoly from industrial property by extending overseas the number of manufacturers of a given patented product.

The Regulation of International Investment

A foreign firm may incorporate a subsidiary in the United States on same terms that Americans can establish a domestic firm. There are few restrictions on the right of foreigners to invest in the United States; they are subject to the same laws as Americans. In this country, as far as international direct investment is concerned, the principle of national treatment of foreigners is virtually absolute.

Restrictions on the right of establishment. Complete freedom of establishment does not prevail in many foreign countries. In some, until recently the colonial possessions of one of the great powers, the fear of colonialism has led them to restrictions on foreign direct investment. Certain of the more highly developed countries of Europe, where nationalism is strong, resent the intrusion of foreigners into their business enterprise system.

Nations where protectionist policies prevail—and often at the instance of their businessmen—like to restrict the establishment of foreign companies. Others profess to accord national treatment to foreign subsidiaries and in many cases are obligated by treaty to do so. These professions of good faith and treaty obligations may be circumvented in a variety of ways, especially by means of administrative harassment.

Although permitting direct investment, countries with balance of payments problems may place restrictions in the way of the repatriation of capital and dividends. Many states regulate the extent of foreign ownership and management by requiring a certain proportion of the capital stock to be vested in residents or by prescribing that nationals must be represented in the management of the firm in certain stipulated proportions. In some countries, the ownership of land and specified resources must remain in the hands of nationals and cannot be alienated to foreigners. In others, laws do not permit foreigners to engage in certain kinds of business or to practice some professions.

Socialism has made progress, especially in the newly-emerging states. Although the socialist movement has not made the gains in Europe anticipated by some, nationalization of enterprises is always a possibility—especially where the business is held to be charged with a public interest.

National attitudes toward foreign investment. In general, United States direct investments are welcome in both the EEC and EFTA areas particularly since they often bring additional capital, advanced technology and innovation. However, policies toward foreign investment vary from country to country; some nations permit virtually all foreign investments while others exercise some selectivity in the types which are permitted or encouraged.

The individual countries vary in the extent of their industrial development and some parts of them are, by their own standards, underdeveloped. The encouragement or the discouragement of United States investments depends upon both the type of investment contemplated and the areas involved.

Italy is especially desirous of seeing industries established in the region south of Rome, the *Mezzogiorno,* which is relatively underdeveloped. Belgium is seeking to attract industries which hold promise of expanding its exports. The Netherlands and Luxembourg, because they are short of labor, do not welcome labor-intensive industries, but the latter country would like to obtain capital-intensive industries, especially those which utilize substantial amounts of steel, its principal industry.

West Germany, which has been making rapid strides industrially, permits, if it does not encourage, foreign investment. Some German private firms desire to attract foreign investment participation, especially where it includes highly-qualified managerial and technical officers. Until recently France accepted United States investment, but, since the acquisition of an old and well-established French automobile company by an American automobile manufacturer, French government officials have shown hostility to United States direct investment, except in specified distressed areas where it is encouraged. In addition, the French government has sought to bring the Common Market to espouse this reticence and discourage widespread American direct investment in the area.

The United Kingdom and Switzerland have had some success in creating a favorable climate for foreign investment. Austria, Denmark and Norway neither encourage nor discourage it, while the hostility of Portugal to foreign capital has been decreasing in recent years.

Inducements for direct investment. Many EEC and EFTA nations offer *special inducements* to foreign capital, especially when it proposes to establish enterprises in the less developed regions as well as those which will increase exports or utilize domestic products. The inducements are varied in form. In exceptional cases, tax concessions and rapid depreciation are granted; thus Belgium, the Netherlands, Denmark, the United Kingdom and Sweden permit stipulated tax-free allowances on reinvested capital gains and provide certain facilities for accelerated depreciation.

Where a part of a country is either under- or overdeveloped industrially, some nations offer inducements to investments in the former or in areas which lie outside the latter. Italy has a program for its distressed regions which includes certain tax exemptions and low interest rates on borrowings. Belgium also provides tax remissions and low interest rate loans for new industries in certain southeast and southwest parts of the country. To induce industry to build outside of the overcrowded Paris region, France offers grants, loans and the remission of certain taxes for foreign industries outside of Paris and in areas of unemployment. American direct investments in France are likely to be less welcome, however, than those of the other Common Market members.

West Germany, less in need of foreign capital than some other European nations, offers little inducement to investment from abroad. The United Kingdom, including parts of Scotland and Wales, provides loans and subsidies to certain new industrial enterprises. Northern Ireland has a program of grants and subsidized buildings designed to attract foreign capital. Norway has established a Development Fund to make low interest loans to new industry. In addition, it remits certain taxes and permits the rapid depreciation of capital of newly-established factories in its northern regions.[5]

Appendix C, "Selected Sources of Business Information on the EEC and EFTA Countries," gives sources to which investors may turn for additional information.

Investment decisions involving substantial amounts of capital or the delicate arrangements of a licensing agreement require careful investigation and analysis especially as concerns the locale, type, form and parties involved. Although opportunities for profitable and rewarding investment in the Common Market abound, there are pitfalls and disappointments which must be avoided.

Direct investment overseas is not only a frequently profitable and satisfying venture for the private businessman or firm, but it also plays an important role in the foreign economic relations of the United States. It is well known that the foreign relations of the United States are carried out by the federal government. What is less well known, but no less true, is the fact that considerable foreign policy is made and carried out on a smaller scale by

United States direct investments abroad. Well managed, successfully operated United States investments in the Common Market serve to cement relations between this country and the EEC and make for a stronger and more effective Atlantic Union.

NOTES

[1] This statement applies principally to those countries with which the United States has a treaty of Friendship, Commerce and Navigation, or a similar treaty, which guarantees "national treatment" to American persons, property and business. As a general proposition, national treatment means that persons, property and businesses of United States residents will receive treatment similar to that accorded to nationals of the nation in which they are located or do business. Since the United States has such treaties in force with all of the EEC and EFTA countries, American business firms should not be at any disadvantage, on this account, in operating inside these institutions.

[2] Cf. Max J. Wasserman and James F. Tucker. "The U.S. Tax Treaty Program," *National Tax Association*, II, No. 2 (March 1949), pp. 33-50. On January 1, 1963, the United States had treaties for the prevention of double income taxation in force with the following EEC countries: Belgium, France, the Netherlands, West Germany; and the following EFTA members: Austria, Denmark, Norway, Sweden and Switzerland. Source: Treaties Affairs Staff, Office of the Legal Adviser, Department of State, *Treaties in Force.* Washington, D.C.: U.S. GPO, 1963.

[3] Computed from data presented in Samuel Pizer and Frederick Cutler. "United States Assets and Investments Abroad," *Survey of Current Business,* Vol. 41, No. 8 (August 1961), pp. 20-26. (A publication of the U.S. Department of Commerce.) Additional data on the financial results of United States direct investments abroad for recent years are given in Samuel Pizer and Frederick Cutler. "U.S. Business Investments in Foreign Countries," a supplement to the *Survey of Current Business.* Washington, D.C.: U.S. GPO, 1960. The profits of United States direct investments in Europe vary widely from country to country. See Emile Benoit, *Europe at Sixes and Sevens: The Common Market, the Free Trade Association and the United States.* New York: Columbia University Press, 1961, p. 195. See also Bruce R. Williams. *International Report on Factors in Investment Behavior.* Paris: The Organization for Economic Co-Operation and Development, n.d., p. IX, 10.

[4] Cf. The United States Council of the International Chamber of Commerce. "Increasing International Trade Through Product Licenses." A special committee report (mimeographed). 103 Park Avenue, New York 17, N.Y., April 1953.

[5] Cf. Morgan Guaranty Trust Co. of New York, *Market Europe,* New York, 1961, pp. 34-36.

6

Investing in the Common Market: Results, Problems and Policies

QUANTITATIVE ASPECTS OF AMERICAN DIRECT INVESTMENT
ABROAD — EXPORT AND INVESTMENT PROS AND CONS — THE
INVESTMENT DECISION

When the United States was a young country, capital from the financial centers of Europe — London, Paris, Amsterdam and Berlin — flowed across its shores to help in the development of railroads, canals, mines, manufacturing and financial enterprises as well as cotton plantations. Although foreign businessmen continue to invest in this country, the *net* flow has been reversed. United States direct investment overseas today exceeds the amount of foreign direct investment in this country several times over.

Table 6.1 shows the movement of United States direct investment abroad and foreign direct investment in the United States for selected years, 1919-1962. By 1962, total American direct investment overseas amounted to about $35 billion. Foreign direct investment in the United States totaled $7.6 billion.

The direct investment interests of American business abroad differ somewhat from those of foreign business in the United States. The former is concentrated in petroleum, manufacturing, mining, utilities, service facilities and agriculture. The latter stresses financial and insurance companies together with manufacturing, especially foods and beverages. About 70 per cent of the total foreign direct investments in the United States are held by Europeans, many of them residents of the United Kingdom, the Netherlands and Switzerland. American direct investments

TABLE 6.1

TOTAL UNITED STATES DIRECT INVESTMENTS ABROAD AND
FOREIGN DIRECT INVESTMENTS IN THE
UNITED STATES, 1919-1962
(In billions of dollars)

	United States	Foreign
1919	3.9	0.9
1930	8.0	1.4
1939	7.0	1.8
1945	8.4	2.7
1950	11.8	3.4
1959	29.7	6.6
1960	29.8	6.9
1961	32.8	7.4
1962	34.7	7.6

Source: Hal B. Lary, *The United States in the World Economy.* (A publication of the U. S. Department of Commerce.) Washington:
U. S. GPO, 1943, p. 123; U. S. Department of Commerce, *U. S.
Business Investments in Foreign Countries.* Washington: U. S.
GPO, 1960, p. 1; U. S. Department of Commerce, *Survey of Current Business.* August 1963, p. 17.

are located principally in Canada, Latin America, Europe, the
Far and Middle East.[1]

Quantitative Aspects of American Direct Investment Abroad

Immediately after its inauguration, the Common Market
attracted the investment of substantial amounts of capital from
American business. This resulted, in part, from the proposed
tariff structure. In addition, the high rate of growth of the EEC,
the relatively low wage scales and the proximity to resurgent
markets were other factors influencing these business decisions.

Table 6.2 indicates total United States direct investments
in the EEC countries in several recent years. Between 1950 and
the signing of the Treaty of Rome in 1957, there was a substantial increase in United States direct capital outflows to the
area. The attraction of the Common Market for American funds
is illustrated by the growth from $1,680 million in 1957 to

$3,671 million in 1962. Germany was the recipient of the largest dollar volume of direct capital outflows in this period.

TABLE 6.2

TOTAL UNITED STATES DIRECT INVESTMENT IN THE EEC,
1950, 1957, 1960-1962
(In millions of dollars)

	1950	1957	1960	1961	1962
Belgium-Luxembourg	69	102	231	261	283
France	217	464	741	857	1,006
Germany	204	581	1,006	1,177	1,472
Italy	63	252	384	483	540
Netherlands	84	191	283	310	370
Total EEC	637	1,680	2,644	3,087	3,671

Totals may not add due to rounding

Source: *Survey of Current Business.* (A publication of the U. S. Department of Commerce.) Vol. 43, No. 8 (August 1963), p. 18.

As Table 6.3 reveals, manufacturing accounted for the greatest share of United States direct investments in the EEC (1962) with a total of $2,063 million; petroleum installations were second and trade third. Neither mining and smelting nor public utilities has attracted much American capital to this area.

Investment in plant and equipment. According to a survey conducted by the United States Department of Commerce, American branches and subsidiaries in all areas abroad plan to increase their investment in plant and equipment in 1963 by 8 per cent (over 1962) for a total of $4.9 billion. The largest investment is planned by the petroleum industry. For 1964, these firms project a slightly smaller investment, $4.5 billion.[2]

Substantial increases in new and additional plant and equipment are also projected by American branches and subsidiaries in the EEC area for 1963 and 1964 as Table 6.4 shows. The planned expenditures are largest in manufacturing, with the heaviest share in Germany. According to the plans of firms in the EEC, the total amount to be invested in plant and equipment will be smaller in 1964 than in 1963.

TABLE 6.3

TOTAL UNITED STATES DIRECT INVESTMENT IN THE EEC, BY INDUSTRY TYPE, 1962

(In millions of dollars)

	Mining & Smelting	Petroleum	Manufacturing	Public Utilities	Trade	Other	Total
Belgium-Luxembourg	n.a.	58	174	1	41	9	283
France	9	257	582	10	122	26	1,006
Germany	x	376	956	3	94	43	1,472
Italy	x	229	232	2	47	30	540
Netherlands	n.a.	163	119	15	59	14	370
Total EEC	9	1,083	2,063	31	361	124	3,671

Totals may not add due to rounding
x Combined in "other" industries
n.a. Not available
Source: *Survey of Current Business.* (A publication of the U. S. Department of Commerce.) Vol. 43, No. 8 (August 1963), p. 18.

TABLE 6.4

PROJECTED INCREASE IN PLANT AND EQUIPMENT EXPENDITURES BY UNITED STATES DIRECT INVESTMENT ENTERPRISES IN EEC COUNTRIES, 1963-1964

(In millions of dollars)

	1963(a)		1964(a)	
	Petroleum	Manufacturing	Petroleum	Manufacturing
Belgium-Luxembourg	15	47	17	61
France	50	99	64	95
Germany	155	265	77	240
Italy	110	56	104	53
Netherlands	56	30	41	33
Total EEC	386	497	303	482

(a) Projected by firms concerned.
Source: *Survey of Current Business.* (A publication of the U. S. Department of Commerce.) Vol. 43, No. 10 (October 1963), p. 15.

Sources and uses of funds. Funds for investment in plant and equipment and other end-uses of the American branches and subsidiaries in Europe (separate breakdowns for the EEC are not available) were derived in 1962, as Table 6.5 indicates, principally from depreciation and depletion allowances followed closely by net income. Capital obtained from foreign sources was more important in meeting the financial needs of these direct investment enterprises than that procured from the United States.

TABLE 6.5

SOURCES OF FUNDS UTILIZED BY UNITED STATES DIRECT INVESTMENT ENTERPRISES IN ALL AREAS AND EUROPE, 1962

(In millions of dollars)

	All Areas		Europe	
	Amount	Per Cent	Amount	Per Cent
Total sources	8,537	100.0	2,426	100.0
Net income	3,833	44.9	648	26.7
U. S. funds	923	10.8	526	21.7
Foreign funds	1,447	16.9	594	24.5
Depreciation and depletion	2,334	27.3	658	27.0

Totals may not add due to rounding.
Source: *Survey of Current Business.* (A publication of the U. S. Department of Commerce.) Vol. 43, No. 10 (October 1963), p. 18.

The sources of funds pattern was different for Europe when compared with the world as a whole. A substantial fraction of the funds, almost 45 per cent, of American direct investment enterprises in all areas was obtained from net income. Depreciation and depletion allowances were a second source.

Investment in property, plant and equipment was the most important use to which the funds of American branches and subsidiaries abroad were put in 1962 in all areas (46.3 per cent), and in Europe (59.6 per cent). The payment of income accounted for about 32 per cent of total fund allocations in all areas, but only about 18 per cent in Europe (Table 6.6).

Sales. The sales of all American direct investment enterprises abroad totaled over $28 billion in 1962 (Table 6.7). Those

TABLE 6.6

USES OF FUNDS BY UNITED STATES DIRECT INVESTMENT ENTERPRISES IN ALL AREAS AND EUROPE, 1962

(In millions of dollars)

	All Areas		Europe	
	Amount	Per Cent	Amount	Per Cent
Total uses	8,537	100.0	2,426	100.0
Property, plant, equipment	3,953	46.3	1,447	59.6
Inventories	644	7.5	244	10.1
Receivables	699	8.2	212	8.7
Other Assets	484	5.6	68	2.8
Income paid out	2,757	32.3	455	18.1

Totals may not add due to rounding.
Source: *Survey of Current Business.* (A publication of the U. S. Department of Commerce.) Vol. 43, No. 10 (October 1963), p. 18.

TABLE 6.7

UNITED STATES DIRECT INVESTMENT ENTERPRISES IN ALL AREAS AND EUROPE: SALES AND EXPORTS, 1962

(In millions of dollars)

	Total Sales	Local Sales	Exports to United States	Exports to Other Countries
All areas	28,129	23,550	1,350	3,220
Europe (a)	11,780	9,295	175	2,310

(a) Data for EEC countries are not available.
Source: *Survey of Current Business.* (A publication of the U. S. Department of Commerce.) Vol. 43, No. 10 (October 1963), p. 20.

of United States branches and subsidiaries located in Europe amounted to about $12 billion. Local sales were substantially greater than the exports of these firms to the United States both for all areas and Europe. Their exports to other areas were larger than those to the United States. These facts lead to the possible inference that the sales of foreign affiliates of United States firms do not replace the domestic trade of American companies to any great extent, but they may hinder some American exports.

United States share of earnings and income received. The

United States share of the earnings of branches and subsidiaries located in the EEC is presented in Table 6.8. It amounted to $344 million in 1961 and $360 million in 1962. United States income from German branches and subsidiaries (Table 6.8) was the largest in both years. That from those located in France was small. In 1961 United States direct investments in the EEC area paid out about 56 per cent of their share of the earnings in the form of income to Americans and almost 69 per cent in 1962.

TABLE 6.8

UNITED STATES DIRECT INVESTMENT ENTERPRISES IN THE EEC: UNITED STATES SHARE OF TOTAL EARNINGS AND INCOME RECEIVED, 1961-1962

(In millions of dollars)

| | U. S. Share of Earnings | | U. S. Income Received | |
	1961	1962	1961	1962
Belgium-Luxembourg	45	41	26	35
France	58	59	26	22
Germany	184	197	103	137
Italy	28	30	23	29
Netherlands	29	34	15	23
Total EEC	344	360	193	247

Totals may not add due to rounding.

Source: *Survey of Current Business.* (A publication of the U. S. Department of Commerce.) Vol. 43, No. 8 (August 1963), pp. 17-18.

Export and Investment Pros and Cons

The Common Market cannot easily be ignored by businessmen in other countries. Directly or indirectly, it is likely to touch the lives of many enterprisers in all areas of the globe. For some American manufacturers, interested in doing business with Europe, the EEC offers a choice between exports to it or the establishment of producing facilities within its borders.

Export prospects. Exports present the signal advantage of benefiting from the promise of the Common Market with a minimum of expenditure. In addition, as pointed out elsewhere, the EEC is an area of growing incomes. This increases the ability of the Market to absorb exports. Its industries are likely to be in the market for raw materials, semi-finished goods and components as well as capital equipment.

Where European consumers or industries demand goods of differing specifications from those manufactured in the United States, American industry must "tool up" to produce exports acceptable to these countries. This is frequently an expensive and disruptive process. If an American manufacturer decides that export disadvantages outweigh the advantages and he still desires to sell his goods in the Common Market, he must decide whether or not to establish manufacturing facilities within the area.

Investment prospects. Of course, the decision to export to, or to manufacture in, the Common Market is not necessarily exclusive. A firm may manufacture some goods in the EEC and export others. Thus some United States automobile companies manufacture European-type vehicles in the EEC and also export some American types to the same market.

Profit opportunities in this Market have been good in the past and promise to continue (at somewhat lower levels) for a number of years to come. Very few American lines of business offer better profit opportunities.

Sometimes, but not always, EEC-located industries are in a better position to supply third markets than American domestic enterprises. This is probably true as far as the Community's associated overseas countries and territories are concerned. American direct investment enterprises in France enjoy the export, import and financial facilities available to firms located within the Franc Zone. Dollar exchange is still a "hard" currency as far as some underdeveloped nations are concerned, while those of some EEC countries are relatively "softer." EEC member nations' currencies are frequently available to those less developed countries which direct a substantial fraction of their exports into the Community. Where an EEC nation has already established good commercial relations with a third country, an American enterprise located within its borders can also reap the benefits which they confer.

When considering investment opportunities in the Common Market, the possible advantages of location in one of the associated overseas countries and territories should not be overlooked. Due to the shortage of skilled workers and sophisticated executives, many of these areas do not offer attractive possibilities for some American manufacturing enterprises. But there may be types of operations where these disadvantages will not prove critical. Local workers can often be trained and executives developed, sent over from the American parent companies or recruited from the EEC countries.

Businessmen frequently complain about government regulation of business in the United States. In many instances, the control which the EEC nations exercise over business may be considerably greater, more pervasive and frustrating than that found in America. Many business acts which are freely performed in America are subject to permits, authorizations and licenses in the Common Market. The amount of paper work which they entail is substantial.

The several Community bureaucracies are of a somewhat different character and generally wield more power than their American counterparts. Except in those departments and agencies which exercise regulatory functions, American government functionaries are schooled to help United States business. They take the attitude that they are servants of the American people and not their masters. Federal agencies perform a number of services, provide information and advice to American business, especially to the smaller enterprises.

The European higher government functionaries are essentially administrators and regulators. The services which they render business and the information they provide are less extensive than those found in the United States. Americans who establish facilities in the EEC will be subject to the same bureaucratic controls as their Common Market colleagues. However, since European businessmen have learned to live under their systems, to make profits and to enjoy business life, why should not Americans do likewise?

Choice of the investment locale. The problem of the choice of a Common Market country in which to invest and the precise location within that country for the facility involves the consideration of factors such as the following:

1. Nature and character of the economy of the country, its suitability for the type of business in question, the attitudes of business colleagues and competitors.

2. The type and nature of the government of the country including its stability, attitude toward business and foreign investment, business laws and regulations, extent to which it applies policies of laissez faire or dirigisme.

3. Cost structures and prices in competing and other industries.

4. The supply and skills of the labor force and executive talent, as well as wage scales, social security and fringe benefits, extent and nature of labor unionism and labor legislation.

5. Proximity to sources of supplies and to market outlets.

6. Capital markets, both long- and short-term, especially access to potential capital requirements, rates of interest and borrowing terms.

7. The transportation system, utilities and energy facilities.

8. Distribution facilities including servicing arrangements.

9. The tax system, especially as it applies to the type of business in question.

10. Anti-trust legislation.

11. Inducements offered by the government to locate in specified areas or to establish certain types of enterprises.

Since a business located in any part of the Common Market will face the competition of those in any other part and since the growth potential of the Market as a whole is of more importance than that of any member nation, these factors have less significance in finding an answer to the question of a specific location within the Community. They are of importance, though, in the decision of whether or not to invest in the EEC area. In deciding upon the locale, accurate and precise information will be required to arrive at a well-grounded and rational decision.

Often the advice of experts in the several fields will prove helpful as will also personal, on-the-spot investigation.

From the point of view of the national economies and that of the EEC, the influx of United States investment may prove of substantial value. Products and technology which have contributed to the strength of the American economy will be added, thereby diversifying and buttressing the EEC. However, the extent to which these advantages will be recognized by the governments of the countries concerned and the institutions of the EEC is problematical.

Choice of products. The apparently bright prospects for enterprises located in the Common Market are not likely to apply with uniformity to all firms, products and business methods. As in the case of any other dynamic economy, the EEC will undoubtedly see some products and their manufacturers rise and others decline. The prospects for certain types of manufactures are, however, encouraging.

Given the probable growth in size and specialization of local EEC enterprises, there appears to be a good market for a wide variety of American-type capital equipment, adapted to European requirements. The demand for certain industrial semi-finished goods and components also seems likely to increase. Higher consumer's incomes resulting from the growth of the Common Market GNP should stimulate the demand for income elastic consumer's goods and durables.[3]

Producer's goods which hold the greatest promise on the markets of the Community may well be those of a labor-saving and cost-cutting type, of demonstrable efficiency and priced within the capital budget ranges of EEC enterprises. They may frequently be of the kind which have produced satisfactory results in the United States. There is every reason to believe that the products which American consumers have come to demand in larger quantities as their incomes increased will also prove increasingly saleable in the Common Market. Such products, however, must be adapted to the European consumer's tastes. In addition, they must be within their purchasing capacities—now smaller than those of American consumers.

The spirit of progress is one of the outstanding features of the Common Market. Hence, products involving innovation are likely to be desired by both EEC producers and consumers. Products and procedures which will assist in automation should be in demand because of the Market's increasing wage scales, social security and fringe benefits. Old-fashioned products, unless they are of established effectiveness and appeal, may well be shunned by Community buyers.

American enterprise has helped to give the inhabitants of this country the highest standard of living of any nation in the world and to attain the nation's role as leader of the free countries. In going abroad American business brings with it a part of this American heritage. The realization of this fact should add another dimension to the satisfactions to be derived from investment in the Common Market.

NOTES

[1] Additional details concerning United States direct investments abroad and foreign direct investments in the United States are given in: U.S. Department of Commerce, *U.S. Business Investments in Foreign Countries.* (A supplement to the *Survey of Current Business.*) Washington: U.S. GPO, 1960 and U.S. Department of Commerce, *Foreign Business Investments in the United States.* (A supplement to the *Survey of Current Business.*) Washington: U.S. GPO, 1962. In addition, the *Survey of Current Business,* published monthly by the U.S. Department of Commerce, usually carries articles in the August and October issues, devoted to the movement and results of American direct investment abroad.

[2] Fred Cutler and Samuel Pizer. "Foreign Operations of U.S. Industry: Capital Expenditures, Sales, and Financing." *Survey of Current Business.* Vol. 43, No. 10 (October 1963), p. 13.

[3] Broadly stated, the income elasticity of a commodity refers to the changes in the amount of it demanded as income rises and falls. Where the amount demanded increases or declines substantially as income rises, or falls, the commodity is held to be income elastic. Where changes in income make relatively little difference in the amounts demanded as income varies, the commodity is said to be income inelastic.

7

Labor in the Common Market

GENERAL NATURE OF THE LABOR AND SOCIAL PROVISIONS—
COST EFFECTS OF THE EEC LABOR PROGRAM—AVAILABILITY
AND COST OF LABOR IN THE EEC—EUROPEAN LABOR UNIONS
AND LEGISLATION

Among the more important features of the European Economic Community are those relating to labor and social policy. The Treaty of Rome specifies that a free movement of labor among the member states of the Community shall be ensured by the end of the transitional period. The Treaty requires that a fund be established to finance the retraining and resettlement of unemployed workers. Finally, it provides for cooperation among member states on such matters as employment, labor legislation and working conditions, social security and trade union rights.

These provisions were considered essential for over-all economic integration. That is, as other provisions of the EEC are implemented, including the establishment of a common external tariff and the elimination of internal trade barriers, production and marketing patterns are changed. Business firms alter their activities in light of new profit opportunities; they might expand operations, transfer to different locations, or merge with other firms. Inefficient producers might be forced to discontinue operations. Insofar as firms do alter their activities in some fashion, it is likely to have an impact on working conditions and job requirements and opportunities.

To alleviate the possible hardships on workers caused by structural changes in the economy of the EEC, and in general

134

to improve the scale of living and working conditions of employees, a labor and social program is being put into effect. Some aspects of this program are stipulated explicitly in the Treaty of Rome. Others are based on general policy statements; they arise as EEC officials, acting upon other economic, political and social developments, devise methods of achieving stated Treaty objectives.

The new policies relating to labor are of significance to American businessmen in a number of ways. In the first place, the competitive position of European firms will be affected by those Community policies which have an impact on wage rates and the availability of European labor. Second, the United States firm which actually initiates productive operations in the EEC must bargain with labor on the basis of new Community regulations.

General Nature of the Labor and Social Provisions

Meaning of free movement of labor. Articles 48 and 49 of the Treaty of Rome stipulate that there should be a relatively freer movement of labor among member countries of the EEC by the end of the transitional period (not later than the beginning of 1970).[1] This does not imply that workers are completely free to move among member states as they are within a state. The phrase "freer movement of labor" means that workers will be able to circulate without restriction to take up offers of jobs anywhere in the Community. Thus workers have the *right* to *move freely* within the EEC *to accept offers actually made.* Before a person can obtain a job in another country he must also be qualified or sufficiently trained for the position.

Regulations permit workers to remain in a country to continue employment and to live there after employment has been secured. The wife or husband of a worker, children under twenty-one years of age, and other wholly dependent members of the family are allowed to accompany the worker. Workers from other states must be treated in the same way as nationals so far as conditions of work and employment are concerned. Equality of treatment extends to membership in trade unions including the right to vote in elections. Any discrimination based on nationality on the part of employers concerning employment, wages or other working conditions is generally abolished.

Significance of labor mobility in the EEC. The EEC countries have employed foreign workers in the past, in many cases on a temporary basis, to meet labor shortages; the practice has not been confined to the use of workers from other EEC countries. As an illustration, West Germany employed persons from over fifteen non-European nationalities in 1962. However, in many of the European countries, Italian workers represent the largest part of the foreign work force.

Developments concerning the free movement of labor in the EEC reflect a trend away from the more typical pattern of selective immigration which was initiated early in the 1900's throughout much of the world. Actually, labor circulation had been liberalized at least partially within Europe in the period following World War II. The Organization for European Economic Cooperation, for example, had promoted labor mobility, and many European countries accepted the idea, at least in principle. In practice, however, foreign workers have generally been permitted to enter a country only temporarily, usually on a seasonal basis or to be used where severe labor shortages existed. These immigrants were normally issued temporary work permits which were not renewed when such labor was no longer needed. Much of the labor migration in Western Europe in the post-World War II period was represented by a movement of Italian workers to Belgium, France and Switzerland.

Permanent mobility of workers in one economic sector was authorized with the implementation of the European Coal and Steel Community (ECSC). Workers in the coal and steel industry of the ECSC were given an opportunity to move among member countries under specified circumstances. Provisions of the EEC relating to labor mobility are similar to those of the ECSC, except that the former applies to all sectors of the area; that is, the former is a far more comprehensive program.

Transitional aspects. In order to avoid sharp structural changes in the European market, the policy concerning the movement of labor is to be implemented gradually. The first Community labor regulation (No. 15) went into force in September 1961 and remained in effect for two years. The initial measures established the machinery whereby job vacancies and applications could be combined. When employment opportunities arise in a member state, workers of that state receive first priority; vacancies unfilled after three weeks must be reported to other EEC states and persons from any member state become eligible to fill them. Workers from other members qualify for exactly the same privileges and benefits as those of the country in which they are working after having been employed in a country for *four* years. Labor-short countries agree to give Community workers preference over non-Community workers.

Action by the Community concerning labor mobility has not ended with the initial regulations. The Commission of the EEC has outlined provisions which it believes are necessary during the second stage of development. In general, the new proposals afford a lower priority for the home labor market. The Commission believes, for example, that the three-week preference period for home labor should be discarded. It also proposes that a worker be treated exactly as a national of the country in which he was working following only *two* years of employment. Eventually, a worker will obtain the right to continue to live in the country of employment even after the loss of the actual job.

It is assumed in the EEC that during later stages of the Community's development the Commission's action will extend beyond that of removing obstacles to the free flow of labor. Ultimately the Commission's task will be a more positive one; it will endeavor to direct the flow of workers into appropriate areas based on the needs of the various labor markets.

The European Social Fund. The EEC not only permits a more free circulation of workers within the area, but actively encourages labor mobility through employment bureaus and through the facilities of the European Social Fund. The function of the European Coordination Office, located in Brussels, is to facilitate the clearing of vacancies and applications for employment. Information concerning job opportunities and applications is channeled through this office. Employment exchanges must not make a distinction between their own nationals and those of other member states as they seek to match unemployed workers with vacancies.

The European Social Fund is similar in many respects to the readaptation scheme which has been employed in conjunction with the European Coal and Steel Community. The Fund, which was set up in 1960, is designed to supply an incentive for workers to accept employment elsewhere—to overcome the natural resistance to a change in occupation or residence, to become part of a different culture or learn a new language.[2] The Fund is engaged in what is termed "joint financing"; it redistributes a certain amount of financial assistance to member states in the form of grants for the resettlement and retraining of workers.[3] Coverage is for all categories of workers, including those in the agricultural sector, and all forms of unemployment rather than being limited to maladjustments resulting from the creation of the EEC.

Grants are made available to offer *occupational* training to unemployed workers for what is called "the link between demographic expansion and technological change." The grants are extended only if it is otherwise impossible to utilize the unemployed workers in new jobs. Furthermore, allowances are paid to member states only after workers have been in productive employment for at least six months in the occupation for which they have been retrained. In a sense, the allowance for the member government is limited to "successful" retraining operations.

Resettlement grants are authorized to encourage workers to move to areas of the EEC where labor shortages prevail. These grants are available only if workers are unable to find suitable employment locally. Member governments are not reimbursed for the specified share of the expenses incurred until the worker has been in productive employment in the new place of residence for at least six months. Resettlement grants need not be limited to country-to-country movements. For example, such an allowance might be made for a labor transfer from southern to northern Italy.

Finally, provision is made for payments from the Social Fund for the benefit of workers whose employment is temporarily reduced or wholly or partially suspended as a result of the conversion of their enterprise to other production; hence they may maintain the same wage level pending their full reemployment.

Extensive efforts are made to distribute information to all workers concerning employment opportunities, facilities for free movement and vocational training. In these ways, the Fund serves to foster occupational and geographical mobility of workers. In addition to promoting an optimum use of the labor force, it helps alleviate adverse consequences of structural changes stemming from rapid economic progress.

During 1961, for example, a program was initiated to retrain some 10,000 Italian workers, most of whom were to be employed in West German construction, metal processing and catering industries. The cost of the training, which took place in Italian training centers, was shared by the governments concerned and the Social Fund.[4]

The Fund operates by refunding 50 per cent of expenditures incurred by member states for resettlement, retraining, and similar purposes. Reimbursement is made only after all the expenditures have been undertaken and after it has been shown that the workers who received benefits have maintained the new type of employment for a period of at least six months. The request for Social Fund aid must come from the state involved. Payments from the Fund are made directly to member states rather than to workers.

By the end of 1961, the Fund had disbursed nearly $26 million. About two-thirds of this amount represented reimbursement for retraining workers; the rest, for resettlement expenses. During 1962, the Fund extended grants totaling approximately $12.29 million to member governments for expenses incurred in retraining and resettlement programs. The largest amount, approximately $4.62 million, was received by France; Italy received $3.73 million; Germany, $2.00 million; the Netherlands, $1.47 million and Belgium, $.46 million.

The operations of the Social Fund in improving the quality of the labor force represent some of the more creative aspects of the EEC. The Fund is scheduled to continue its functions for at least the duration of the transitional period (that is, until the EEC is fully implemented). At that time, depending upon the decision of the EEC authorities, a part or all of its activities may be extended, or it may be assigned new tasks relative to the development of the Community labor force.[5]

Social security benefits. The provisions relating to social security benefits are another aspect of the EEC labor program. One of the earliest provisions, in force since the beginning of 1959, permits workers to retain social security benefits when they move to another member state.

Article 118 of the Treaty of Rome requires close collaboration between member states in reference to social security benefits. One objective of the EEC authorities is to bring about greater uniformity in national systems of social and labor legislation. This would tend to remove a possible obstacle to the free movement of labor. It would also reduce the significance of what is known as "distortions of competition." That is, insofar as social security and other fringe benefits differ from one member state to a second, they represent a greater cost burden on firms in one country than in others. Hence firms in the first country are, in a sense, at a competitive disadvantage. For example, much of the cost of social security benefits might be borne by employers in Italy and a small share financed out of general tax revenues, whereas the opposite situation might prevail in Belgium. Under these circumstances the Italian firm would face a cost disadvantage.

In view of this problem, the EEC Commission has undertaken to promote changes in national legislation through voluntary cooperation of member governments with the objective of the harmonization of social systems (Article 117). Harmonization is to occur in an upward direction rather than as a simple "averaging" process. That is, an effort will be made to raise standards in all countries, rather than lowering them in some countries, to achieve similar systems.

Harmonization of social security programs is likely to be a relatively long-run process. As noted later in this chapter, the differences in programs from country to country are quite significant; they cannot be eliminated easily within a short period of time.

Principle of equal pay. Article 119 of the Treaty of Rome calls for "equal remuneration for equal work as between men and women workers." The equality of pay principle, which is applicable to both the piece-rate and time-rate methods of payment, is slated for full implementation by the end of 1964. In the interim, the differences are to be reduced in successive stages. By mid-1962, any differences were to be reduced to a maximum of 15 per cent; by mid-1963, to 10 per cent; and by the end of 1964, all discrimination is to be abolished. The principle of equal pay is of greatest interest in countries such as France where there is a high percentage of females in the labor force.

The equality of pay principle has applicability only in reference to the sex of the workers. Firms retain the right to utilize wage differentials based on usual criteria such as seniority, productivity and family considerations.

Seasonal and frontier workers. A special set of proposals and regulations applies to seasonal and frontier workers, since they cannot be as readily covered by social benefits as other workers. Seasonal workers are those employed periodically, on a temporary basis, in a country other than that of residence. Many seasonal workers are Italians who typically are hired for a period of time in France and Germany in the building and farming sectors.

Frontier workers are those living in one country but regularly employed on a full-time basis in a second country. One example is the worker residing in Belgium near the French border who is employed in the French iron and steel industry.

Efforts have been made by the EEC authorities to make the rights and privileges of these workers both explicit and uniform throughout the Community. This is primarily a matter of getting member countries to agree which country, the one of residence or the one of employment, is responsible for a particular aspect of a worker's social rights. In practice, the provisions are implemented in such a fashion that the country of residence assumes responsibilities under some specified circumstances, the country of employment, in others.[6]

Cost Effects of the EEC Labor Program

The basic objective of the EEC labor program is to create a framework within which an optimum use of human resources is possible. The promotion of geographical and occupational mobility is considered a prerequisite for continued industrialization and rapid technological change. One effect of the program is that it could theoretically alleviate some of the upward pressure on labor costs and thus render European production more competitive. It may have the effect of encouraging foreign direct investment in the EEC to take advantage of relatively favorable labor cost conditions.

One reason why the EEC labor program may increase productivity and reduce pressure on wage rates is that there is a greater likelihood that the Community labor force will be more fully utilized. Freedom of workers to move from one state to another should reduce the extent to which unemployment constitutes a burden in one area of the EEC at the same time that labor shortages exist in other areas. Southern Italy, for example, has experienced chronic unemployment through much of the period since World War II; in contrast, the predominantly industrial areas, especially in West Germany, have vacancies in manufacturing which exceed the number of unemployed workers. The scarcity of human resources in some areas is reportedly one of the factors which has curbed investment in the EEC.

In the selection of a site for operations, a business firm must take several factors into consideration—proximity to natural resources and sources of energy, transportation facilities, the finished product market, the availability of labor, among many other factors. As a result of the Common Market labor program, firms are given the opportunity to recruit workers from beyond the frontiers of national markets. Insofar as labor mobility is actually encouraged, along with the free flow of products, business firms have somewhat greater freedom in locating their operations where it appears that profits are greatest.

The EEC has undoubtedly increased labor efficiency by promoting occupational mobility. The Social Fund furnishes vocational retraining assistance in an effort to aid in the productive reemployment of workers who must change jobs. The existence of structural unemployment is not limited to Western Europe; many of the industrial countries of the world are finding relatively high levels of unemployment in some sectors at the same time that a substantial number of vacancies exist in other sectors of their economies. The problem, at least in part, is that unemployed workers lack the skill or training to fill existing vacancies.

In early 1963, the Council of Ministers adopted several principles concerning the nature of vocational training. In general, an effort will be made to afford everyone the right to improve his skill throughout his entire career. Another important factor is that an attempt will be made to offer training facilities in advance of the requirements of the Community. Insofar as the EEC training program succeeds in achieving its objectives, the labor force will be more productive.

The compilation of annual reports on employment trends in the Community is an important function of the EEC Commission and these are likely to foster a more efficient use of the labor force. The reports are fairly detailed, showing conditions by country and by sector in the employment market. Forecasts of manpower requirements and availabilities are also provided. The reports are of great value to the businessman who contemplates the initiation or expansion of productive activity and who wishes to determine the employment situation in a particular geographical area of interest.

The EEC and wage structures. One of the basic features of the Community will be the absence of internal trade barriers. Ultimately, EEC traders will be able to export and import freely with other member countries. According to economic theory, a region tends to export items which embody its abundant factor of production and to import those goods which embody the scarce factor. One result is that a free flow of commodities tends to equalize commodity prices and the relative returns to the factors of production in the various trading areas. Accordingly, commodity movements serve as a substitute for factor movements. Yet it is generally accepted that unrestricted commodity trade alone cannot completely equalize factor prices.

A factor of production, such as labor, will tend to move to areas where productivity is highest. One result is that the movement serves to equalize returns to the factors of production in the regions involved. Thus one effect of the free movement of commodities and of labor in the EEC is the creation of relatively similar wage structures in the various member countries.

Complete wage equality is not expected, however. In the first place, workers do not enjoy *complete* freedom of movement. They can emigrate only if they are unemployed, and if job opportunities are available elsewhere. Second, imperfect knowledge, transportation costs and other factors tend to preclude perfect equality. Finally, national languages, culture, prejudices and other potential obstacles will remain long after the EEC is fully implemented; the free circulation of labor is impeded by many factors other than government imposed restrictions.

Results of the EEC labor policy. The introduction of the initial steps to further a free movement of labor among member countries has proved to be a difficult task. Fortunately, the general absence of unemployment in most member countries has resulted in conditions favorable to the implementation of policies. Opposition to immigrants is typical in areas where jobs are not plentiful. Even in the United States, workers moving into a new area, particularly if in substantial numbers, meet with resistance on the part of workers already there. The EEC's application of the principle of equal remuneration may avoid to an extent the friction stemming from "cheap labor," which frequently characterizes the settlement of new immigrants in an area. Actually, geographical immobility of workers in the EEC has stemmed at least partially from a housing shortage. It is not expected, however, that the mobility of workers and their families will ever be as great among countries as within a national labor market.

The implementation of initial provisions of the labor program and structural changes stemming from normal growth have caused shifts in the relative shares in employment among different sectors of the EEC. The portion of total employment in the agricultural sector declined from 22.7 per cent in 1958 to 19.5 per cent in 1962. Employment in the services sector rose from 35.3 to 37.4 per cent during the same period. Industrial employment increased from 42.0 to 43.1 per cent for the same years.[7] It is interesting to note that, unlike the trend in Europe, the share of workers in industrial employment in the United States has *decreased* noticeably during the past several years.

Availability and Cost of Labor in the EEC

The American firm, in deciding to invest directly in the EEC, must determine if the supply and cost of factoral inputs are conducive to a satisfactory rate of profit. In most instances, the wage bill represents the major cost for the operation of an enterprise.

Size of the EEC labor force. The labor force in the EEC is roughly equal in size to that of the United States—about 73 million workers—despite a smaller population in the EEC. This is because the labor force participation rate (the share of total population in the labor force) is somewhat larger than in the United States. The participation rate differs significantly from one member state to another; it is relatively high in West Germany and low in the Netherlands.

In addition to a higher participation rate in Europe, the work-week is longer than the 40-hour week in the United States. In most EEC and other Western European countries, the legal work-week has ranged from 44 to 48 hours. One exception is France in which the 40-hour week has been legal since before World War II. The actual work-week in France has generally exceeded 40 hours, thus resulting in overtime payments.

Another factor determining the availability of labor to the business firm is the share of workers in non-agricultural sectors. The agricultural sector of Europe (as well as of the United States) has been releasing workers for other occupations which are more productive. In 1958, for example, almost 23 per cent of the EEC labor force was in agriculture; by 1962, it had fallen to less than 20 per cent. As a result, an increasing share of workers is available for manufacturing and the service industries. This trend is expected to continue; it is projected that only about 16 per cent of the active population will be in agriculture by 1970. Retraining provisions of the European Social Fund may be used to make certain that the rural workers acquire the training and skills needed in non-agricultural pursuits.

EEC unemployment. In most areas of the EEC, unemployment is at a low level. In some regions, a shortage of skilled workers appears to have curbed the volume of private capital formation. The European Commission noted in its *Third Annual Report,* for example, that the gap between labor supply and demand was retarding the growth rate in certain sectors, and that there had been a sizeable increase in the number of unfilled vacancies. West Germany, as an illustration, has been characterized by a severe labor scarcity. The number of unemployed workers averaged about 150,000 during 1961 and 1962; job vacancies averaged about 550,000 throughout the same period. Job opportunities have also greatly exceeded the number of unemployed in the Netherlands.

In a few areas of the EEC, especially in southern Italy, unemployment remains relatively high, although the rate has been decreasing in the past few years. As noted earlier, extensive efforts are being made to retain workers and to resettle them where vacancies exist.

The unusually low rate of unemployment in the EEC is the result of a high level of consumer, business and government spending. It also stems from efforts on the part of the EEC to retrain and resettle workers. In 1962, the unemployment rate in Belgium was 2.2 per cent; Germany, .8 per cent; Italy, 3.0 per cent; and the Netherlands, .9 per cent. For the United States during the same year, unemployment amounted to 5.6 per cent.[8]

Projected labor statistics. Although the current labor situation in the EEC is of major importance, conditions in the future are perhaps of greater significance to American business. Fortunately, projections have been made by the EEC for the years 1965 and 1970 which shed some light on this matter.[9] These statistics have been computed for five EEC states; Luxembourg is not included.

The employable population of the EEC is projected to increase to 75.6 million in 1965 and to 77.9 million in 1970. The proportion of workers to population is estimated to fall from 43.4 per cent in 1960 to 42.8 per cent in 1970. The decrease in the labor force participation rate will be the outgrowth of longer school attendance and earlier retirement.

Unemployment is projected to continue at a relatively low level. By 1970, it is expected to drop to one million. In addition, the average length of the working week will be reduced throughout the Community. An annual average of 40 hours per week is anticipated as a result of a shorter working day and of longer holidays.

The level of output and income is calculated to remain at a high level. Per capita productivity of the working population is expected to increase by nearly 50 per cent during the ten-year period. Average gross output per worker in 1960 was the equivalent of about $2,500; this is expected to increase to approximately $3,750 by 1970 (in constant dollars).

Statistics for individual countries. Projections relating to the availability of labor in individual EEC countries are presented in Table 7.1. The size of the labor force and population is projected for five member countries (excluding Luxembourg) for 1965 and 1970; for purposes of comparison, the actual labor force and population figures are given for 1960. The three major determinants of the labor supply for each country are the size and growth of total population, the share of the population actively working or seeking employment, and net migrations.

Some of the results of retraining and resettlement allowances from the Social Fund are reflected in the figures in this Table. Additions to the labor force through migration are greatest for West Germany and France; both Italy and the Netherlands would experience a net outflow of workers.

The labor force participation rate is projected to decrease

significantly in West Germany. In the other member states, it will remain more constant.

For the Community as a whole, employment is projected to increase by about 7 per cent during the ten-year period. It will expand as much as 14 per cent in the Netherlands and as little as 3.5 per cent in West Germany.

TABLE 7.1

EEC POPULATION AND LABOR FORCE PROJECTIONS—1965 AND 1970

West Germany	1960	1965	1970
Population	53,382	55,476	57,607
Natural increase		54,476	56,107
Migration		1,000	1,500
Labor force	25,570	26,057	26,466
Labor force participation rate	47.9	47.0	45.9

Belgium	1960	1965	1970
Population	9,153	9,429	9,688
Natural increase		9,364	9,558
Migration		65	130
Labor force	3,670	3,725	3,855
Labor force participation rate	40.1	39.5	39.8

France	1960	1965	1970
Population	45,542	47,148	49,450
Natural increase		46,378	47,907
Migration		770	1,543
Labor force	19,180	19,870	20,730
Labor force participation rate	42.1	42.1	41.9

Italy	1960	1965	1970
Population	49,250	50,777	52,353
Natural increase		51,520	53,853
Migration		−750	−1,500
Labor force	20,645	21,311	21,992
Labor force participation rate	41.9	42.0	42.0

TABLE 7.1 (Continued)

	Netherlands		
	1960	1965	1970
Population	11,507	12,153	12,836
Natural increase		12,211	12,939
Migration		−58	−113
Labor force	4,224	4,551	4,833
Labor force participation rate	36.7	37.4	37.7

Source: European Economic Community Commission: *Economic Development Prospects in EEC from 1960 to 1970.* (This report is the English Summary of *Les Perspectives de Développement Economique dans la C.E.E.* Rapport d'un group d'experts, 1962, pp. 23-27).

Labor costs in the EEC. The United States firm investing in the EEC and hiring European workers will discover not only that wage rates are substantially lower than in the United States, but that the rate differs from one EEC member to the next.

Because of the low level of unemployment and other factors, labor unions have demanded substantial pay increases in the EEC countries and wage rates have risen rather sharply during the past few years. As shown in Table 7.2 the greatest change in wage rates since 1958 has been in France and Germany. In relative terms, wage gains in all EEC countries have exceeded those in the United States during the same period. EEC wage rates are likely to continue to rise more rapidly than in the United States because of the low European unemployment rate.

It is difficult to make an accurate comparison of labor costs among the EEC countries. There are problems involved because of the existence of different types of taxes, social security, and fringe benefits. In some cases, it appears that the wage differentials within a country may be as significant as those between countries. Wage discrepancies between industries also appear to be as great as that between countries. The promotion of occupational and geographical mobility will presumably reduce wage differentials throughout the Community. However, the United

States firm contemplating direct investment in the EEC should investigate industry labor costs as closely as country labor costs. Furthermore, other production expenses, such as raw material, energy and transport costs, as well as interest and rent payments must be considered.

TABLE 7.2

PERCENTAGE CHANGE IN WAGE RATES, THE EEC AND THE UNITED STATES, 1959-1962, AND FIRST QUARTER OF 1963[1]

	1959	1960	1961	1962	1st qtr. 1963
Belgium	2	4	3	8	7
France	7	7	10	9	8
Germany, West	5	9	10	12	7
Italy	2	3	4	8	8
Netherlands	2	8	5	8	10
United States	4	3	3	3	2

[1] Annual figures are percentage changes from preceding year; quarterly figures are percentage changes from first quarter of 1962.
Source: Adapted from recent issues of International Monetary Fund. *Annual Report*. Washington, D.C.

An early, but fairly comprehensive wage survey covered fourteen branches of industry and at least 30 per cent of wage earners in all manufacturing industries in five of the EEC countries (excluding Luxembourg). This survey included all direct and indirect labor charges facing the employer. For the year under consideration, 1959, average hourly wages were found to be highest but roughly equal in Germany, France and Belgium—the equivalent of about $.80 an hour. In the Netherlands and Italy, hourly wage rates were about 20 per cent lower.[10]

Generally, hourly wage rates for most of the major manufacturing industries are highest in West Germany; lowest in Italy. Rates in other EEC countries tend to fall between these extremes. Hourly wage rates are also highest in the automobile and shipbuilding industries; lowest in pottery, and the cotton and wool spinning industries.[11]

A substantial amount of data concerning labor costs is being compiled and published by the Statistical Office of the EEC. One recent and relatively detailed study, for example, consists of a comparison of workers' real incomes for thirteen of the Community's major industries.[12] Studies of this type suggest not only the relative cost structure, but also the potential demand for consumer goods and services.

Nature of wage costs. Non-wage costs account for a larger share of total labor costs in the EEC than in the United States. Table 7.3, for example, indicates that direct wages account,

TABLE 7.3

HOURLY LABOR COSTS IN THE EEC IRON AND STEEL INDUSTRY, 1961

(in U.S. dollars)

	West Germany	France	Italy	Nether-lands	Belgium	Luxem-bourg
Total	1.37	1.11	1.04	1.40	1.26	1.47
Direct wages[1]	.94	.63	.60	.78	.90	1.03
Bonuses, overtime, & incentive pay	.07	.04	.05	.11	.03	.08
Pay for hours not worked	.09	.06	.06	.11	.10	.10
Social Security contributions	.20	.24	.26	.24	.21	.21
Social taxes	—	.04	.01	—	—	—
Labor recruiting costs	.02	.02	.01	.07	.00	.01
Payments in kind	.02	.06	.01	.05	.01	.01
Other social contributions	.03	.02	.04	.04	.01	.03

[1] Wages paid for hours worked, but not including pay for apprentices.
Source: Statistical Office of European Community, Siderurgie, Issue no. 5/6, Luxembourg, 1962. Reproduced in United States Department of Labor. *Labor Developments Abroad.* January-March 1963, p. 4.

roughly speaking, for only about two-thirds of total wage costs in the EEC iron and steel industry. Various types of indirect costs, particularly social security contributions, represent a large fraction of the total wage bill.

Table 7.3 shows that the total hourly wage cost in Luxembourg was about 40 per cent higher than in Italy. These figures are for the year 1961; it is likely that the degree of discrepancy in wage rates will be reduced as the Community policy for labor is implemented.

Social security arrangements. The American direct investor must recognize that EEC social security systems differ markedly from those in force in the United States. As a general proposition, European systems are more comprehensive (in terms of types of programs) than those in this country, and, as noted in Table 7.3, contributions toward the programs in the EEC constitute a large share of the indirect labor cost. The relative importance of welfare programs can be shown for different countries by comparing the value of social security benefits to national income. In 1954, the ratio of social security benefits to national income was 15.1 per cent in Belgium, 17.5 per cent in France, 18.3 per cent in West Germany, 13.7 per cent in Italy, and 12.0 per cent in Luxembourg. The comparable ratio in the United States for fiscal year 1953-54 was 5.2 per cent.[13]

Welfare programs have existed in Europe for many years. They serve to provide at least a minimum level of living, to protect workers against risks over which they have no control, and in general to ensure social justice and promote equality of opportunity. Equally important is the fact that the programs serve to promote a continued high level of consumer spending.

The welfare systems of individual EEC states vary considerably, although it is the intention that they be harmonized. Most social security benefits in the EEC are under state control, although some complementary private arrangements do exist. In most EEC countries, employers contribute the greatest share toward the financing of benefits; much of the remainder is financed by employee contributions and out of general tax receipts. The share of social security benefits contributed by employers has been highest in Italy and France; it has been substantially lower in the other EEC countries. The social security systems represent a burden on employers insofar as they must bear part of the costs; this burden is higher than in the United States, but is perhaps offset by lower direct wage costs in the EEC. Social security expenditures are incurred in most European countries for sickness, maternity, employment injury, old-age, survivors, and unemployment.

An unusual type of welfare program which has been utilized in some form by all of the EEC countries (and in Europe in general) is the family allowance. The family allowance represents a regular payment, normally by the government, to the head of the family based on the number of children in the family. Typically, these benefits are directly related to the size of the family; they are not related to wages or worker productivity, although in some cases, they are tied to a cost-of-living index. Most of the financial resources for the family allowance are derived from a special tax on employers.

European Labor Unions and Legislation

The United States firm conducting business in European markets will encounter labor organizations which, in some respects, operate in a fashion similar to those in this country. In many other ways, European labor unions are unique and significantly different from those in the United States. Equally important is that the techniques, relative strength and organizational structure of the EEC labor unions vary considerably from one member country to another and thus preclude extensive generalization.

Union ideology. One factor which differentiates the European labor movement from that of the United States is that the former tends to be identified with a particular political or religious ideology. In many European countries, Protestant, Catholic, Socialist or Communist unions exist which are adjuncts of political parties. Catholic unions, for example, are of major significance in Belgium, France and Italy. Communist strength is greatest in France and Italy. Socialism, which has held little appeal for American workers, has flourished among Western European labor organizations. The most closely united trade union movement exists in West Germany in which the dominant federation is social democrat.

Another significant factor is that there is an endeavor on the part of European unions to strengthen the solidarity of the working class as a group. Class consciousness is strong and deeply rooted, and is reflected in the attitudes of the European worker. The efforts of organized labor to retain featherbedding and to resist technological developments and certain other managerial efforts to raise productivity, especially in the older industries, are much stronger in Western Europe than in the United States. Some observers feel that social stratification is slowly breaking down in Europe.

Labor legislation. One of the most important characteristics of European unions, perhaps the result of their ideology, is that they rely extensively on political action to achieve their objectives. As a result of this approach, matters which would be subject to collective bargaining in the United States or Great Britain are subject to statutory regulation in the EEC—but this varies considerably from country to country. Political action is strongest in France or Italy. The wide range of social security benefits (collective security) available to the European worker reflects emphasis on a political approach. The American method, particularly, is in the nature of "business unionism" and direct negotiations with the employer to achieve economic objectives. American workers have discounted the value of securing broader changes in the structure of society. However, political action has by no means been ignored in this country.

Collective bargaining is most efficient and highly developed in Germany, Belgium, and Luxembourg. In others, especially France and Italy, where unions lack a strong organizational structure, legislation is more important as a source of rights and obligations of employers and employees. An extensive body of law has developed in most EEC countries relative to the health, safety and welfare of workers. Heavy political involvement of European unions reflects their belief that this is the practical approach to economic and social gains.

Centralized negotiations. One of the more important characteristics of European labor which may affect the United States firm operating in the Community is that collective bargaining is relatively centralized or consolidated. That is, negotiations are likely to encompass a broad geographical area, such as on an industry-wide basis, in both the management and labor structure. In Italy and France, for example, few contracts are negotiated on a plant basis, since the local unions are not adequately developed. In general, the union structure has been strongest on the high organizational levels, and this has been conducive to bargaining on an industry-wide basis.

A distinctive feature of collective bargaining in Europe is that much of it is undertaken by employers' associations. The structure of these organizations varies; it may cover an industry, a region, or consist of several industries. In some countries, the employer organization tends to parallel that of the unions. The American firm in Europe will, of course, be required to bargain in "good faith" and may find it necessary to participate in an employers' association.

Industrial unions—those operating on a plant basis—tend to be more pervasive than craft unions; this trend is expected to continue. Unions have also gained membership during the post-war period, primarily the result of low unemployment rates.

Although it is possible to make certain generalizations concerning the European labor movement and legislation, there are so many differences on a national basis, and changes are occurring so rapidly that it is of little value to examine the detail of the situation. The United States firm, of course, must necessarily be concerned with labor unions and legislation; it will be influenced in its decision to locate in a particular country by many other factors—nearness to the market, availability of resources and similar conditions.[14]

The EEC and unions. The EEC has little immediate and direct influence on the nature and operations of unions in member countries. It does not, for example, interfere with the labor-management collective bargaining processes which are regulated by member states. One factor, however, is the provision for the participation of union representatives on a few of the official advisory and administrative committees of the EEC. For example, one advisory committee which assists in the administration of the Social Fund is composed of representatives of trade unions, employers' associations, and governments.[15]

It is expected that as internal trade restrictions are removed and as European industries tend to become oriented to Community-wide rather than nation-wide activities, unions will be compelled to follow a similar pattern. Unions have already established coordinating organizations, on both a Community and an all-European basis. Union congresses of the six countries have been held for the purpose of laying a foundation for coordinated activity throughout the Community.

Union attitudes toward regionalism. Generally, the major labor unions have favored the type of regional integration embodied in the EEC; in most cases, their ideas have paralleled those of their respective governments. Actually, it appears that many European unions support even broader integration; they have been staunch supporters of integration on all levels—economic, political and social. They believe that labor will achieve the greatest gains when all aspects of social policy of the EEC are harmonized or coordinated.

Some labor unions have been critical of certain features of the Treaty of Rome. They feel, for example, that labor interests are not adequately represented on a sufficient number of the Community's consultative and administrative bodies. They also assert that the Treaty of Rome has less value for the working class because it does not make full employment an explicit economic objective.

The Treaty of Rome contains many provisions which were developed specifically to benefit workers and labor unions. It is obvious that the framers of the document recognized the importance of gaining acceptance on the part of the working group.

NOTES

[1] The free movement of services, also provided for in the Treaty of Rome, is distinct from the movement of labor. It is examined in chapter 9.

[2] The scope and operations of the Fund are specified in Regulation No. 9, which was adopted by the Council in 1960. The establishment of the Fund was provided by Article 123, Treaty of Rome.

[3] Article 125, Treaty of Rome.

[4] Financial contributions of member states to the Fund are fixed according to the following scale: Belgium, 8.8 per cent; Germany, 32.0 per cent; France, 32.0 per cent; Italy, 20.0 per cent; Luxembourg, .2 per cent; and the Netherlands, 7.0 per cent.

[5] Article 126, Treaty of Rome.

[6] For details of these regulations, see the two publications of Official Spokesman of the EEC, *Information Memo.* Brussels. One is dated February 25, 1963; the other, March 26, 1963.

[7] See European Economic Community, "Social Developments in the Community in 1962." *Information Memo.* Brussels. July 1963, p. 3.

[8] See International Labor Organization. *International Labor Review.* Statistical Supplement. Vol. LXXXVII No. 5, May 1963.

[9] Statistics in this section were derived from the EEC Commission's *Report on the Prospects for Expansion in the EEC From 1960 to 1970.* November, 1962. Some of the statistics are reproduced in the EEC's *Bulletin from the European Community.* January 1963, p. 13.

[10] See EEC. *Bulletin from the European Community.* March-April 1962, No. 52, pp. 7-8.

[11] One source of information on relative labor costs is the *Yearbook of Labor Statistics,* published by the International Labor Organization.

[12] See *Statistiques Sociales, No. 3, 1962: Revenues des Ouvriers.* CEE, 1959.

[13] See International Labor Organization. *The Cost of Social Security.* Geneva, 1958, pp. 161-164.

[14] For a description and analysis of recent labor developments in several European countries, see Galenson, Walter, *Trade Union Democracy in Western Europe.* Berkeley and Los Angeles: University of California Press, 1961.

[15] Article 124, Treaty of Rome.

8

The Economic Harmonies
of the Common Market

COMMON COMMERCIAL POLICY—HARMONIZATION OF TRANS-
PORT POLICY—ENERGY POLICIES—FREE MOVEMENT OF
CAPITAL—COMMON MARKET CAPITAL REQUIREMENTS—FIS-
CAL POLICIES AND TAXATION—MONETARY POLICIES—BALANCE
OF PAYMENTS QUESTIONS—FULL EMPLOYMENT AND SOCIAL
POLICIES

Common Commercial Policy

Any consideration of common commercial policy in the
European Economic Community necessarily reflects one of
the key concepts in its creation, i.e., the idea of unified, general
policies applicable both within the area and in relation to outside parties. Jean Monnet, a founding father and chief architect
of present day attempts at European unity, has commented in
this connection:

"What have the 'six' done in creating a European Community? They have created a customs union certainly. But they
have done much more. They have agreed to consider as common, affairs which in the past were regarded as essentially
national. To do this they have set up common rules and set
up common institutions to apply them. And so, whereas in the
past problems were dealt with as aspects of the balance of
power, now they are dealt with as common interests."[1]

If Common Market objectives desired by Monnet and others
who share his views are to be fully attained, mere willingness
to deal with economic problems as matters of common interest

must be implemented by exhaustive efforts to bring about harmonization of policy in a wide range of areas. Even when the customs barriers fall and discrimination based on nationality is removed, there are broad sectors in the economic life of each country where national policies must be brought into line if member states are to be successfully merged into a single economy. In some areas general coordination of policy will suffice. In other cases harmonization or approximation of national laws or policies will be required. In still other situations, actual uniformity of the laws may be necessary.

The development of the Common Market has tended to increase awareness of the interdependence of national economies, of commercial interests held in common, and of the need for coordination in commercial policies.

Commercial policy related to common external tariff. A common commercial policy follows as the necessary adjunct to a fully established common external tariff as well as for more complete economic integration. It is this common tariff together with a common commercial policy which will ultimately make the EEC a single trading unit in relation to the rest of the world.

The tariff, then, is a fundamental instrument in the commercial policy of the EEC. Coupled with it, and also basic in the commercial policy of the Community, is the requirement that all tariff and trade negotiations, by the end of the transition period, are to be conducted by the Community as a whole, i.e., by the Commission with the mandate of the Council of Ministers and the advice of a special Committee created for the purpose.

Treaty provisions. The Treaty directs that common commercial policy take into account the favorable incidence which discarding customs duties between member states is likely to have on the competitive strength of enterprises in those states.[2] Member states are directed to coordinate their commercial relations with third countries in such manner as will facilitate the implementation of a common foreign trade policy.[3] The Commission is charged with formulating proposals, for consideration by the

Council, to establish common action and a uniform commercial policy.

The Council's actions with regard to the initiation and conduct of tariff negotiations with third countries and the adjustment of member states' liberalization lists and tariff agreements with these countries were discussed in chapter 4. In addition, subsidies on exports to third countries are to be harmonized by the end of the transitional period to the extent necessary to prevent unfair competition between enterprises within the Community.[4]

In summary, ultimate common commercial policy will be based on uniform principles as to changes in the common external tariff, conclusion of tariff and trade agreements, standardization of liberalization measures and export policy, and commercial protective measures relating to dumping and subsidies.[5] Provision has been made to avoid such diversion of trade and other economic difficulties as might arise during the transitional period as a result of actions taken in forming a common trade policy. The Commission is authorized to take preventive and corrective measures, and in an emergency the individual member states may act on their own, subject to subsequent Commission approval.

After the end of the transitional period members are required to take a common stand in international economic organizations, and may proceed only by way of common action. This provision is fundamental to the very concept of a common market.[6]

Foreign aid; harmonizing credit policy. The problem of aid to underdeveloped countries has an important bearing on commercial policy because such exports are often subsidized by the state, and distortion of competition within the Community may follow as a result. In this area members are seeking to coordinate policy through mutual consultations in a permanent committee, the Development Aid Group, formed for the purpose.

In the interests of eliminating inequities in the trading positions of enterprises in the different member states, some progress has been made in harmonizing policies relating to the extension of trade credit, credit insurance and export credit guarantees. Where policy is to extend credit to importers for long periods, traders have an advantage over their counterparts elsewhere where credit policy is more stringent. Similarly, where a state partially or totally guarantees long-term credit on an exporter's shipments, the exporter is favored over those in other member countries where state guarantees are not available.

Harmonization of Transport Policy

European transport in crisis. Transportation poses especially difficult problems in attaining over-all integration. In the first place, the problem of integration—in itself difficult enough—is complicated by the generally unsatisfactory situation of transport throughout Europe, particularly rail transport. In the recent years only Dutch and Swiss railways have operated profitably. Elsewhere the railroads have run up staggering deficits. Thus in Belgium, with the most dense rail network in Europe, the railroads spend $1.50 for every dollar taken in. A third of the railroads' total revenue is provided by the government as a subsidy to cover deficit operations! Italian railroads are similarly plagued with bulging losses. Elsewhere officials running these nationalized lines face problems of near crisis proportions.[7]

Basic problems must be solved. Each country in the EEC has a somewhat different approach to the solution of the transport problem. Political influence and meddling, excessive government regulation, unrealistic pricing policies and inequality of treatment of the carriers have complicated the picture.

Fundamental agreement must be reached on such specific problems as pricing policy, rate and fare regulation, taxation, user charges on road and water transport, and harmonization of divergent internal policies; a common external transport policy must also be forged.

The EEC Commission has pointed out that transport in the member countries is characterized by conditions of imperfect competition and exhibits such objectionable features as these:

". . . Public authorities intervene in 'infrastructure' matters, especially in financing and constructing roads and waterways.

". . . Obligations are frequently imposed (on railroads, especially) to perform public services such as carrying anything offered by anyone, maintaining operations on deficit lines, and hauling some passengers and goods at enforced reductions in prices.[8]

". . . Transport's structure is peculiar in that widely differing enterprises are providing similar services, and 'definite inelasticity' exists in the way transport demand reacts to changes in price."[9]

Physically the EEC transport problem differs in many ways from the American problem. Total population of the EEC is almost the same as that of the United States, but the land area of the former is only one-sixth as large. Shipping distances are thus much less—the longest distances within the Common Market are no more than 600 to 700 miles—and EEC annual freight volume per person is only one-seventh that in the United States. Too, air transport in Europe plays a minor role in intercity traffic. It is only about 1 per cent of intercity rail traffic. Finally, the short distances tend to favor road carriers over railroads for freight movement in many instances.[10]

Need for common transport policy. Lack of a common transport policy can easily nullify present and future progress in establishing the Common Market. Secret transport charges and discrimination in transport rates can readily replace the tariffs, quotas and other barriers to free trade which are being removed within the Community. As one writer has expressed it, "With customs duties and quota restrictions and all discriminations by nationality in either the sale of goods or services to be abolished between the member countries, it is most important that national transport systems should not reintroduce such barriers and discriminations by the backdoor."[11]

In a sense, transport constitutes the focus of European integration. A free flow of labor, enterprise, goods and capital is possible only through physical means supplied by railroads, automobiles, boats and aircraft.

Even before the organization of the Common Market, about a third of the total import-export trade of the six member countries was done within the Market area (1956). In the first three years of the EEC (1958-1960), the value of intra-Community trade increased by 50 per cent. Combined industrial production during the same years increased by 25 per cent (compared to an 8 per cent increase in the United States), and subsequent increases through 1963 have been impressive. Obviously, the transport system must be able to cope with these demands of the economy.

Treaty provisions on transport. The Treaty of Rome lays down only the broad objectives of a common transport policy. Specific methods to be employed in arriving at such a policy are not defined. The Council is empowered to establish common rules applicable to international transport effected from or to the territory of a member state, or crossing the territory of a member state or states. It can also prescribe conditions for the admission of nonresident carriers to national transport services within a member state. A common transport policy is to be established by the end of the transitional period.[12]

Member states may not discriminate against carriers of other member states under existing legislative or administrative provisions, and members may introduce no new discriminatory legislation.[13]

By the end of the second stage of the transitional period, carriers may not discriminate as to transport rates or conditions, in respect of the same goods conveyed under the same circumstances, because of the country of origin or destination of the goods carried.[14]

Other articles in the Treaty prohibit transport subsidies for particular enterprises or industries, unless authorized by the Commission, and prohibit charges by a carrier in excess of normal transport rates for the crossing of frontiers unless such charges are reasonable in the light of actual costs incurred.[15] The effect of the latter prohibition is to do away with charges for an unloading and reloading at frontiers which does not in fact take place. Thus the cost of crossing a frontier between member countries cannot act as a barrier to trade.

The provisions of the section on transport in the Treaty apply to transport by rail, road and inland waterway.[16] The Commission regards pipelines as within these provisions. While the transport section does not apply to ocean shipping and aviation, other provisions of the Treaty do apply.

Progress toward transport goals. In 1961 a special Memorandum prepared by the Commission defined Community aims as requiring (1) elimination of any obstacles which transport may place in the way of establishing the over-all Market; (2) integration of transport policies on the Community level; and (3) organizing the transport system within the whole Community. Equalization is to be sought for the regulatory and cost conditions under which carriers compete with one another, and investments are to be "coordinated" to avoid waste, duplicated construction and excessive competition.[17]

Specifically, the Memorandum stated that "Infrastructure (roadway) costs must be equitably distributed; the administrative and operational organization improved, and some of the obligations incumbent on public services relaxed. Those which continue must be compensated and the charges resulting from (enforced) tariff reductions equitably reimbursed.

"As and when these corrective measures are applied and produce their effects, the conditions of competition in transport will come closer to those existing in the other sectors (of the economy). It will therefore be possible to allow transport to benefit to a greater degree from the advantages flowing from competition."

The 1962 Action Program. In May 1962 the Commission submitted to the Council a comprehensive "Action Program" devised to further the early realization of common transport policy. Major objectives of the program centered around (1) giving nonresident carriers access to and rights in the transport market, both national and international; (2) establishing a system of prescribed freight rates and passenger fares, and (3) harmonizing fiscal, social and technical legislation which pertains directly to transport.

Since the railroads have long had detailed arrangements governing international shipments, this part of the program applies primarily to highway transport. Basically, the Commission recommended liberalization of international truck competition. Railroad managements have objected, in this connection, that carriers should be placed on an equal cost footing prior to freeing international motor transport if competition generally is not to be further distorted.

The proposed program envisages the removal of restrictions on the right of establishment of such activities related to transport as travel agencies, agents and brokers by 1963, and removal of restrictions on the establishment of transport companies and business by 1967 (see also page 213). A system of Community licenses to be functioning by 1969 is also in the planning stage, and all discriminations based on nationality in the granting of such licenses are to be removed by 1972. The program also makes extensive recommendations relating to procedures for granting licenses for international highway transport, liberalization of some aspects of international passenger traffic moving over highways and the gradual removal of various other restrictions on nonresident carriers.

Fixing transport charges poses a particularly difficult problem. Truckers' freight rates have not usually been regulated in the past; railroad freight rates have been. Completely uncontrolled competition is likely to result in chaos. *Some* rate regulation is generally agreed to be necessary. The Action Program, in attempting to decide *how much*, proposes a system of brackets consisting of maximum and minimum rates for all rail, road and water shipments. Within the defined limits, carriers will be free to set their own charges to meet competitive conditions. The regulations, if adopted, will not apply to loads under five metric tons or to distances shorter than 50 kilometers. Upper and lower rate limits, at first probably quite wide, will ultimately be narrowed as harmonization proceeds.

Another requirement for a common transport policy is that the various laws relating to taxation of fuel and vehicles must be harmonized, and there must be a tax system which will assure equality of treatment among the three types of carriers. In the technical field, regulations relating to vehicular construction standards and use, traffic movement, and insurance laws and highway codes, to mention only a few, must be harmonized. Social legislation governing hours of work, safety requirements, social security and similar matters must also be brought into line before a common policy can become a reality.

In general, the approach of the EEC in pursuing its goals has emphasized freedom of competition among the carriers and equal treatment of all carriers by government. Ultimately the objective is to place all carriers on an equal cost and tax basis with more autonomy and pricing freedom to avoid distortion of competition.

Physical changes in transport network. The foregoing comments indicate the general direction of the efforts of the EEC Commission to create a common transport policy by removing discrimination based on nationality, coordination of practices, and the harmonization of laws. The work of the Commission, however, must go beyond this. The original national transport systems evolved to meet primarily national needs. Today, purely national needs are rapidly being submerged in the larger perspective of Community requirements. A permanent transport network must be devised to serve the expanded needs of the enlarged Community. Extensive studies have been undertaken by the Commission to this end, and numerous specific proposals and recommendations have been made to integrate and link up the individual national systems in order to handle the increased trade which establishment of the Common Market has brought about.

Among these proposals are the linking up of the Rhine and Rhone River systems, electrification of portions of Belgian and German rail lines in order to provide a completely electrified system for the heavily traveled Paris-Liege-Cologne route, modernization of the Modane station facilities in France to accommodate increased traffic, construction of river port facilities in Luxembourg in connection with the canalization of the Moselle River, and construction of a Paris to Brussels super-highway.

Progress in physical facilities to hasten economic integration is already marked. Among the symbols of such progress are "the Trans-Europ Express system (TEE) of high-speed day trains between 70 major cities, the TEEM network of fast merchandise trains which began operating in 1962 over 31 routes, the luxurious Europabuses operated jointly under 14 rail administrations, the Interfrigo Company for Europewide refrigerator car services, the 'Europ Pool' of 203,700 freely exchanged freight cars and the Eurofima Company for pooling finances to purchase new freight cars."[18]

Coordinating investment in transport. Waste of transport resources can be controlled initially if original investment allocations are wisely made. Just as in the United States, Europe has surplus carrier capacity in relation to actual traffic requirements. Needless duplication of equipment, roadways and services aggravates the problem. The objective of EEC policy is to consider each investment proposal in the light of what is best for the *overall* Community transport system. This is necessarily so if the Community is to create the conditions necessary for the development of an efficient transport system capable of satisfying, at minimum cost to the public and under the best conditions, the requirements resulting from economic expansion.

Energy Policies

Absence of treaty provisions. There has been less progress toward a common energy policy for the Community than in other fields. Several reasons may be cited. None of the European treaties relating to energy provides for a common policy. In the absence of specific treaty requirements, individual countries have been slow to assume the initiative. The various fuel and power industries have been brought under three different coordinating authorities. General provisions of the Treaty which created the EEC apply to oil and gas. But atomic energy comes under Euratom,[19] and coal under the ECSC.[20] The power industry is extremely complex and highly technical, and the individual nations have sharply conflicting interests. Thus, Germany seeks to protect her extensive coal mining industry. France wants to sell Sahara oil to the Common Market. Italy has some natural gas and facilities for refining imported oil, but has no domestic sources of either oil or coal.

Need for a common energy policy. Obviously, as the EEC attains greater economic unity and industry continues to expand, an adequate and reliable supply of low cost energy must be provided if development is to proceed at a maximum pace. Yet today there are wide differences in the costs and prices of fuel, in fiscal policies relating to the power industry, and in national policies designed to protect or develop one or another of the fuel and power industries. These and similar factors have a distorting effect on competition within the Market—an effect which must be minimized and then eliminated. The need for a common policy was formally acknowledged in April 1962 by an unofficial meeting, in Rome, of the Ministers of Fuel and Power of the member states.

Joint effort for common progress. The authorities of the EEC, ECSC and Euratom are aware of the need and of the many problems which must be resolved before a common policy can be created. Its ultimate form and even the means by which it can best be attained are still conjectural, but a start has been made. Initial studies of the problem were launched by the ECSC in 1957. Subsequently, after the EEC and Euratom were formed, the responsibility for this activity was shifted to an Inter-Executive Energy Committee composed of representatives from EEC, ECSC and Euratom.[21] In 1961 this group tendered preliminary proposals to the Council of Ministers. These were debated and, although never formally adopted, the European Parliamentary Assembly in early 1962 passed a resolution approving a broad policy very similar to that embodied in the original Inter-Executive proposals. The need for a common policy having been acknowledged, the Inter-Executive set about working out a time schedule for the implementation of such a policy. By mid-1962 specific proposals were forwarded to the Council.

Essentials of the plan involved the following points:

—energy requirements of the Community will increase rapidly from 1960 to 1975.

—coal, which supplied half of energy requirements in 1960, will supply less and less of total needs.

—other forms of energy should be supplied as cheaply as possible; the price of these fuels should not be inflated in order to keep coal competitive, rather, the production of coal should be subsidized, though "nothing should be done to give the more costly forms of energy *lasting* protection against the more economic forms."

—oil will be the main source of energy until 1970, and thereafter atomic power will probably become competitive.

—a common market in energy should be in effect by 1970 and restrictions on the import of oil should by then be removed, except for quotas on oil imports from Eastern Europe (this provision is designed to prevent increased dependence on imports from Communist countries from reaching proportions inimical to the security of the Community should these supplies be cut off for political or military reasons).

—internal taxes on gasoline should be harmonized by 1970.[22]

When the Council considered these proposals in October 1962, they were rejected. There were still too many objections. Reconciliation of conflicting national interest appeared impossible. In March 1963 the Council designated two groups—one technical and one political—to work with the Inter-Executive in a further effort to salvage some form of common policy.

Present prospects for a common policy are not very bright. A considerable period of time may elapse before a workable plan evolves. Even as the individual member states go their own way in the energy field, there are limits imposed by other general provisions of the Treaty which prevent irresponsible action. No member is likely to act with total disregard for the interests of the others. To this extent, at least, there is some pressure in the direction of the original objective, that is, to ensure the free movement of energy products and the supply of energy at the lowest possible price.

Free Movement of Capital

Treaty objectives. The free movement of capital, as a necessary factor in production, can be achieved only through the realization of common financial policies among member states. Any approach to the problem is complicated by the fact that freeing capital movements can have an important effect on the strength of individual national currencies.

The Treaty requires members mutually to abolish restrictions on the movement of capital belonging to residents and discriminatory treatment based on the nationality of the parties, their place of residence or the location of the capital. These measures are to be taken insofar as is necessary for the proper functioning of the Common Market. Current payments have already been freed of restrictions in accord with Treaty requirements.

Member states are not to discriminate in applying domestic provisions, in respect of the capital market and credit system, to the movements of capital which have been freed under Treaty provisions. Exchange authorizations are to be granted in the most liberal manner possible. Loans for the financing of a member state or its territorial subdivisions are not to be issued or placed in another state in the Community except where the latter has agreed.

Exchange policies relative to the movement of capital between member states and outside countries are to be progressively coordinated and liberalized. New exchange regulations are not to be introduced which make existing rules more restrictive as they relate to the movement of capital.

Where capital movements result in disturbances in the capital market of a member state, the latter may be authorized to take appropriate protective measures. Where the need is urgent, a member may take independent action. The Commission must be advised and may require the member to change or abolish the particular measures taken.

In addition, a member, in case of serious difficulties in any sector of the economy, may seek authorization from the Commission to take extraordinary measures in order to restore the situation. Such emergency measures may even run contrary to Treaty provisions if the Commission decides this is necessary.[23]

Progress in freeing capital movements. To date considerable progress has been made in freeing capital movements. At the end of 1958 the currencies of all the member states were substantially convertible. Direct investments (for example, financing a branch with which the investing parent company or partnership retains a permanent relation), medium- and short-term financing of trade, investments in real property and movements of funds for personal requirements (except loans) are now unrestricted, as is the reinvestment of profits. Securities quoted on a stock exchange in the EEC may be bought and sold freely, whatever the residence of the buyer or seller. This is only partially the case with new issues and stocks not listed on the exchanges. Such transactions have been liberalized conditionally by several members and may again be subjected to restrictions if the absence of controls endangers achievement of the economic objectives of the country concerned.

Freedom of movement of short-term funds is still lacking. Liberalization in this connection must await greater harmony in present national monetary policies. Premature liberalization could result in the flow of so-called "hot money" from areas of less interest return to areas of greater return. The export of such funds from one country affects that country's balance of payments and may have an inflationary effect in the recipient nation. Liberalization measures are likely to come slowly. There is no time schedule set up in the Treaty for the termination of such other restrictions as remain on the freedom of capital movements. Some are closely tied in with fiscal and monetary policies which must necessarily be considered at the same time.

The European Investment Bank. As the Common Market continues to develop, capital requirements continue to grow.

Financing is required for various purposes. It is necessary for various projects which are primarily of Community-wide interest, where the Community as a whole is likely to benefit, and where individual states or private capital sources are unlikely or unwilling to supply the necessary funds. Capital is also required to finance the increasing amount of trade within the Market and between the Market and outside countries. Capital is needed as well for the undertakings of private industry, public utilities and the various divisions of government.

The European Investment Bank, which was created by a Protocol to the Treaty and has its headquarters in Brussels, is concerned with the first category of financing just mentioned. Its purpose is to contribute, by calling on the capital markets and its own resources, to the balanced and smooth development of the Common Market as a community.

It is empowered to grant loans and guarantees on a nonprofit basis for financing projects in less developed areas within the Community. It is charged with aiding modernization projects and new facilities necessary for the development of the Common Market where, by their nature or cost, these cannot be readily financed by individual states. The Bank is also concerned with the financing of undertakings which are of common interest to more than one state where individual states are unable or not inclined to finance such projects in their entirety. The Bank exercises strictly financing functions. It does not hold equity issues of the projects it finances.

An initial capital of 1,000,000,000 *units of account* was set up by the Protocol. Each unit has the same gold content as that of the United States dollar. The original capital was subscribed by six member countries, one-fourth in gold and three-fourths in the currency of the contributing country. The Bank is empowered to raise additional capital funds by various means including loans in the international capital market or in the internal money markets of the members. It has, for example, floated a loan through a Dutch bank and in 1961 a public issue of 4.5 per cent bonds was offered.

The Board of Governors of the Bank consists of three Ministers appointed by the member states. There is also a Board of Directors of twelve members. A Management Committee conducts the current affairs of the Bank.

Loans are made at interest rates only slightly lower than those prevailing on the markets and are ordinarily for less than the total amount required for the particular project being financed. They have been granted to small business as well as large. Among the earliest loans of the Bank were those for chemical and power projects in southern Italy and in the south of France—relatively underdeveloped areas. Transport loans have been made for railway modernization and electrification in Italy, France and Germany. A rural electric power network in Brittany received a loan, and there have been numerous loans for the construction of factories and other industrial facilities ranging from a clothing factory to an iron and steel works. The amounts of individual loans have varied from a few hundred thousand units (dollars) to 25 million.

Common Market Capital Requirements

For ordinary business and investment needs, the European Investment Bank does not constitute a source of capital funds nor, as just noted, was it so intended. The capital needs of the Common Market must be met elsewhere. In some of the countries there has been what might be termed a chronic insufficiency of domestic investment capital. Such capital shortages have in some measure, particularly in West Germany, been reduced by retaining some industrial earnings rather than paying out all such earnings to stockholders. Meeting capital needs in this way tends to reduce yields on common stocks (3 to 3.5 per cent in West Germany—excluding the steel industry for example—as opposed to yields of up to 5 per cent on prime stocks in Great Britain), but it does result in the creation of corporate capital funds which may later be used by the corporation as the need arises or for financing other companies.

Demand for capital buoys interest rates. These capital shortages create heavy demand for funds, and this continuing demand keeps interest rates high. In West Germany government securities provide yields of 6 per cent while yields on prime debt securities of first ranking corporations range slightly higher. Thus a $50,000,000 public bond issue of German Federal Railways maturing serially 1968 to 1982 bears a 6 per cent interest rate. A $15,000,000 debenture issue of a Danish utility, Copenhagen Telephone Company, was a 1962 offering in the U. S. market for a yield of 5.95 per cent.

Long-term borrowing rates generally run from 5 to 7 per cent for prime companies in the EEC. Netherlands is a possible exception. The Dutch opened their capital market to loan issues by firms in other EEC countries in 1961 and the rates are lower. Government and prime corporate debt securities yield about 4.5 per cent over the long-term, but the amount of Dutch money permitted to foreign borrowers is still strictly limited.

The demand for capital in Western Europe is so great that these relatively high interest rates appear likely to continue for an indeterminate period.

The British money market. To what extent will the financial houses of Lombard Street meet capital requirements of enterprises in the EEC? The British capital market is one of historically high investment yields on both equity issues and bonds. To produce these yields, a relatively large proportion of corporate earnings has traditionally been paid out. Compare typical British yields of 5 per cent on prime stocks with 3 per cent in the Netherlands and even less in Belgium and France. Today there is some tendency in Britain in the direction of retaining more industrial earnings and of smaller payouts to stockholders as a means of raising capital internally.

At the same time, a high interest policy in Great Britain has served to combat inflationary tendencies and attract foreign investment funds. In the early 1960's government bond yields were around 5.5 per cent and long-term industrial money cost from 6 to 6.5 per cent. It appears evident that the cost of money on the London capital market is no less than within the EEC itself, and, in addition, the United Kingdom has its own balance of payments problems and a pound which has weakened in relation to the currencies of EEC nations.

Are European capital sources adequate? Ultimately the source of new capital funds is found in the savings of investors in these nations. But will these historic sources of capital in Britain, France, Germany and the Netherlands be adequate to meet Common Market needs? British capital resources are only a fraction each year of the 50 billion dollars saved annually in the United States. Annual savings in the EEC are in turn only a fraction of British annual savings. Aside from the question of the size of the capital markets in London, Paris, Amsterdam, Frankfurt, Brussels and Rome and their ability to supply the needs of European trade and industry, there is still the question of restrictions remaining on the movement of capital even after the steps described earlier in this chapter have been taken. Progress has been made, as noted, and the basically reciprocal nature of the EEC undertaking logically points to an ultimate relaxation of controls over existing money markets within the Community. Not all government restrictions have been removed, however, nor are they likely to be entirely removed for several years to come.

A super stock market for Europe? Is there the possibility that existing decentralized European money markets will somehow be able to pool their resources in a single financial center to service the financial requirements of an integrated Common Market economy? Present prospects are not very bright. Aside from government regulation and widely divergent monetary and fiscal policies within the several member states, there are differences in custom, practices and organization of the individual exchanges. Each financial center thus far retains its own stock exchange, gold market and foreign exchange market. Each market has its particular system of dealing (e.g., the bidding system used on the Paris exchange differs from the practice in Amsterdam), different legal requirements as to disclosure, different quotation systems, varied degrees of government regulation, etc.[24]

Europe seeks American capital. With basic limitations on the size of European capital markets, heavy demand for funds, existing controls and restrictions on the international flow of investment funds, Europe will continue to look to America for capital. United States investments in European manufacturing operations during 1962 amounted to $968 million according to the U.S. Department of Commerce. From 1957 through 1962 American investments in Europe aggregated some $4.5 billion. The total of foreign dollar bonds offered in New York during 1962 amounted to almost $1.4 billion, twice the 1961 amount. In 1963 both American and foreign investors were again lured by the relatively high yields available (5.5 per cent and more), and American purchases of foreign securities in the first half of 1963 amounted to almost $1 billion.[25]

Foreign investment and U. S. balance of payments. As pointed out in chapter 6, American investment in foreign securities has had an effect upon the United States balance of payments. Dollars sent abroad eventually return in part in the form of income and interest payments, and in part in the form of exports. Even now the return on American investment abroad and foreign borrowings here about equals outgo. But the short-term effect of the dollar outflow is to increase the balance of payments deficit. A United States Secretary of the Treasury, at a session of the International Monetary Conference, has expressed concern "with the increasing use of the various mechanisms of the New York capital market by European borrowers to raise funds for their own internal purposes." He has urged Western European nations with capital surpluses to accept new responsibility in meeting these capital needs. American policy has traditionally favored the free movement of capital. Government financial authorities want open and expanded financial markets in Europe to enable Common Market countries better to meet their own needs and also to enable American business to borrow there just as European business can and does borrow in the United States.

Recently several steps have been taken toward finding a way to reduce the United States balance of payments deficit. The Federal Reserve's discount rate has been raised from 3 per cent to 3.5 per cent, the ceiling on bank interest paid on time deposits has been increased to 4 per cent, and an export promotion drive has been inaugurated, among other measures. The purpose of these steps is to minimize short-term capital outflows resulting from the fact that interest rates abroad have been higher than in this country. In 1962 such transactions accounted for $623 million of the total $2,200 million payments deficit. In addition, a 15 per cent excise tax on American investments in foreign securities bought from foreigners has been proposed. How effective these and other devices will be in improving the balance of payments situation remains to be seen, but they will undoubtedly have an effect upon the availability of American capital for financing purposes within the Common Market. Application of extensive capital-outflow curbs would not seem likely to bolster confidence in the dollar, and the point of view has even been expressed that the dollar is overvalued in terms of European currencies and that this constitutes a major impediment to effective policy making by government authorities in the international economic field.[26]

EEC investment peak passed? Aside from whatever American government regulations or fiscal policies as will in the future alter investment in the Common Market, there are other factors which may operate to slow down somewhat the tempo of the last few years. Britain, for example, was denied entry into the Market and this in effect decreased the potential size of the great supermarket which had been envisaged earlier. The French have sought to curtail entry of outside, and in particular U. S., capital into French industry. Economic growth of the Common Market nations has slackened in some measure. The United States is in one way or another discouraging investment of American capital in developed nations.[27] Too, there has been some decline in overseas expansion by American companies.

Nonetheless, the Common Market is still a vital and growing market with large rewards for the American businessman and American capital.[28]

Fiscal Policies and Taxation

Early in 1963 the EEC Commission published the report of a Fiscal and Financial Committee concerning problems existing within the Common Market in the field of taxation and finance. Articles 99 and 100, of the Treaty of Rome, require the Commission to establish the necessary conditions for a Common Market in the field of taxation. The report surveyed the effects of existing fiscal and financial systems and measures and of the possibilities of harmonizing them. Specifically the Committee studied the question as to whether and to what extent existing differences in the financial systems of the member states hinder or even preclude the establishment of a Common Market. It also studied the problems of securing and guaranteeing conditions corresponding to those of an internal market and surveyed such possibilities as exist of removing those differences which constitute a particular hindrance to the establishment and functioning of the Common Market. The report examined the effects of public revenue and expenditure policies on competition and pointed out the direction which financial policy should take if distortion of and restraints on competition are to be avoided.

The fact has been established that a number of existing national tax regulations may distort competition in the Common Market and thus seriously impede the integration of national economies. This is likely to be increasingly so as more and more internal customs barriers are removed. A further fact which has been developed is the need to include all the taxes under existing systems in any discussions on harmonization, even if the necessity, urgency and degree of harmonization vary from case to case.

Differences in the total tax burden may well affect the conditions of competition. Taxes directly affecting the exchange of goods and services in the Common Market were examined in detail by the Committee. The report expresses the view that existing turnover and company taxes and those taxes that directly affect the movement of capital (taxes on capital transactions and on interest and dividends) should largely be harmonized to secure equal competitive opportunities for everyone and to guarantee the allocation of productive resources according to profitability as well as capital movements unimpeded by taxes. (See also the section on business taxation in chapter 9.)

The report also states that capital movements should not be hampered by taxes on capital transactions and that where these taxes cannot be completely abolished they should at least be made uniform.

Because the various taxes affecting transport have a direct effect on the transportation of goods and in some cases may seriously impair it, the study gives special attention to these taxes and points out that some alignment of automobile and transport taxes is inevitable.

Harmonization of personal income tax, to any substantial extent, is not considered necessary, but a formal standardization of income tax techniques has been urged. The preference is expressed for a special type of income tax which should be levied in all member states together with a moderate annual tax on net wealth, levied only on individuals and not on companies. The tax on net wealth should make it possible to tax property income more easily and at the same time facilitate the control of income tax assessment.

It appears that the harmonization of special consumer taxes can be taken up at some time in the future without materially affecting the functioning of the Common Market. There are very considerable differences in the special consumption taxes in the individual member states and these differences do not permit the immediate removal of tax frontiers, which is the ultimate objective. Therefore some standardization in fiscal policy will be necessary.

The measures proposed by the Fiscal and Financial Committee are to be supplemented by a multilateral double-taxation agreement between member states based on the Organization for Economic Cooperation and Development (OECD) draft proposal; by a number of supra-national measures of mutual financial compensations to even out the budgetary effects of tax harmonization; and by coordination and harmonization of the principles determining member states' financial policy.

Monetary Policies

Need for harmonization. The various forms of regulation and control relating to capital movements, discussed earlier in this chapter, and fiscal policies relating to taxation constitute important aspects of a nation's financial system. National monetary policies must also be brought into harmony if an integrated Common Market economy is to emerge. The manipulation of interest rates and changes in exchange rates are of foremost importance in this area. If one member of the Community changes its policy as to bank credit, boosts the rate of interest or revalues its currency, each of the other member states is likely to be affected in some degree and the functioning of the over-all economy of the Market may be subjected to severe strains and imbalances.

The need for early action in the monetary sector has become increasingly apparent as financial controls have been dropped in order to provide greater freedom of movement for capital and as the result of increasing harmonization in other, non-financial, sectors of the economy. A recent resolution of the European Parliament acknowledges that "A common monetary policy is an essential condition for achieving the economic and political unity of Europe."

Treaty provisions and the Monetary Committee. Provisions of the Treaty require each member state to treat its policy as to exchange rates as a matter of common interest. Unilateral action on the part of one member must not result in injury to another, contrary to Community interest. If one country alters its exchange rate and as a result the balance of payments equilibrium within the Community is endangered or conditions of competition are distorted, the EEC Commission may authorize appropriate counteraction on the part of other member states[29]. Similarly, changes in interest rates can result in serious difficulties. A marked increase in rates can result in the flow of "hot money" into states offering relatively high returns on short-term investment funds. The transfer of such funds in turn affects the balances of payments between the countries. Under the Treaty, members may (subject to prescribed circumstances) take the action necessary to avoid such balance of payments difficulties.

The Treaty provides for a Monetary Committee which is charged with keeping under review the monetary and financial situation of member states and of the Community and also the general payments systems of member states. It renders regular reports to the Commission and to the Council and in addition conducts studies and formulates opinions relating to the problems involved. It is composed of two representatives from each of the member states and two from the Commission. Policies concerning bank credit, interest rates and exchange rates have been given special consideration. Specifically the Committee has the duty "to promote the coordination of the policies of the member states in the monetary field in so far as is necessary for the functioning of the Common Market."

It must be noted that the Committee is an *advisory* body. It has *consultative* status only. However urgent the need for harmonization in financial matters, and some of these problems must be solved before there can be complete freedom of capital movement within the Community, the Committee can only recommend or suggest. There is still a long way to go before a common policy will become a reality. There are differences in banking structures, in traditional practices, in relations with outside countries and conflicting interests among the nations themselves. Monetary policy will become an increasingly important means, however, of directing the economy as restrictions on the flow of goods and capital are progressively lifted.

EEC reserve bank for the future? In spite of the obstacles, progress is being made. The present emphasis is upon coordination of national policies looking toward the ultimate evolution of Community-wide common policy. One major proposal—still in an embryonic stage—urges a common reserve bank for the EEC. This idea was put forward several years ago by Jean Monnet's Action Committee. In 1962, the Economic and Financial Committee of the European Parliament passed a draft resolution along similar lines.

Such a reserve bank could be created if central banks in the individual countries were to transfer a fixed proportion of their respective reserves to a common reserve fund. The proportion could then be increased from time to time until all reserve funds were held by the central reserve bank under supranational control. The resulting institution would be similar in some respects to the Federal Reserve Bank system in the United States. Such a bank could make a contribution of great value in stabilizing the financial system of the Community and in dealing with balance of payments problems. Eventually, and there is no present plan in this direction, a common currency might even be created. For now, it must be admitted that both a reserve bank and a common currency are objectives to be attained well in the future, if at all.

EEC monetary problems and world finance. Policy on EEC monetary matters must obviously be forged within the matrix of the present world monetary system. Aside from purely internal questions which arise from interrelationships among member states, a common monetary policy must take into account the interrelationships which exist between members and existing monetary institutions.

At the core of the present system of international finance is the International Monetary Fund. Some analysts hold that it has a long-term restrictive influence on world trade resulting from fixed exchange rates and a shortage of international reserves. In theory the system permits individual nations to alter their exchange rates and provides sufficient liquidity to float countries over temporary balance of payments difficulties. In practice, however, exchange rates have generally been maintained at fixed levels even when this has resulted in severe inflationary or deflationary pressures in the internal economy of the nation involved.[30]

Some authorities feel that the existing system could be improved by increasing liquidity or by discontinuing the system of fixed exchange rates. Neither of these means is presently regarded with favor by many monetary authorities and both steps would in turn bring on other problems. Central banks in the system have kept it operating by the drawing rights procedure brought into use to overcome deficiencies of liquidity. A nation with a balance of payments deficit is able to draw on the Fund to secure the particular currency necessary to meet its obligations.

National wage policies are also tied in closely with the problem. Monetary authorities have urged that wages should be kept at levels which will avoid increases in production costs to the point where a country's export goods are priced out of the world market. When this happens, imports exceed exports and the country experiences a balance of payments deficit.[31]

EEC monetary policy must also take into account the role of the United States dollar as an international key currency. The dollar is the principal money used in international trade. It is used as a means of payment for many international transactions regardless of where they take place. The dollar, too, constitutes well over 50 per cent of the international reserves of the world's trading nations. So long as it remains a key currency the members of the Common Market will be vitally concerned with the position of the dollar in international financing operations, and its strength or weakness will both reflect and influence developments within the Community.

Anyone concerned with trading with the Common Market, or with other nations, is aware that much of the increased liquidity that world trade has enjoyed in years recently past has been supplied by the United States. Following the end of World War II the pound sterling was no longer able to shoulder the burden as the leading international reserve currency. With decreasing availability of gold, other nations have increasingly held United States dollars as their reserve currency. In short, the United States has become banker to the world.

This responsibility, together with heavy financial commitments abroad for aid and defense, has had some embarrassing consequences so far as the United States balance of payments is concerned. However cavalier some economists may be about the American deficit position on balance of payments, the deficit continues to exist. It is substantial—by the end of the second quarter, 1963, it was running at a seasonally adjusted annual rate of $5.2 billion. And, it has failed to respond to the politically expedient but often ineffective short-term palliatives which have been administered thus far.

As one means of overcoming the deficit, EEC countries have been urged to assume greater responsibilities in meeting problems of liquidity in world trade and in extending aid to underdeveloped nations. If and when this responsibility is assumed, and aside from the question as to the extent of the benefit to the United States, the collective influence of the Common Market countries in international financial policy is likely to be felt to a much greater extent than it is today. There is today a discernible shift in the balance of world economic power in the direction of Europe. American views, policies and solutions in world monetary matters may very well carry less weight as time goes on and the EEC countries adopt and put into effect supranational policies of their own.[32]

Balance of Payments Questions

The general concept of a country's balance of payments is widely understood. A more precise definition of balances of payments might be that they are "statistical tabulations of economic transactions between residents of one country and the residents of the rest of the world, another country or group of countries."[33] They define a nation's economic relationships with the rest of the world or with another nation or groups of nations. The manner in which nations adjust these balances has an important effect upon their economic growth.[34] Individual countries in the EEC thus have a balance of payments in relation to each other and also in relation to outside countries.

The elimination of major imbalances between member nations is essential if freedom of capital movement is to be assured. In the past, quotas (import restrictions), currency controls and various other means have been utilized by individual governments to bring their external accounts into balance. The Treaty now prohibits these means, under most circumstances, and as a result monetary authorities in the several states must depend upon budgetary controls and the adjustment of interest rates, along with other fiscal and monetary policies, to rectify imbalances in external accounts.

Treaty provisions.[35] Each member is responsible for its over-all balance of payments equilibrium with other nations. Equilibrium is to be maintained while at the same time ensuring stable prices, confidence in the national currency and a high level of employment. In addition to the coordination of economic policies among the members necessary to accomplish these objectives, the Monetary Committee has pointed out (Third Annual Report) that the active cooperation of all countries of the West will be required.

Each member continues to control its own exchange rate, but policies consistent with the common interest must be followed. If a member changes its exchange rate contrary to the common interest and conditions of competition are thereby seriously distorted, the Commission may authorize other members to take counteraction.

If a member gets into serious balance of payments difficulties as a result of a persistent deficit or because of the kinds of currency it has as a part of its international reserves, and these difficulties threaten the functioning of the Common Market, the Commission will then examine the situation and propose corrective action to be taken by the member. If such action proves inadequate, the Council may then direct that *mutual assistance* be provided. This may take any of several forms. Aid may be extended by concerted action of the other members in or through an international organization (as the IMF, if such aid is otherwise available). Import restrictions may be authorized with respect to third countries while at the same time protection is afforded the country's export volume. Grants of credit may also be made by the other members. If all this fails to resolve the difficulty, the Commission may authorize such other and more drastic emergency measures as may be necessary.

Where a sudden crisis in a member's balance of payments occurs, the member may act on its own to remedy the situation. Such steps must result in minimum possible disturbance to the operation of the Market economy, and the Council may subsequently require the member to amend, suspend or abolish the measures which have been adopted.

Full Employment and Social Policies

As already noted in chapter 7, Treaty provisions require complete freedom of movement of labor by the end of the transitional period. At that time a laborer may not be discriminated against on the basis of his nationality so far as his employment, remuneration or working conditions are concerned. These requirements contrast in marked degree with the rules which have prevailed regarding work cards, immigration and entry permits and the various other forms necessary for a citizen of one state to pursue employment in another.

The removal of barriers to the free movement of labor has enabled countries experiencing labor shortages to draw on manpower available elsewhere. This in turn has facilitated increases in production which have generally characterized industry in the Common Market from its very inception. Although Europeans as a rule are reluctant to leave family ties and their home villages, there has in fact been a considerable migration from labor-surplus areas into labor-short areas. Employment has been increased over what it might otherwise have been.

The coordination of labor policy continues, and even certain of the labor unions have now opened discussions aimed at creating federations throughout the Common Market area.

One result of tariff reduction has been to admit goods into an area from outside countries where such goods have been produced at lower costs. As noted elsewhere in the book, inefficient producers within the EEC have from time to time found it necessary to merge with more efficient producers or discontinue operations altogether. This has naturally resulted in some unemployment.

To meet this problem, and to ensure satisfactory conditions relating to working conditions, retraining and social security, regulations implementing the Treaty have been careful to provide that workers enjoy the facilities of closely coordinated employment bureaus, a common vocational training policy administered on the Community level and opportunities for retraining and resettlement where this is necessary.

NOTES

[1] A special message from M. Monnet to the Mount Allison Summer Institute, reported in *Canada, the Commonwealth and the Common Market*, W.B. Cunningham (Ed.). Montreal: McGill University Press, 1962, p. 1.

[2] Article 110, Treaty of Rome.

[3] Article 111.

[4] Article 112.

[5] Article 113.

[6] Article 116.

[7] For an up-to-date and authoritative account of transport problems in Europe and elsewhere, see Sites, James N. *Quest for Crisis — A World-Ranging Search for Clues to the Transport Future*. New York: Simmons-Boardman Publishing Corporation, 1963. Chapter 10, "New Transport Policies for the New Europe," deals with the Common Market.

[8] Sites, *supra*, notes concerning the subsidy of the Belgian government to its nationalized railroads that, "This is being paid out for a wide range of losing services which are required by government to be performed for social and political purposes. For instance, special passenger fare reductions are made available to city commuters, veterans, military men, students and even journalists. The reductions range up to 75 per cent of full fare—'which virtually no one pays any more.'

"As one result of these low-low fares, 'we lose money on every ticket,' declares a discouraged railroad official. . . . 'To run railroads under the Belgian system is like pumping water into a wicker basket. The more efficiently you run the system, the less money you get in state subsidies. The less efficiently you run the system, the more you get in subsidies. It doesn't make any difference how good a job we do — the subsidies are always there.' " (p. 74.)

[9] Sites, James N., *op. cit.*, quoted with permission from a summary of the 1961 EEC Memorandum on transport, p. 102.

[10] Sites, James. N., *op. cit.*, p. 100.

[11] See Clark, Colin. *British Trade in the Common Market*. London: Stevens & Sons, Limited, 1962, p. 125.

[12] Articles 74 and 75.

[13] Article 76.

[14] Article 79. Regulation 11 (see *Journal Officiel des Communautés Européennes*, August 16, 1960) implements this provision and prohibits all such discrimination on and after July 1, 1961. It requires that all shipments made within the Community are to be accompanied by a delivery memorandum, in duplicate, showing the name and address of the shipper, description and weight of the goods, place and date of acceptance of the

goods, destination, and itinerary or distance where necessary to justify a rate other than the normal transport rate, and frontier crossing points if any. There are certain exemptions available under the rule.

[15] Articles 80 and 81.

[16] Article 84.

[17] Sites, James N., *op. cit.*, pp. 101-102.

[18] *Ibid.*, p. 100.

[19] European Atomic Energy Community, with headquarters in Brussels, created by a treaty signed March 25, 1957 by Belgium, France, Federal Republic of Germany, Italy, Luxembourg and the Netherlands.

[20] European Coal and Steel Community, with headquarters in Luxembourg, created by a treaty signed April 18, 1951, with the same signatories as Euratom.

[21] The EEC and Euratom were set up simultaneously, but separate treaties were signed for each community.

[22] For a detailed account of the entire fuel and energy problem see chapter 4, "Energy: Three Communities, One Problem," in Shanks, Michael, and Lambert, John. *The Common Market Today — And Tomorrow.* New York: Frederick A. Praeger, 1962, pp. 106-125.

[23] Treaty provisions summarized in this section, relating to the free movement of capital, are contained in Articles 67, 68, 70, 71, 73 and 226.

[24] For a discussion of practices on various foreign exchanges and foreign investment in general, see Gilbert, R. A. *International Investment.* New York: Simmons-Boardman Publishing Corporation, 1963.

Various other efforts are underway to develop a coordinated European capital market. In London, the Times on February 21, 1964 reported the formation, for example, of a new organizaztion called the American Research and Development Corporation. with the participation of 12 European and 4 American banking groups. The object of this new institution was stated as being that of creating new or developing old companies with growth possibilities in Europe. (*The Times,* February 21, 1964, page 17).

[25] See also, "Where the Money Is," *International Management,* Vol. 18, No. 7 (July 1963), pp. 18-20.

[26] Johnson, Harry G. "An Appraisal of Kennedy's International Economic Policies," *Business Horizons,* Vol. 6, No. 2 (Summer 1963), pp. 81-86. The 15 per cent excise tax (H.R. 8000, generally referred to as the "equalization" tax) on the purchase of foreign securities from non-U.S. persons, had passed the House of Representatives at the time of this writing (March 9, 1964) and was before the Senate Finance Committee. Although the Senate had not yet acted on the bill, the possibility of its passage and its retroactive features operated during the last half of 1963 and early 1964 to reduce the volume of securities purchases of this type in a major way.

[27] For example, the 1962 U.S. Revenue Act has curbed companies seeking tax havens in European countries, and government policy appears to encourage licensing arrangements in Europe as opposed to other direct investments. Note also provisions of the recently enacted 1964 U.S. Revenue Act.

[28] For a detailed discussion of American investment abroad, see Mikesell, Raymond (Ed.). *U.S. Private and Government Investment Abroad.*

Portland: University of Oregon Books, 1962. For a brief, timely discussion of the effect of American investment abroad on U.S. balance of payments problems, see *The Morgan Guaranty Survey*, August, 1963.

[29] Article 107.

[30] For a discussion of the organization and functions of the IMF, see Wasserman, Max J. and Hultman, Charles W. *Modern International Economics*. New York: Simmons-Boardman Publishing Corporation, 1962, pp. 424-429.

[31] See the paper contributed by Professor H. G. Johnson, of the University of Chicago, reported in *Canada, the Commonwealth and the Common Market*, W. B. Cunningham (Ed.). Montreal: McGill University Press, 1962.

[32] For a discussion concerning the need for reforming the existing international monetary system, see: Machlup, Fritz, "Plans for Reform of the International Monetary System." *Special Papers in International Economics*, No. 3, International Finance Section, Department of Economics, Princeton University, 1962; and Harris, Seymour E. (Ed.), *The Dollar in Crisis*. New York: Harcourt, Brace and World, Inc., 1961.

[33] Wasserman, Max J. and Hultman, Charles W., *op. cit.*, p. 35. See also Wasserman, Max J., Hultman, Charles W., and Zsoldos, Laszlo, *International Finance*. New York: Simmons-Boardman Publishing Corporation, 1963, pp. 55-80.

[34] For a critical review of current theoretical explanations of the balance of international payments and the effects of the international balancing process on economic development, see Letiche, John M. *Balance of Payments and Economic Growth*. New York: Harper & Brothers, Publishers, 1959.

[35] Articles 104-109.

9

Business Practices and Regulation Under the Common Market

RULES GOVERNING COMPETITION—COMMON PATENT, TRADE-MARK AND DESIGN LEGISLATION—FREEDOM OF ESTABLISHMENT—BUSINESS TAXATION

Rules Governing Competition

As tariff barriers within the EEC have declined and the potential market for goods has increased, manufacturers and producers have sought to take advantage of this larger market by securing the means of increased output and by protecting themselves from increased competition. Many small and inefficient firms, which have been protected in the past by high tariffs, are unlikely to survive in the fully established Common Market. Many will be, and already have been, absorbed in bigger firms with more capital—firms faced with the necessity for growth in order to compete with what were formerly "foreign" producers. Mergers between firms, sell-outs, creation of joint subsidiaries, trading agreements and combinations of one kind or another have occurred as a logical and inevitable effect of bringing the Common Market into existence.

Antitrust legislation. Those who drafted the Treaty of Rome were aware that the formation of these business combinations and the inevitable emergence of larger and more efficient firms geared to reap the benefits of a huge consumer market would involve the problem of assuring that consumers, as well as producers, gain from the advantages of large scale production. Accordingly, the Treaty of Rome charges the Commission with responsibility for implementing enforcement of the provisions which have been made to ensure freedom of competition within the Community. Specific rules have been provided for the regulation of trusts and other business combinations familiarly referred to in Europe as cartels or *ententes*.

The further problem of the monopoly firm, which is able by reason of its size to dominate a particular industry at the expense of the community, and a wide range of restrictive practices were considered and appropriate regulatory steps devised.

Before examining antitrust and monopoly policy within the Community in detail, some historical perspective will be useful in understanding why solving the problem of ensuring free competition—as required by the preamble to the Treaty—has been particularly difficult.

Municipal laws vary widely. Antitrust regulations within the individual countries composing the EEC have varied widely in scope and legislative form. German regulatory policy has required the registration of all agreements tending to restrict competition illegally, and this approach in general has been adopted in the Treaty provisions. French law, in contrast, leaves it to the state to discover and prove such agreements and practices but provides for full-scale investigation where restrictive practices are suspected. The latter provision for investigation has also been carried into the EEC rules. Other nations have still different policies.

National regulation of *intrastate* cartel operations is not prohibited by the Treaty provisions, which provide only that agreements or practices which are likely to affect trade *between member states* and which *result in restricting or distorting competition* are null and void and come within the existing EEC regulatory mechanism. Thus the subsidiary of an American firm established in the Common Market, for example, must observe the municipal law of the member state in which it is organized as well as the EEC antitrust laws. "Municipal law" is used here in a legal sense and refers to the national laws of the individual member states. A third body of law also pertinent even when the American subsidiary is located within the EEC is United States antitrust law, which may very well be applicable (see page 205 following).

Antitrust tradition lacking in Europe: a Dutch example. Ensuring free competition in the Common Market has also been complicated by the fact that there is no antitrust tradition in these European states as there is in America. In the Netherlands, for example, an entirely different attitude has existed on the question of competition and antitrust regulation. For centuries the Dutch enjoyed the advantages of trading guilds and concerted trading. The first Dutch law relating to restrictive practices is as recent as the period of the depression in the 1930's. Before that time there were no curbs on either cartels or monopolies. Competition was assured because Dutch industrialists and trading businesses had to compete in world markets for export trade, and there were many foreign competitors in the domestic market. This "natural" climate of competition diminished somewhat with increased industrialization after World War I. Even so the benefits of cartelization appeared to outweigh the disadvantages, and cartels (e.g., that in the printing industry which was formed in 1914) were unmolested.

Cartel legislation of the 1930's had a mixed effect. On the one hand, and this required an amendment to the Dutch Constitution,[1] the government was enabled to create bodies representative of occupations, groups of occupations or the whole of economic life and to grant these bodies rule-making and legislative power. Far from discouraging the formation of cartels, their formation was actually encouraged to enable the Dutch to cope with depression-inspired foreign protectionist policies raised in world trade. During this period of trying business conditions there was thought to be too much competition. Cartels helped to maintain prices and halt the downward trend of wages, or at least this was believed to be the case. Cartelization was viewed as necessary to balance production and consumption. In some cases the law was used to require

non-participants to adhere to a cartel agreement, while in others
it simply provided grounds for an action against a member who
failed to observe the cartel's provisions. In general, the government's power to make cartel agreements binding was not used
very extensively.

But the benevolent regard of government for these cartels
was accompanied by legislative provisions designed to ensure
that while the function of the useful cartels could not be negated
by a minority of non-participants in the cartelized industry, the
cartel could not pursue its own interests to the detriment of the
consumer. Up to World War II and German occupation, the
government did not use its power to annul agreements. In general these principles have been observed in later years, although
their application in specific cases has changed considerably.
Cartelization, in fact, did not solve the economic problems of
the depression. The 1935 law was replaced on November 5,
1941 by a decree promulgated during the German occupation
under which cartels were controlled directly by the occupation
government. Immediate post-war cartel policy for the most part
represented a return to the economic policies of the 1930's. The
government could set maximum prices, it could license business
enterprises to ensure competent management and authorize or
annul labor agreements (the Industrial Organization Act and
Works Council Act).

A new law, in 1951, provided that no regulation should
constitute an impediment to fair competition, and this provision
was carried over into the Economic Competition Act which was
passed on June 28, 1956. Under the latter Act, the state has
power to create mandatory cartels and also to annul or prohibit a cartel. Agreements regulating competition (but not those
concerned with labor relations) have to be registered with the
government unless specifically exempt. The Act provides that
regulation of competition by agreements between owners of
enterprises may be declared non-binding. Conversely, the state
can make a regulatory agreement binding on everyone in an
entire industry, provided the regulation is requested by at least

one party to the agreement and it is in the public interest to do so.

Today Dutch cartel policy has as its objectives to keep production costs and prices low; to strengthen the competitive position of Dutch industry in world trade; to raise productivity; and to enhance the quality of production. It opposes cartelization where its effects are not in the general interest, and what is or is not in the public interest is left to administrative decision. There is no presumption in Dutch law that even substantial restriction of competition is necessarily objectionable. Dutch policy does not seek to eliminate the cartels; rather it seeks to modify cartelization by terminating and preventing activities which are contrary to the public interest. There are thus in existence today in the Netherlands various restrictive agreements for the limitation of production, profit-pooling, price control, business allocation and even controls on admission to a particular trade.

Regulation of competition in Belgium. In Belgium, cartels and monopolies have been the subject of special legislation since 1924. In addition, there are pertinent provisions in the Belgian Constitution (Article 20) which guarantee freedom of association, the Civil Code (Article 1382) which creates liability for damages done to others by reason of illicit competition, and the Penal Code (Article 311) which makes punishable the raising or lowering of prices by fraudulent means.

The 1924 law prohibited raising or lowering prices abnormally by minimum-maximum price agreements or by agreements to restrict the production or free circulation of goods, excepting resale price maintenance contracts made between a producer and his distributors. Royal decrees of 1934, 1935 and 1937 were aimed at curbing abuses of economic power, dishonest competition and protecting small retailers from the growing size of department stores. Belgian policy during the depression permitted mandatory cartels under certain circumstances (though the power of the state to create these compulsory cartels was used sparingly) where these strengthened the position of Belgian industry in world markets or enabled producers to take part in international cartels. This policy continued up to the beginning of the 1960's but, on balance, only a relatively small number of mandatory cartels was established and these were not infrequently in such relatively unimportant industries as window glass, floor covering and putty. Among the reasons for the rejection of proposed cartelization schemes were that the agreement imposed more restrictions on those who did not participate in the cartel than on those who did, and that it involved an unconstitutional delegation of state authority to private persons. The cartelization plans that were approved often revolved around problems of Belgian participation in world markets.

In 1952 the law was amended. The new regulation acknowledged that while restraint of competition is not wrong per se, it has objectionable potentials from the point of view of public interest and therefore should be curtailed. The focus of cartel policy was less upon the exercise of economic power than upon *abuses* in the exercise of this power, i.e., such things as abuse of the public interest and the cartel's abuse of the rights of its members.

A new bill was introduced in parliament in 1959 following extensive investigations carried on by the Belgian Council of State, and a law was enacted which became effective May 27, 1960. It depends for its enforcement upon administrative procedures, and there is no appeal to the law courts. The Treaty of Rome was concluded in 1957 and the Belgian authorities were aware that some aspects of their national law might conflict with the rules on competition as laid down in that document and as they were to be subsequently implemented by the EEC Commission. There are certainly elements common to both the Belgian and EEC approaches to the problem, and in this respect the provisions of Article 86 as to monopoly undoubtedly influenced the Belgian law. In any event, the administrative procedures to be employed in applying the Act were not promulgated until October 1961, several months after which the first EEC implementing regulation was published (February 1962) and it was some months after that until a case under the 1960 law was actually completed.

In summary, Belgian experience with cartel laws has not been entirely satisfactory even to the Belgians. Their policy has been to promote Belgian export trade where necessary by cartel arrangements, to protect Belgian industry from foreign competition, to permit restrictions on production in time of depression in order to prevent oversupply with consequent price decreases, lowered wages and loss of capital resulting from over-investment. Cartels have been permitted where higher quality and technical progress would result. Practical advantages gained from this policy have left something to be desired. Few requests for mandatory cartels have been concerned with improving quality or advancing technical progress. Too, Belgian industrialists have generally preferred private cartelization in order to avoid the risk of state interference and government regulation in mandatory cartels established under the enabling legislation.

Regulation of cartels and monopolies under the provisions of the Treaty of Rome does not apply to business conducted entirely within a state nor to the trade of a member state with third parties outside the Common Market. As may be seen from the examples of Dutch and Belgian law just given, member states will continue to have individual antitrust laws of their own. American businessmen operating in Common Market countries must be familiar with such laws and must be guided by them in appropriate circumstances. It is the effect of these national laws on trade among the member nations that has been of primary concern to the authors of the Treaty and to the EEC Commission in formulating common regulatory legislation designed to ensure free competition within the Community.

Restrictive practices. Article 85 of the Treaty prohibits and makes null and void all agreements, decisions and concerted practices likely to affect trade between member states which are aimed at or result in the prevention, restriction or distortion of competition within the Common Market. These include in particular restrictions entailing the direct or indirect fixing of prices; limitation or control of production, markets, technical development or investment; market sharing; discriminatory terms which place the parties to transactions at a competitive disadvantage; and, tie-in sales.

There is an escape clause in the Article, however, under which these prohibitions may be declared inapplicable where the agreement, decision or practice contributes to the improvement of production or distribution of goods or to the promotion of technical or economic progress, provided, *interalia,* that the arrangement does not subject the concerns in question to restrictions which are not indispensable to the achievement of the objective, that the consumer receives an equitable share of the resulting benefits, and that such agreements or practices do not eliminate competition in respect of a substantial proportion of the goods concerned, i.e., create a monopoly position.

Monopoly. Article 86, which deals with monopolistic and oligopolistic practices, forbids one or more firms to take improper advantage of a dominant position within the Common Market or within a substantial part of it, to the extent to which trade between member states would be affected thereby.

Implementing regulations. Implementing provisions relating to these rules on competition have been published pursuant to Article 87 of the Treaty. Their purpose is to secure enforcement of the rules, assure their uniform application, and provide the necessary administrative procedures. The first such provisions were embodied in Regulation 17, which became effective on March 13, 1962[2] and from which date the prohibitions contained in Articles 85 and 86 of the Treaty came into effect.

Notification. The regulations set up the procedures under which agreements and practices falling within the Treaty provisions are to be notified to the Commission. Notification is not compulsory. *But,* the regulation provides (Article 5) that agreements, decisions and concerted practices existing at the time the regulation came into effect or (Article 4) coming into being thereafter, *and in respect to which exemption from the prohibitions specified in Article 85 of the Treaty is desired,* must be notified to the Commission. If no notification is made, there is no way in which the Commission can grant a declaratory decision exempting the agreement or practice from the prohibitions of Article 85. This power rests exclusively in the Commission, although subject to review by the Court of Justice.

There are certain exceptions to these requirements of notification. They are the situations wherein no trade between member states is involved, or where only two enterprises are involved and the sole effect of the agreement is to impose on the immediate purchaser conditions as to which goods acquired under the agreement are to be resold, or as to limitations involving patent or other industrial property rights, or where the object of the agreement relates only to developing uniform standards or to joint research aimed at bringing about technological improvements.

The requirement for notification of restrictive agreements and practices stems from the fact that the Commission is obliged by the Treaty to investigate every such arrangement. By contrast, under United States antitrust law it is up to the Justice Department and the Federal Trade Commission to discover restrictive trade practices and to decide which such practices are to be investigated and, if a violation is found to exist, prosecuted. Under the EEC, all such practices are null and void unless brought under the exemption provisions of the Treaty. To do this the agreement or practice has to be notified to the Commission in the manner and form prescribed by the implementing regulations if the desired exemption is to be had. Under United States antitrust law the burden of proof is on the government to show that the practice is restrictive of competition and illegal. Under the Common Market policy the burden of proof is on the enterprise to show that a particular practice is not. If there is an actual infringement of the Treaty rules concerning competition, however, notification in no way operates to cure it.

From the point of view of the businessman, the purpose of notification is that it is a necessary step to establishing that the escape clause in Article 85 applies to the particular agreement, decision or practice being notified. Failure to notify has a twofold effect. First, it is impossible for the Commission to make a dispensatory declaration under the escape clause. Second, heavy fines or penalties may be incurred for negligent or wilfull infringement of the rules, which might have been avoided if there had been notification and subsequent recommendation by the Commission that the agreement or practice be terminated. Without notification, then, a restrictive agreement or practice (even if it satisfies the requirements of the escape clause) is necessarily prohibited and is subject to all of the ensuing administrative and civil consequences including fines, penalties, nullity and damages.

In summary, an agreement, decision or practice either does or does not infringe the provisions of the Treaty as to freedom of competition. If it does infringe these provisions, and it *does not* qualify for exemption under the escape clause, it is null and void and it must be terminated or modified to the extent necessary to bring it within the exemptions. If it infringes the provisions of the Treaty and *does* come within the exemptions in the escape clause, then it must be notified to the Commission if a declaratory decision stating that the exemptions of the escape clause do apply is to be obtained.

"*Negative clearance.*" Suppose that it is not clear as to whether an agreement or practice falls within the prohibitions of the rules as to competition. In this event, the Commission may be asked for a "negative clearance" (Article 2 of Regulation 17). This is a statement by the Commission that there are, under Articles 85 and 86 of the Treaty, no grounds for it to intervene with respect to the particular agreement, decision or practice.

The procedure operates only upon request, and negative clearance is granted purely on the basis of the information given to the Commission on the application. The discovery of further facts at some later date may result in reopening the entire question. The negative clearance in no way operates to bring the arrangement under the provisions of the escape clause of Article 85, nor does it extend the time within which notification must be made.

Terminating violations. If the Commission finds that there is an infringement of the rules against competition, it can require the offending party to terminate the infringement. This action can be taken on the request of a member state or third party with a justified interest in the matter or on the Commission's own initiative. The Commission has the power to request information from member states and from individual enterprises in connection with restrictive practices or monopolistic practices relating to competition. It can investigate individual enterprises or even entire sectors of the economy where competition appears to be restricted or distorted, can request the authorities of member states to conduct appropriate investigations or can conduct its own investigations. In the latter case, Commission personnel are vested with a broad range of powers which include the power to examine books of account and other business documents, copy them, require explanations and have access to all premises of the business.

The Commission is required to maintain close liaison with the authorities of the member states in conducting these investigations of infringements and must also supply copies of the pertinent requests and documents involved to officials in the state concerned.

Fines and penalties. If a business or association furnishes false or misleading information in an application for a negative clearance or in a notification or in reply to a request for information, or fails to submit to an investigation as ordered, fines of $100 to $5,000 may be imposed, and in cases of continuing default, fines may be levied for each day of default. Where an enterprise or association of enterprises wilfully or negligently violates the rules in the Treaty as to competition, fines of $1,000 to one million dollars, or even a larger amount equal to 10 per cent of the turnover of the preceding business year, may be imposed. Provision has also been made for penalties where there is a delay in ending an infringement following the Commission's directive to do so. The Court of Justice has jurisdiction to decide proceedings instituted against Commission decisions fixing these fines and penalties and may cancel, reduce or increase them.

FORMULAIRE B 1

FORMULAIRE POUR LA NOTIFICATION SIMPLIFIÉE

Le présent formulaire doit être fourni en un seul exemplaire, sans annexe et sans modification du texte imprimé.

Si ce texte ne convient pas pour la notification à faire, il y a lieu d'employer le formulaire normal B.

A LA COMMISSION DE LA C.E.E.
Direction générale de la concurrence
Direction «Ententes et Monopoles»
12, avenue de Broqueville
Bruxelles 15

NOTIFICATION SIMPLIFIÉE D'UN ACCORD DIT DE «CONCESSION EXCLUSIVE»

en application des articles 4 et 5 du règlement n° 17 du Conseil et de l'article 4, paragraphe 2 bis, du règlement n° 27 de la Commission

Le soussigné (1) ....

agissant en qualité de (2) ....

de l'entreprise (3) ....

(4) ....

déclare que cette dernière a conclu un ou plusieurs contrats visés à l'article 4, paragraphe 2 bis, du règlement n° 27 de la Commission (contrats dits de concession exclusive) pour les

produits suivants : ....

....

....

....

Les contrats en question sont mentionnés ci-dessous :

A. S'il s'agit d'un *contrat-type*, c'est-à-dire d'un contrat que l'entreprise déclarante conclut habituellement avec d'autres entreprises

a) indiquer le nombre des contrats-type signés jusqu'à la date de la notification ;

b) indiquer le nom et l'adresse d'un des concessionnaires avec la date de la conclusion du contrat (5)

----

(1) Nom, prénom et adresse du déclarant.
(2) Propriétaire, président, directeur général, gérant, etc
(3) Raison sociale et adresse.
(4) Activité de l'entreprise.
(5) Ce contrat doit être tenu à la disposition de la Commission aussi longtemps que le contrat-type est utilisé.

B. S'il ne s'agit *pas d'un contrat-type* (1) :

Nom et adresse du concessionnaire	Date du contrat

Le déclarant certifie

1. Qu'il n'a pas été établi de concession exclusive réciproque de la distribution de produits concurrents fabriqués par le concédant et par le concessionnaire,

2. Que l'octroi de la concession exclusive n'a pas pour effet de restreindre la possibilité
— pour les intermédiaires ou utilisateurs de se procurer les produits faisant l'objet des contrats auprès d'un autre concessionnaire ou de tout autre intermédiaire établi dans le marché commun,
— pour le concessionnaire de vendre également à des clients établis en dehors de sa zone contractuelle ;

3. Que les accords ne comportent pas d'obligation, pour le concessionnaire, de respecter un prix de vente minimum fixé par le concédant.

Le soussigné déclare que les renseignements fournis ci-dessus sont conformes aux faits.
Il a pris connaissance des dispositions de l'article 15, paragraphe 1, alinéa a, du règlement n° 17.

Le soussigné se réserve de faire valoir que l'accord notifié n'est pas visé par l'article 85, paragraphe 1.

...., le ....

Signature

(¹) Les renseignements demandées sont à fournir pour tous les contrats conclus.

Further implementing regulations. Regulation 27[3] relates to the procedure and forms to be followed in applying for a negative clearance and in giving notification of an agreement, decision or concerted practice under Regulation 17.

Regulation 59[4] made changes in the filing dates for notification. Regulation 153[5] further modified Regulations 17 and 27 and set out a simplified form of notification of certain exclusive distribution agreements.

Exclusive Agency Contracts. Subsequent statements (see pp. 2919/62 and 2920/62, *Journal Officiel des Communautés Européennes*) relating to notification of exclusive agency contracts made with commercial agents have excluded these particular agreements from the prohibitions laid down in the Treaty. If the commercial agent is in fact an agent and undertakes no transactions on his own account, and assumes no credit risk on his own account in connection with the transactions he concludes on behalf of his principal, then such contracts need not be notified to the Commission because the conditions requisite to application of the Treaty prohibitions do not exist. Note, however, that if the commercial representative is an independent trader who has an interest, either directly or indirectly, in the transactions, or performs services following the transactions, or maintains a stock of the goods, or can fix the price of the goods, then the agreement should be notified to the Commission.

The use of a commission agent as a regular method of sales contact is well established in Europe; hence the importance of these particular provisions as to notification. Because a large portion of tax income in many European countries is derived from the "turnover tax" (a tax levied whenever title passes from one level of production or distribution to the next), rather than from income, corporate profits and other taxes, European firms often sell direct to retailers through commission agents who make the sales contacts and arrange the sales. This keeps changes of title in the goods and the consequent turnover taxes at a minimum.

United States antitrust law may apply. As noted earlier in the chapter, municipal antitrust law continues to govern competition in trade that is completely intrastate and in no way involves commerce between the member states. It also governs trade between a member state and a non-member nation. Treaty provisions and the implementing regulations just mentioned must be observed where business activity involves trade between member states of the Common Market. The subsidiaries of American firms established in the Market have a further concern with antitrust law in that they may still be subject to provisions of United States statutes relating to competition. Even though the subsidiary has received a "negative clearance" by the EEC Commission as to a particular restrictive agreement or practice pursuant to the exemption clause in Article 85 of the Treaty, this does not in itself insulate the American company from prosecution under the Sherman and other antitrust acts.

While acknowledging that this is still "an extremely fuzzy area of American law," an early work on the Common Market published by the American Management Association cautions: "To be on the safe side, company managements should look hard and carefully at the implications of this question before entering into any patent license containing restrictive clauses or cross licenses with foreign competitors; before making any agreements with foreign companies fixing the territories for distribution or fixing retail prices; before entering into partnership arrangements with foreign companies, particularly if the foreign partners are actual or potential competitors; before agreeing to restrict exports from or imports into the United States, even though that agreement is between an American parent and a foreign subsidiary; before becoming a member of any foreign trade association which exercises control over production, sales, imports or exports; and, finally, before complying with a request from a foreign government to restrict or control exports from, or imports into, the United States."[6]

With the growth in importance of the Common Market and passage of the Trade Expansion Act (1962), increased attention in Washington has been focused on the activities of American companies trading or operating overseas. The Justice Department has recently set up a special office, the Foreign Commerce Section of the Antitrust Division, to coordinate investigations and prosecutions involving United States companies selling or operating abroad.[7]

Public enterprises and state monopolies. Not all restrictions on freedom of competition arise in the private sector of the economy. The practices of public enterprises may also have a restrictive effect as do the state fiscal monopolies which have existed in Germany (matches and spirits), France (tobacco, newsprint, petroleum, etc.) and Italy (salt, tobacco, cigarette paper, etc.). These tend to place enterprises in one state at a disadvantage competitively in relation to enterprises in another. As to both state monopolies and public enterprises, the Treaty requires members not to introduce any measures contrary to the general rules of competition which have just been discussed. State trading monopolies are required to remove all discrimination, in the course of the transitional period, among Community producers and consumers. Where states have granted special rights to state monopolies or industries, the rules relating to restrictive practices, dumping, and state aid apply with full force. Thus, consumers in a nation where there is a state monopoly on the manufacture or supply of a particular commodity, such as salt, for example, must have a free choice between the salt supplied by the monopoly and salt imported from other EEC countries.[8]

The Commission is empowered to recommend that dumping practices be terminated and, where they continue, to authorize protective measures on the part of injured member states. The Treaty does not define "dumping," but by agreement among the Commission and representatives of the member states its meaning is held to be that supplied by Article VI of GATT, i.e., the practice of introducing the products of one country into the commerce of another at a price less than the price in the ordinary course of business in the exporting country. Goods dumped into a state must be re-admitted to the state of origin free of all customs duties or other quantitative restrictions (the so-called "boomerang" clause).

Government aid and subsidies. In order to encourage the development of a particular industry or to make it competitive with similar foreign industry, governments frequently provide subsidies to these industries. Such aid, if it distorts or threatens to distort competition, is prohibited to the extent that it adversely affects trade between member states. Among exceptions to this general rule are subsidies of a social character granted to individual consumers, subsidies necessitated by natural catastrophe and aid to certain regions in Germany which have been adversely affected by the division of that country. Other exceptions which *may* be allowed include aid to underdeveloped regions or areas of serious underemployment, aid extended in connection with major projects of common European interest and certain other situations specified by the EEC Council.

A continuing surveillance of systems of aid existing in the several member states is maintained by the Commission,[9] and any state subsidy which impedes the progressive development or functioning of the Common Market is to be eliminated.[10] In enforcing an order for termination of an improper aid or subsidy, the Commission may have recourse to the Court of Justice.

Common Patent, Trademark and Design Legislation

Another area of importance to American businessmen with interests in the Common Market relates to the protection of industrial property rights. Although patents are not mentioned directly in the Treaty of Rome,[11] both the general program concerning removal of restrictions on freedom of establishment (see page 212) and that concerning removal of restrictions on freedom of supply of services (see page 216)—both adopted October 25, 1961—establish the right to acquire, exploit or dispose of industrial property and the rights thereto attached. Heretofore patent laws have been strictly national; no patent is in force except in the county issuing it. United States companies with operations abroad have obtained protection by securing patents under the national laws of each of the countries concerned.

While earlier treaties (especially the Paris Conventions of 1883, 1934 and the recent Lisbon revision of 1958 which has not yet gone into effect) have had some influence in the direction of unifying the laws relating to industrial property, there are substantial conflicts in the municipal laws of the several Common Market countries. Thus Germany requires a strict examination of novelty and subject prior to granting a patent, while France does not. Again, while Dutch patent law grants protection to pharmaceutical and chemical processes, Italian law does not. In two states (Netherlands and Luxembourg) there is no protection at all for designs and models. The duration of the protection also varies among the different states as do examination procedures and tests for novelty.[12] As a result of their study of the problem, the coordinating committee set up by the EEC Commission has come up with a program which is quite new so far as the member states are concerned.

Proposed European patent law. Under authority of Articles 100-102 of the Treaty of Rome,[13] the Commission has proceeded to have drafted a uniform European patent law. The proposed new law will not replace the laws of the individual countries but will make it possible for an inventor or manufacturer to secure a patent valid for all of the Common Market countries and in such others as may subsequently join. It will not impair the right of the contracting states to maintain their domestic patent law along side the European patent law, if necessary measures of adaptation are carried out, nor will it in any way void commitments of the contracting states under other international treaties, in particular the Paris Convention of 1883 for the protection of industrial property. Such a law will be the first to offer international rights to an invention.

A draft of the convention to establish the European patent has been published (November 1962) to enable prospective signatories to study it, but it is not yet in final form, nor are the draft conventions on trademarks and designs. The final agreement is to be ready for signature early in 1964, by which time regulations to implement the convention will also be prepared. Although the present draft still contains alternative clauses and various reservations, which have yet to be resolved, the broad outline of the direction in which harmonization is proceeding is clear.

One point of great interest to the American businessman,

which is still undecided in the draft, involves the question as to whether or not non-citizens of the member states will be able to secure the European patent. If American firms can secure the patent, either directly or through their foreign subsidiaries, they will gain extensive additional protection for property rights in the Common Market area. Unfortunately, to accord inventors outside the signatory countries the protection of the European patent may involve a conflict with an older treaty for the protection of industrial property, the Paris Convention of 1883, to which the United States and all six EEC countries are signatories.

Patent law administration. The draft of the convention provides for a European system of patent law and the granting of European patents valid in all member states. A European Patent Office and a European Patent Court will be set up to administer the new law and provide for its interpretation and enforcement.

The former will consist of examining sections, examining divisions and patent administration divisions. Above these divisions there will be boards of appeal to decide appeals from the decisions taken by the sections and divisions, and revocation boards to rule on applications for revocation of European patents and on applications for compulsory licenses.

The European Patent Court will hear appeals on points of law from decisions of the appeal boards and revocation boards of the Patent Office and, in addition, will decide questions of interpretation under certain circumstances in infringement proceedings being tried by domestic courts under municipal law. (See section following on infringement proceedings.)

Procedure for granting patents. When an application for a patent is filed it will be first examined on points of form by the European Patent Office. A novelty report will then be drawn up by the International Patent Institute in The Hague. On the basis of these inquiries a *provisional European patent* will be granted approximately 18 months from date of application, and published along with the novelty report.

Under the draft convention the provisional patent lapses five years from date of publication thereof, unless within that period an application has been made (by the holder or any third party) to the European Patent Office for examination of the provisional patent. When such an application is made, the Patent Office examines the provisional patent as to its novelty and degree of inventiveness and then, where appropriate, confirms the provisional European patent as a *final European patent.*

Term of protection, lapsing, revocation. The *term* of European patents will run for 20 years from date of application, with protection commencing on the date of publication of the provisional patent. The patent *lapses* when the period of protection expires and also if the holder surrenders it or if renewal fees are not paid. It may be *revoked* if the Patent Office subsequently finds the subject matter was not patentable or the specification of the invention was insufficient.

Compulsory licensing. A compulsory license will be granted in the case of a European patent by the Patent Office by reason of non-user, interdependence with earlier patents or in connection with provisions of the Euratom Treaty. Such licenses are effective throughout the entire Common Market area. Individual member states may also issue compulsory licenses under European patents where such licenses are in the public interest, but in such cases the licenses are effective only within the territory of the issuing states.

Infringement proceedings. An action alleging patent infringement may be brought in any domestic court with jurisdiction to hear cases dealing with infringements of domestic patents. Such courts will apply municipal law in deciding the case, with the following exceptions: "If the validity of a provisional European patent is contested during proceedings for the infringement of that patent, a decision establishing an infringement may only be taken after the provisional European patent has been confirmed as a final European patent. If during an action for infringement of a final European patent the defendant questions the validity of the patent, the court shall stay proceedings pending a decision by the revocation board of the European Patent Office. If questions of interpretation arise in infringement proceedings, domestic courts from whose decision there is no . . . . appeal under muni-

cipal law must, and lower courts may, submit them for an inter-
locutory decision by the European Patent Court."[14]

Co-ordinating committee groups are also at work on the
harmonization of existing municipal laws on trademarks, designs
and models.

Freedom of Establishment

The right of laborers to take jobs anywhere in the Common
Market has already been noted in chapter 7. Business management, too, is guaranteed freedom of movement in the Community. All restrictions on the freedom of establishment of
nationals of one member state in the territory of another member
state (including the associated overseas territories) are progressively being abolished in the course of the transitional period,[15]
and no new restrictions are to be introduced.[16]

Concept defined. Freedom of establishment includes the
right of nationals of one member state to engage in and carry
on non-wage-earning activities[17] and to set up and manage enterprises and companies in another member state free of restrictions
based on nationality. It extends also to companies[18] duly constituted under the public or private laws of a member state and
having their registered office[19] or central management or main
establishment within the Community, and to their setting up of
agencies, branches or subsidiaries in the territory of any of the
member states.

By assuring freedom of establishment and the free movement
of capital, no opportunity for economic development within the
Community should be lost as a result of restrictions on an entre-
preneur who might otherwise have moved in to exploit it.

In implementing these provisions, an attempt has been made
to give priority treatment to activities in regard to which freedom
of establishment will promote the development of production and
trade. Under the general program for abolishing restrictions on
freedom of establishment a four-stage plan was laid down.[20] By
the end of 1963, restrictions on freedom of establishment or the
supply of services (which see, below) in certain of the textile
industries, coal mining, chemicals, metalworking, construction

and several others must be abolished. Those in certain of the beverage and food industries, and in accountancy and auditing, among others, must be removed by the end of 1965; in the transportation industry, in fishing, tobacco manufactures, etc., by 1967; and, all remaining restrictions on the freedom of establishment and the supply of services by 1970.

Ultimately, directives will be issued relative to the mutual recognition of diplomas, certificates and other qualifications.[21] These will presumably involve bringing some uniformity into the curricula of institutions of higher learning and other training programs as well as in the qualifications required in order to enter the professions.

Freedom of establishment creates business opportunities. Freedom of establishment, so far as individuals are concerned, applies to *nationals* of a member state. So far as *companies* are concerned (and these include limited partnerships and all corporate entities, excepting only non-profit companies), if they are duly constituted in accordance with the law of a member state there is no requirement that the place of actual control of the company be within the Community or that the members of the company or its management or directors or the owners or holders of the company's capital be nationals of one of the member states. Hence, an American subsidiary established in one of the member states has the advantage of being able to conduct business in any of the other member states. That American firms are receptive to this expanded opportunity is evident from the increasing number of American firms which have established subsidiaries and branches within the Community. In the first three years following the creation of the Common Market more than a thousand American companies established operations within the six member states. DuPont, for example, established nine operating subsidiaries or affiliates in Western Europe between 1957 and 1961. International Telephone and Telegraph Company in the past three years (1961-1963) has built 13 new telecommunication plants in 12 of the 13 Common Market and EFTA countries.

The reasons for establishing these subsidiaries by no means

depend solely upon the business climate created by the Community's efforts to remove restrictions on freedom of establishment. The opportunity to avoid tariff and other trade barriers obviously is a more basic motivation. Or an American company may find, for example, that the product it manufactures is so heavy or bulky that high freight costs preclude its being exported profitably into the Common Market. Again, a product may be so labor intensive that it cannot be manufactured profitably in the United States for export at prevailing wage levels. These factors favor establishing a subsidiary within the EEC to take advantage of a favorable tariff arrangement, of lower transportation costs in getting to market and lower wage levels.

While formerly such a subsidiary might operate only in France, for example, it can now conduct business in all of the member states as the result of the removal of restrictions on freedom of establishment.

A further effect of the removal of these restrictions has been to permit the regrouping or dissolution of many "subsidiaries" which were required under national company law but which served no economic purpose. Such companies are being replaced simply by agencies or branches in many instances.

On the other hand, a course of action made desirable for purely business reasons is not infrequently frustrated by tax or other considerations at home. Thus, in recent years the Department of State has tended to encourage American business to establish foreign subsidiaries—first to help rebuild the European economy following World War II and more recently to aid in the fight against Communism in underdeveloped nations. At the same time, the tax views of the U.S. Treasury Department have sometimes tended to discourage or penalize investment abroad. Tax laws can obviously impede companies from putting profits into overseas expansion or building up overseas sales operations. What will the tax rate be in 1970 on companies with subsidiaries abroad? Will subsidiaries be able to deduct taxes paid abroad to EEC member states? Will the view that investment in subsidiaries in developed nations increases the American balance of payments deficit prevail over the longer-term view that benefits in the form of earnings will tend to redress this deficit? Will sound long-term economic policy prevail over political expedients of the moment? It is difficult to see how either capital, in the long-term, or industrial employment is drained away from the United States into EEC nations when an American firm builds a plant abroad in order to compete in the Common Market by producing goods that cannot be produced in the United States at a cost that will permit the goods to compete price-wise in that market!

Obstacles to freedom of establishment. While a company or subsidiary in one member state will be free to establish itself in another member state when all restrictions are finally removed, it does not thereby automatically gain legal recognition as a company in the latter state nor is it exempt from the laws of that state as they relate to company management. This follows from the fact that company formation and operation are governed by the laws of the several member states. These laws vary widely as to the nature of the company created, its powers, requirements as to number of members, minimum capital, status of directors, meetings of shareholders, auditors, registration and in many other respects. The procedures involved in forming a company vary from the very minimum formalities required in Luxembourg to the elaborate steps necessary to form the *Aktiengesellschaft* in Germany or the *Societa per axioni* in Italy.

A parent company seeking to form a branch or subsidiary must be familiar with the wide range of legal technicalities involved in the several nations. And, there are other problems. Mergers and combinations of companies formed in different member states are often extremely complicated. A company seeking to move from one country to another may have to liquidate in the country of first establishment and then re-form in the other.

To require that all company law in the several states be made uniform has not been feasible, nor does this seem necessary to the creation and functioning of a common market, any more than it has been in the United States where business corporations are formed under the laws of the several states rather than by federal charter.

A common form of European company? While restrictions

on freedom of establishment *are* gradually being removed, resid-ual problems still have to be worked out. One proposal to facilitate their solution which has been made[22] is that of a com-mon form of European company, that is, a single new form of company which would be recognized and permitted to exist along with those created under individual national laws. The existence of such European companies would solve many of the problems just mentioned, would facilitate the movement of companies from one member state to another, would simplify mergers and provide an alternative to *unification* of company law among the EEC states.

Freedom to provide services. Restrictions on freedom of sup-ply of services within the Community are progressively being abolished. *Services,* as the term is employed within the context of the Treaty, means simply remunerative activity to the extent that it is not covered by Treaty provisions relating to the free movement of goods, capital and persons, and includes in partic-ular professional services, the services of artisans and industrial and commercial activities. Among these are medical and consult-ing services, tourism, entertainment, motion picture films, etc. The supply of services is in a sense regarded as a temporary activity as opposed to the concept of establishment which carries with it a connotation of continuity. Thus an auditor may serve several firms, and serve each for intermittent periods only. A manufac-turer of electronic devices, on the other hand, comes within the concept of establishment because of the continuous character of the business activity.

Just as in the case of freedom of establishment, a general program for the removal of restrictions on the freedom of supply of services has been approved.[23] By 1970 all such restrictions of an economic nature, or legislative or administrative provisions which in any state govern the entry, departure or residence of nationals of other member states, if these impede the supply of services by such nationals, will have been removed and the nationals of the several states will receive equality of treatment so far as supply of services is concerned.

Business Taxation

Differences in both the rate and types of taxation levied on businesses in the several member states obviously affect the competitive position of those businesses. A firm operating in a state which gains extensive revenues from business taxes operates under a disadvantage when compared with a firm which does its business where the state draws revenues from primarily non-business sources. In a recent year, for example, company taxes amounted to almost 16 per cent of total tax receipts in Luxembourg and only 3 per cent of total tax receipts in Italy. Disparities existing among the different tax systems can distort conditions of competition in the Common Market and accordingly must be harmonized.

Company taxes. In Germany the company tax *(Körperschaftsteuer)* generally amounts to 15 per cent on distributed profits and 51 per cent on undistributed profits. In France the rate is 50 per cent on actual profits; in the Netherlands, from 42 per cent to 45 per cent depending upon the amount of profit; in Luxembourg, about 40 per cent of total profit.

There are similar differences in the rates of other taxes levied on business. In France payroll taxes and the employer's contribution to social security presently amount to almost 40 per cent of the gross wages bill. In Italy social security charges paid by the employer amount to almost 52 per cent of total wages paid. In Luxembourg the figure is about half that in Italy. The tax rules relating to depreciation allowances are also important. These are particularly liberal in the Benelux countries, less so elsewhere.

Problems raised by differences in tax rates are compounded by the effect of additional taxes which are incident in some instances to only a particular country within the Community (e. g., certain of the schedular taxes in Italy, or the directors' tax in the Netherlands). Either harmonization or approximation of the laws relating to business taxation in the Community will require much effort and very probably a considerable period of time.

Turnover taxes. In addition to direct company taxes and income taxes, a considerably more important tax in most continental European countries is the business turnover or transactions tax. This is an indirect single- or multi-stage tax levied at various stages in the production and distribution of goods and on the performance of services. It varies in character from the so-called "waterfall" or "cascading" tax in Germany, and elsewhere, levied at each stage of manufacture or distribution to an "added value" tax *(taxe sur valeur ajoutée)* employed in France.

In the first case, the tax is cumulative and the final price of goods reflects the cost of the component parts plus the number of transactions taxed in bringing the raw materials to finished product. Because of differences in the tax in the several states, the disparity in price of goods has to be adjusted when goods are exported into another state within the EEC if inequities in trade are to be avoided. Under the French system, the tax is not cumulative. It is levied at a fixed rate, multi-stage, and paid only on the value added to the goods at a particular stage.

In a recent year, turnover and transport taxes varied from 16 per cent of total tax receipts in Luxembourg to almost 35 per cent of tax receipts in France (see Table 9.1). The rate of the turnover tax also varies widely among the several member states.

TABLE 9.1
Taxes Levied by State and Subordinate Bodies in EEC Member Countries

	Per cent of Total Tax Receipts					
Type of Tax	Germany	France	Belgium	Netherlands	Italy	Luxembourg
Income Tax	23.0	13.7	} 34.2	38.8	20.0	30.6
Company Tax	8.4	9.7	}	13.5	3.0	15.8
Turnover & Transportation Taxes	25.3	34.7	29.1	19.0	20.4	16.2
Customs Duties	4.1	2.3	5.3	7.7	5.5	3.9
Capital Gains Tax & Tax on Capital Movements	2.8	5.5	6.0	3.8	7.0	2.3
All other Taxes	36.4	34.1	25.4	17.2	44.1	31.2

Source: Adapted from data contained in the 1962 Report of the Fiscal and Financial Committee of the EEC Commission. Percentages are for the year 1959.

Article 99 of the Treaty specifically directs the Commission to submit proposals to the Council for the issuance of directives (under Article 100) to bring about the harmonization of turnover taxes, excise duties and other forms of indirect taxation, including compensatory measures applying to exchanges between states.

An important problem is that of determining how much the turnover tax has added to the cost of the final product in order to set an amount of compensatory refund (or "drawback") on the product, when it is exported to other EEC states, that will be fair to competitors in those states and not favor producers in the exporting state.

Harmonization of business taxes. The basic problem is to arrive at an approximation of tax laws in the several states, or at least sufficient harmonization in fiscal policies to prevent tax levies from operating inequitably upon producers and firms in the several member states.

In spite of the complexity of the problems involved, a start has been made toward finding solutions. The 1963 report[24] of the Fiscal and Financial Committee of the EEC Commission recommends that cumulative turnover taxes presently in force should be abolished. In their place an added-value tax to be levied at all stages up to and including the wholesale stage would be introduced and supplemented, if necessary, by an autonomous tax on retail trade or by an extension of the added-value tax to the retail level. After the proposed reform, tax frontiers would be abolished so far as the turnover tax is concerned. This proposal has already had some consideration in that the Commission submitted to the Council a draft directive late in 1962 aimed at the harmonization of turnover taxes. The proposed directive provides for an added-value tax applied uniformly by the member states to all stages of production and wholesale trading. Since the rate of the tax will be the same in each country, no export drawback will be involved.

As already stated, differences in the taxation of companies can have the effect of discouraging a company from setting up or operating in a particular state where the tax is high and will also affect its competitive position in relation to companies in other member states. To meet these problems a uniform company tax is proposed with differential rates for distributed and undistributed profits. A proposed tax of about 50 per cent on undistributed profits is under study. The Fiscal and Financial Committee has also proposed a system of deducting taxes on interest and dividends at the source on the grounds that this would facilitate administrative problems involved and tend to eliminate tax evasion.

Certain excises on goods which can be used for either production or consumption purposes create special problems if tax frontiers are maintained, since rates of compensatory taxes and tax refunds can be ascertained only with difficulty. In order to prevent distortion of competition the report of the Committee points out that such taxes should either be combined with the added-value tax or allowed to be deducted from it.

NOTES

[1] Articles 149(a) to 149(e), *Constitution*, Koninkrijk der Nederlanden.

[2] Voted by the Council of Ministers at Brussels, February 6, 1962, and published at p. 204 *et seq.*, *Journal Officiel des Communautés Européennes*, Number 13/62, February 21, 1962.

[3] Effective May 11, 1962, *op. cit.*, p. 1118, Number 35/62, May 10, 1962. The regulation together with the prescribed Form A (Application for negative clearance under Article 85, part 1, of the Treaty) and Form B (Notification of an agreement, decision or concerted practice) are available in English in *Supplement to Bulletin of the EEC*, No. 5, 1962.

[4] Effective July 11, 1962, *op. cit.*, p. 1655 *et seq.*, Number 58/62, July 10, 1962.

[5] Effective December 25, 1962, *op. cit.*, 2918 *et seq.*, Number 139/62, December 24, 1962.

[6] Ball, George W. (contributor), "The Treaty of Rome and Its Provisions," *The European Common Market*, New York: American Management Association, 1958, pp. 53-54.

[7] See also Crosby, R. W., "Antitrusters Aim New Actions at Mergers and Foreign Ties," *Iron Age*, Vol. 191, No. 2, January 10, 1963, pp. 28-30.

[8] See Article 37 (commercial state monopolies) and Article 90 (public enterprises) Treaty of Rome.

[9] See Article 93, Treaty of Rome.

[10] Many subsidies have in fact already been eliminated, among them the German subsidy to synthetic rubber producers, and major changes have been made in the subsidies granted heretofore in France and Italy to the shipbuilding industry.

[11] Article 106 of the Treaty does specify, however, that member states may not introduce new restrictions among themselves on transfers of payments connected with certain invisible transactions listed in Annex III to the Treaty, among which are listed patents, designs, trademarks and inventions including the assignment and licensing of rights pertaining thereto.

[12] For a concise summary of existing municipal laws relating to patents, trademarks, models and designs in the Common Market member states see paragraphs 1008-1013 in Campbell, Alan and Thompson, Dennis, *Common Market Law*, London: Stevens & Sons, 1962.

[13] These articles provide for the promulgation of such directives for the approximation of legislative and administrative provisions of the member states as have a direct incidence on the establishment or functioning of the Common Market, for the elimination of disparities in legislative or administrative provisions of the member states which distort conditions of competition in the Common Market, and for the avoidance of such distortion as might arise from the enactment or amendment of legislative or administrative provisions of the member states.

[14] See EEC Information Memo P/10159, *Draft Convention on European Patent Law*, dated November 14, 1962. Since work on the drafts of these conventions, undertaken under a general agreement relating to the establishment of international industrial property rights, is still continuing, EEC information memos and bulletins provide an indispensable source of the most recent developments and should be consulted where current information is essential.

[15] See Article 52, Treaty of Rome.

[16] See Article 53, Treaty of Rome.

[17] The right of establishment does not apply to wage-earners or to salaried people. It does apply to self-employed individuals, entrepreneurs, partners, sole proprietors and company directors, as well as to companies as such.

[18] This includes co-operative companies. Non-profit companies are excluded because the Treaty is commercial in its objectives, but member states (by Article 220) are urged to negotiate with one another to bring about mutual recognition of these organizations.

[19] Maintaining a registered office in one of the countries (as might be done, for example, with a Belgian or Dutch company with a registered office in one of those countries, but with the entire activity of the company carried on in an outside country not in the EEC) merely in order to come within the provisions of this Article is insufficient. The business activity of the company must show a *continuous and effective link with the economy of a member state*.

[20] Approved by the Council on October 25, 1961.

[21] See Article 57, Treaty of Rome.

[22] See Article 220 of the Treaty which provides for "the mutual recognition of companies . . . etc."

[23] Approved October 25, 1961.

[24] For a brief summary of the report, see *Press Release*, EEC, IP (63) 18, dated January 31, 1963. The full report is available from EEC national sales offices.

10

The Impact of Common Agricultural Practices and Policies

GENERAL NATURE OF THE COMMON AGRICULTURAL PROGRAM
—FUTURE UNITED STATES EXPORTS TO THE EEC—JOINT SOLU-
TION OF AGRICULTURAL PROBLEMS—PROMOTION OF AGRICUL-
TURAL SALES TO THE EEC

The national agricultural policies which were being pursued at the time of the formulation of the Treaty of Rome by
the future EEC members differed significantly in methods, importance and objectives. It was believed that an extension of these
separate programs would provide a continuous source of friction among the European nations and thus preclude economic
harmonization in other sectors of the region. Accordingly, a
common farm program came to be accepted as an integral
part of close economic integration on the part of members of
the European Economic Community.

The six countries had traditionally protected and subsidized
their respective agricultural sectors. Thus, they had become
increasingly self-sufficient in foodstuffs due to the growth in
farm output since World War II, despite a significant expansion
in consumption. The severe shortage of food during World
War II represented a major factor which contributed to the
promotion of agricultural protection and self-sufficiency. Another
reason for continued protection is that the agricultural sector
in the Community remains a strong political force; approximately
20 per cent of the labor force is in agriculture. The comparable
share in the United States is less than 10 per cent. An equally
important consideration which has led to special farm legisla-

tion is that, since one farm organization usually dominates in a country, agricultural interests are unified in the EEC countries. These organizations are active in the development of farm policy and in the joint administration of agricultural programs. The feeling generally persists that a political party cannot remain in power without farm support.

General Nature of the Common Agricultural Program

The Treaty of Rome (Article 39) calls for a common agricultural policy (CAP), but progress in this direction has been slow. Agricultural integration was excluded from the first stage of the Community's development because members were unable to conclude an agreement. It was not until January 1962, four years after the EEC commenced operations, that the Council of Ministers adopted a series of regulations on the basic aspects of this program. This initial step was considered necessary before the Community could enter the second stage of development.[1] Many aspects of the CAP remain uncertain, some have yet to be formulated, and still others may be changed in coming years. It is also conceivable that the member countries find it impossible to implement fully the program which they are designing.

As specified by the EEC Commission, the new CAP has four major objectives: to provide a fair income to farmers; to stabilize agricultural markets; to achieve balance between supply and demand within the Community and in its external trade; and to ensure a fair deal to consumers through reasonable and competitive prices.

Methods of attaining objectives. To help accomplish these objectives, certain basic agricultural prices are to be maintained at a level high enough for farmers to earn a living. Reliance will not be placed on direct government subsidies but on managed price levels to raise farm income. Insofar as domestic prices exceed world prices on agricultural products, protection is afforded to prevent a large volume of cheap imports from non-member countries. For the important basic products, protection is accomplished through a system of variable levies, although for some agricultural commodities a fixed tariff applies.

A European Agricultural Guidance and Guarantee Fund has been established to administer various provisions of the program. It will be used to introduce modernization and structural improvements, and will intervene with support purchases (especially for grains) to maintain minimum price levels. It is authorized to make refunds on exports to third countries; these export subsidies may be necessary for shipments abroad in instances where EEC prices exceed world prices. Financial resources for the Fund will be derived from contributions of member states.

The CAP is quite complicated; however, it does replace an even more complex structure of national quotas, tariffs, taxes, and support policies. As is true of most other features of the EEC, the agricultural program will be implemented gradually over a period of seven and one-half years beginning in mid-1962 through the end of 1969. During this transitional period, widely divergent national farm plans will be merged into a common plan and a unified market will be gradually developed within which farm products can move freely at a common price. A new set of restrictions will go into effect on imports from non-member countries and joint decision-making will be required for the solution of various problems relating to agricultural production, prices and marketing.

In late 1963, the Commission of the EEC proposed that some aspects of the farm program be instituted in less than one year rather than gradually over the remainder of the period through the end of 1969. This would eliminate a series of transitional regulations and provisions which otherwise would be applied by individual members through the end of 1969. France, in particular, favored such an approach while Germany, with a relatively inefficient agricultural sector, provided strong opposition. A broad agreement was finally reached on common prices and policies for rice, beef and dairy products. This agreement represented a compromise in which Germany accepted a lowering of prices on these items in exchange for other concessions relating to both agriculture and industry.

Significance of the CAP for individual EEC members. By American standards, the EEC agricultural sector is generally considered to be economically inefficient. European agriculture has been subsidized in various ways since before World War II. Germany's farm prices have been maintained at the highest level—about 20 per cent above the lowest, which have existed in France. Agricultural prices in the other four member countries have generally fallen between these two extremes. As illustrated in Table 10.1, supports have also exceeded those in the United States for some products.

TABLE 10.1

SUPPORT PRICES OF SPECIFIED PRODUCTS IN THE EEC
AND THE U. S. (1960-61)

Support price per bushel:

Country	Wheat	Rye	Barley
Germany	$2.97	$2.52	$2.12
Italy	2.82	—— (a)	—— (a)
Belgium	2.56	—— (a)	—— (a)
Netherlands	2.33	1.94	1.62
France	2.22	1.66	1.42
United States	1.78	.90	.77

(a) No price supports.
Source: Adapted from *Toward Maintaining and Expanding Markets in Western Europe for U. S. Farm Products.* U. S. Department of Agriculture. February, 1963, pp. 3-8.

European agricultural inefficiency is partially the result of small-sized productive units; of an estimated nine million farms, over five million are twelve acres or less in size. Inefficiency also stems from fragmented land holdings which characterize the EEC countries. Widely-spaced holdings hamper the full utilization of many types of machinery and farm buildings. They result in a considerable amount of waste of time and effort for the farmer who must travel from one area to another.

France, Italy and the Netherlands represent the most important exporters of farm products to other EEC members; they have been the major proponents of freeing trade in farm products and of establishing uniform agricultural prices through-out the Community. Resistance to rapid implementation has been provided by West Germany.

The elimination of internal trade barriers, a part of the CAP, will have the effect of accelerating the movement of farm commodities among countries. Much of the gain from the program will accrue to France as it obtains easier access to other EEC markets for grain and livestock, but especially for poultry, eggs, beef and dairy products. The increase in French exports will come largely at the expense of shipments from non-member countries. Over one-half of the Community's arable land—including the most fertile—is held by France.

Italy will be able to increase exports of fruits, vegetables and nuts; the Netherlands should be able to expand sales of dairy products, poultry, eggs, and certain livestock products. Greece, as an associate member, obtains preferential tariff treatment in Community markets. This relationship will simplify its exports of tobacco, fruits and cotton. Belgium is principally an importer of farm products and will secure an increasing share of its total needs from other EEC members.

West Germany, the largest EEC importer of food and fiber products, has relatively high agricultural support prices. Germany's farm sector is small (less than 15 per cent of the population) and relatively inefficient, even by European standards. The new EEC support price for some products is scheduled to be lower than the German price and is certain to cause a degree of hardship to the West German farm sector. Its consumers, of course, will benefit by lower food prices. Germany will continue to import large quantities of wheat, feed grains, fruits, various types of meats, and many other items. An increasing share of its food and fiber imports will come from other EEC members.

Although the agricultural program has been initiated, many critical issues remain unresolved. Some observers are dubious of continued internal agreement and eventual success of the plan. One problem, for example, relates to the establishment of a uniform target price for grain. France, in contrast to other members, has a preference for a relatively low rate on the theory that this should discourage agricultural production in other regions of the Community. Controversy has also arisen over the ultimate use of revenue collected from the variable levy system.

Future United States Exports to the EEC

The Common Market has, in the past, provided a major outlet for United States agricultural production. As shown in Table 10.2, the value of shipments to the seven countries in fiscal year 1961-1962 totaled about $1.2 billion; this represented almost one-third of all *dollar* sales abroad. Sales to the EEC are primarily for dollars, which is in contrast to shipments to many other parts of the world where local currency transactions are permitted. The desire of the United States to retain European agricultural markets stems from two particularly important factors. One is to continue a high level of exports and thus prevent the United States balance of payments deficit from becoming more severe. The second reason is that a large volume of for-

TABLE 10.2

U. S. AGRICULTURAL EXPORTS TO EEC MEMBERS,
FISCAL YEAR 1961-62
(in millions of dollars)

Country	Value
Belgium-Luxembourg	$130.3
France	99.2
West Germany	415.3
Italy	191.5
Netherlands	347.7
Greece	21.8
Total EEC	1,205.8
Other countries	3,934.8
GRAND TOTAL	$5,140.6

Source: Adapted from data in U. S. Department of Agriculture. *Foreign Agricultural Trade of the United States.* July-August, 1963, pp. 28-41.

eign sales is necessary if the size of the huge government inventory of surplus agricultural products is to be held within reasonable limits. This inventory is now valued at about $8 billion.

Factors affecting the value and composition of exports. Since protective national agricultural programs existed prior to the Treaty of Rome, of what significance is the European Economic Community to United States agricultural production and exports? The pattern of United States agricultural trade with the Community has been changing during the past several years; it is likely that the pattern of trade would have continued to change even in the absence of the Community and its common agricultural policy.

At the same time, the change in the volume and composition of agricultural trade is likely to be more noticeable because of the European Economic Community. Three major factors may be cited in this respect:

(1) One factor is that the common agricultural policy may be more protective than earlier national programs. It appears that this has been the case during the early phases of the Community farm program. Although the barriers applicable to some products—including wheat, corn, poultry—are higher now than they were before the agricultural program went into effect, it is too early to determine if the Community will continue to be more protective. American access to the European market for these items is subject to future negotiation; trade developments are expected to be reviewed within the coming years. The whole problem of agricultural production, trade and protection is to be studied at an early session of the General Agreement on Tariffs and Trade.

(2) A second factor is that the elimination of internal trade restrictions will facilitate a more effective use of Community agricultural resources insofar as different areas shift to the type of production for which they possess the greatest cost advantage. This may permit the Community to become more self-sufficient in agricultural production with no increase in the use of resources. It also means that each member will acquire preferen-

tial treatment in other members' markets. Thus, for example, a net exporter of some primary commodities, such as France, will hold a prior claim in the German market over all non-member countries. A change in trade patterns of this nature is due to the customs union effect. The elimination of internal barriers and the establishment of a common external barrier will place the United States farmer at a competitive disadvantage.

(3) The Common Market may affect United States agricultural exports in another way. The third factor is that economic integration will promote specialization and greater industrial productivity within the Market. The increase in economic activity, greater purchasing power and higher standards of living should create a much stronger dollar market in the Community for United States goods and services. Increases in purchasing power have already altered consumer preferences and spending patterns. One noticeable change has been the per capita increase in consumption of high protein foods, such as red meats, poultry, and frozen foods, and a decrease in consumption of potatoes and other starchy foods. However, the demand for most agricultural products (especially the non-meat agricultural products) is believed to be income-inelastic. Even if the Community does continue to foster a high growth rate, their agricultural imports would not expand as rapidly as their imports of finished and manufactured goods.

The way in which the CAP will affect United States agricultural shipments to the EEC depends upon the type of commodity involved. Some exports will be affected adversely, some favorably. Most agricultural commodities fall into one of three categories in this respect. In the first category are several products the output of which can be expanded relatively easily within the EEC and which are subject to the Community's system of variable levies. The second group includes agricultural products on which the Community has imposed a fairly high fixed tariff. A third category includes commodities for which the EEC is heavily dependent upon the rest of the world and for which no, or relatively low, tariffs are imposed.

Variable levy commodities. In the first category are several commodities which are produced in substantial quantities within the EEC and in which the EEC has already and is likely to continue to become increasingly self-sufficient. Items in this first category include grains, pigmeat, poultry and eggs—products which, as shown in Table 10.3, have accounted for over 30 per cent of the value of agricultural shipments to the EEC.

TABLE 10.3

TYPES OF U. S. AGRICULTURAL PRODUCTS EXPORTED
TO THE EEC, 1961

Commodity	Value[1]	Per cent of total
Wheat and flour	$185.6	15.58
Feed grains	195.0	16.37
Poultry and eggs	48.3	4.06
Pork	.6	.05
Rice	15.1	1.27
Tobacco	96.5	8.10
Fruits, vegetables	70.1	5.88
Vegetable oils, expressed	33.4	2.80
Lard and tallow	34.6	2.90
Soybeans	121.5	10.20
Cotton, including linters	238.2	20.00
Food for relief, etc.	30.6	2.57
Other	121.6	10.21
TOTAL	1,191.1	100.00

[1] In millions of U. S. dollars.

Source: U. S. Department of Agriculture. *Foreign Agricultural Trade of the United States.* October 1962, p. 8.

Although emphasis of the Community agricultural program centers on grain production, it also involves a number of related products. Minimum prices will be maintained for certain types of grains through support purchases and variable import levies in an effort to raise farm income. The variable import levy, a chief component of the program, is designed to offset the difference between the EEC support price and the world price; it will generally replace other types of restrictions at the Community border.

The crucial effect of the variable import levy system is that the United States and other non-member countries are destined to become residual suppliers of those commodities protected by the system. Only after the full amount of agricultural production forthcoming at existing Community support prices is exhausted are external suppliers likely to be able to enter the European market. The variable levy affords unlimited protection; regardless of how efficient foreign agriculture becomes, it can not compete with EEC producers for Community markets.

The variable levies for grains and some grain conversion products are, in a sense, neutral. The most important factors determining the extent to which the United States retains its historical share of the European market for these products are the level of the common support prices, and the way in which Community farmers respond to these support prices. The support prices, which eventually are to be uniform throughout the Community, will be higher than existing prices in some countries (such as France) and lower in others (such as Germany). The effect of the Community support price and variable levy is quite unpredictable. Present indications are that they will have the effect of stimulating over-all agricultural output for products in this category.

Under these circumstances, the amount of variable levy commodities sold to the EEC countries by United States exporters depends upon EEC consumption and production. United States sales might be expanded if Community consumption increases more rapidly than production; the variable levy prevents the United States exporter from competing with local producers through more efficient efforts.

Thus, continued United States sales of variable levy commodities will depend to a great extent upon whether or not the United States government can persuade the EEC to pursue a liberal approach in implementing the Treaty of Rome. This country may be required to bargain with the EEC under the Trade Expansion Act of 1962 in order to retain the European market. Unfortunately, the EEC's system of variable levies is not adaptable to the usual tariff bargaining. Thus it may be necessary for the United States to negotiate for its "historical share of the market." The market for variable levy commodities is causing Americans the greatest concern. The new CAP represents a serious threat to a $400 million export market.

Commodities with high fixed tariffs. For a few types of agricultural commodities, the EEC has imposed relatively high *fixed* tariffs. Tobacco is probably the most important United States agricultural export to face a fairly high EEC tariff; vegetable oils, a less important export, also are included in this category. The common external tariff on tobacco imports is considerably higher than the rates which were in effect prior to 1957. However, it does not appear that the new tariff poses an immediate threat to United States tobacco exports as most shipments to the EEC are of a high quality. This type is used primarily in cigarettes and its output cannot be readily expanded in the EEC and in associated territories in Africa. The United States is the only country in the world with the appropriate combination of soil, climate, skill and experience to produce substantial amounts of certain types of tobacco of superior quality. Exports from this country are primarily flue-cured or burley tobacco.

A poorer quality of tobacco which is grown in the associated African states can be substituted for the United States product in cigarettes. Such a substitution is likely if the import duty becomes even more protective. Greece, an associate member, grows an oriental-type tobacco which may also be used more widely in the EEC since it will enter duty-free. More recently, Greece is attempting to develop a type which will compete with that produced in the United States.

The United States government is expected to negotiate under its Trade Expansion Act in an effort to induce the Community to lower its fixed tariffs on tobacco. In any event, the ability to export this item will depend upon willingness and capacity to produce a high-quality leaf.

Low duty commodities. It does not appear that there will

be a major change—at least not a decrease—in the Common Market's agricultural import requirements of several types of commodities. Principal items in this category include cotton, soybeans, linseed, industrial tallow, oilcake, hides and skins and a few other less important products. Most of these products are admitted into the Common Market either duty free, or at a small fixed tariff. At the 1960-61 tariff conference of GATT, the EEC agreed to bind or reduce the common tariff on a number of these agricultural commodities.

These particular items are not produced in sufficient quantity within the Community and their output cannot be readily increased in the future. As shown in Table 10.3, the items in this category presently account for about one-half of total United States agricultural exports to the Community. As long as the United States remains competitive in the world economy, it will in all likelihood retain the existing share of the market for these products. For some items, such as cotton and soybeans, the market will probably become larger.

Affect on sales in third countries. The common agricultural program will have the greatest impact on United States shipments to EEC countries, but it may also affect shipments to other parts of the world. Provisions have been made by the Community for the payment of subsidies on exports to non-member countries should internal agricultural surpluses develop. The extent to which the Community competes with the United States in third country markets will depend upon the extent to which the common agricultural program encourages the expansion of internal production. Should production increase more rapidly than consumption, with a consequent development of surpluses, the EEC will employ export payments in order to sell commodities in world markets. The United States government has paid export subsidies for many agricultural products for similar purposes.

Agricultural imports from the EEC. Although the greatest impact of the EEC will be on United States exports, it may have some effect on agricultural *imports* from the EEC. As shown in Table 10.4, in a recent year, 1962, a relatively small volume was imported from the EEC. Approximately 6 per cent of all United States agricultural imports originate in the EEC.

TABLE 10.4

U. S. AGRICULTURAL IMPORTS FROM THE EEC, BY COUNTRY[1]
(in thousands of dollars)

Country	Value
Netherlands	76,594
Italy	62,132
France	51,878
West Germany	29,359
Greece	29,259
Belgium and Luxembourg	9,266
TOTAL	258,488

[1] Fiscal year 1962.

Source: Adapted from *Foreign Agricultural Trade of the United States: Annual Supplement Trade by Countries.* United States Department of Agriculture. April, 1963, pp. 4-5.

Many of the imported commodities are specialty items; their greatest value is that they contribute to the variety in American diets. Some of the principal imports include Dutch hams, Italian vegetables and fruits, French and Italian wines and many other items. There is little reason for these particular imports to be affected as a result of the establishment of the EEC.

Joint Solution of Agricultural Problems

Members of the Community have found that a mutually acceptable *agricultural* program has been the most difficult to formulate. It appears, at least initially, that member countries have been overly protective toward what is generally recognized to be a relatively inefficient sector. The agricultural policy which is being pursued was one of the first aspects of the EEC to pose a threat to close and friendly business relationships between the Community and the United States. The United States could lose part of its agricultural markets, especially for the variable levy commodities, as the CAP is implemented.

Officials of the EEC do not seem to be unduly concerned about United States criticism of the protective movement toward agriculture. The United States government has found it difficult to take a strong position on this issue in view of the degree of protection and subsidization (of both production and exports) afforded the American farmer. For example, the United States had to obtain a waiver from the General Agreement on Tariffs and Trade (GATT) in order to establish quotas to prevent agricultural imports from undermining the domestic price support program. GATT condones quotas only when domestic production is restricted. United States action in this matter has weakened its GATT bargaining position as well as its influence over the nature of the agricultural program undertaken by the EEC.

Promotion of resource mobility. International solutions are perhaps required for national agricultural problems. In view of the long-run trend in world agriculture to exceed substantially population growth, a greater resource movement into the secondary and tertiary industries may be economically desirable.[2]

The use of programs, both in the United States and the EEC, which are designed specifically to promote the mobility of agricultural workers into other sectors of the economy would be a basic solution in view of agricultural surpluses in many countries. In the immediate future, at least, programs of this nature are certain to be more successful in the EEC than in the United States because of sufficient job opportunities in other sectors. The number of vacancies in manufacturing and service industries is probably the most important determinant of the rate of movement into urban areas. The high industrial unemployment rate in the United States is presently one factor retarding the movement to urban occupations. If the EEC is to make a realistic effort to raise per capita income, resource mobility may have to be encouraged in view of the inefficient agricultural structure and the scarcity of industrial workers. A severe shortage of workers has had the effect of hindering EEC industrial investment.

It is to be expected that rural-urban mobility in the EEC will be promoted somewhat with the implementation of the policy to increase geographical labor mobility. That is, the common social legislation and the ability of workers to move freely from country to country may also be conducive to rural-urban mobility.

There has already been a noticeable shift of workers among different sectors. In 1958, an estimated 22.7 per cent of employment was in agriculture; in 1962, it had fallen to 19.5 per cent. The share in agriculture in individual countries varies from a high of almost 30 per cent in Italy to a minimum of less than 10 per cent in the Benelux countries.

The Community makes provision for the establishment of an Agricultural Guidance and Guarantee Fund with one of its functions that of helping achieve necessary structural changes within the Community. The nature of this provision has not been made explicit by the Community planners; presumably, it might be employed to encourage labor mobility.

Another institution is the European Social Fund (examined in chapter 7) which makes financial assistance available for the resettlement and retraining of workers. It is not likely, if self interest prevails, that the Community will continue in the long-run to employ practices which retain resources in an inefficient sector, at least if such resources are desperately needed in other areas of the Market.

The Trade Expansion Act of 1962 is likely to play a major role in inducing a liberal policy toward United States agricultural exports. Presently, the United States exports about $1.2 billion worth of agricultural products to the EEC annually, but imports only about $250 million worth from that area. Non-agricultural imports from the EEC, however, amount to about $2 billion each year.

If the United States succeeds in concluding an agreement with the EEC it is likely to be on a "package" basis. This country is likely to offer concessions in the non-agricultural field, in order to obtain agricultural concessions. Negotiations are to be conducted under GATT in mid-1964; it has been agreed that farm products will be included in the discussions.

World-wide commodity agreements. Another general approach to agricultural problems is through the establishment of international agreements on certain commodities, especially grains. Such agreements embody the regulation of prices, production, trade and stock-piling practices of agricultural products. They would have to be far more comprehensive and regulative than those presently in existence. It is not likely, for example, that the Common Market will be willing to impose production controls in its agricultural sector unless the United States is prepared to institute similar basic changes in its domestic agricultural program. International commodity agreements will require membership on the part of all major producing, consuming, importing and exporting nations. Agreements of this nature have been proposed by the United Kingdom and appear to be acceptable to the Community.

It is difficult to say how United States agriculture would fare under such arrangements. Typically, the exporting countries agree to divide the markets in the importing countries in some acceptable fashion. The bargaining power and position of the United States government would be the crucial factor determining its share of the market. In many instances in the past, however, markets have been divided on the basis of historical shares, with each exporting country retaining its traditional overseas markets.

Promotion of Agricultural Sales to the EEC

The United States government has, in recent years, participated in efforts to facilitate the sale of agricultural products in foreign markets, including the EEC.[3] Market development has been emphasized in Japan, Western Europe and Italy, but has been conducted on a smaller scale in many other countries. Promotional and educational work assumes many forms, including cooperative activities in conjunction with United States trade and agricultural groups, exhibits at international trade fairs, and marketing and product utilization research. These efforts have served to introduce new commodities to foreigners, to acquaint United States exporters with marketing techniques and needs abroad, and to indicate in other ways how this country might maintain, expand or develop foreign markets for food and fiber products.

Financial resources for these programs are partially derived from the local currency proceeds accumulated as a result of the Agricultural Trade Development and Assistance Act of 1954 (P.L. 480). Title I of P.L. 480 authorizes the United States government to sell domestic agricultural products abroad in exchange for the currency of the purchasing country. Section 104a of P.L. 480 specifies that a part of the currency proceeds accruing to the United States under the Act be used by the Department of Agriculture to develop new markets abroad for United States agricultural products. Following the enactment of P.L. 480 in 1954 through the end of 1962, the Department of Agriculture and cooperating trade groups initiated almost 700 projects with local currency proceeds in nearly 70 foreign countries for this purpose. In addition, local currency has been used to underwrite exhibits at international trade fairs, and to finance contracts for market research and commodity utilization.

Much of the promotional activity has been limited in the past to countries which participated actively in the P.L. 480 program; these were principally the soft (inconvertible) currency countries. Activity in hard (convertible) currency areas such as Western Europe was dependent primarily upon the extent to which accumulated local currencies could be converted into hard currencies. Because of the problems inherent in local currency conversion, Congress has extended a dollar appropriation to the Department of Agriculture to buy convertible currencies for financing promotional activities. As a result, the promotion of agricultural markets in Western Europe is no longer limited to the availability of currencies arising under P.L. 480.

Cooperative program. Under the cooperative program, the United States Department of Agriculture and private United

States trade and agricultural groups work together to promote agricultural sales abroad including Western Europe and the EEC. By mid-1963, more than forty private associations representing producers and processors were participating in the activities. The projects, which are financed jointly, take a variety of forms depending upon the type of commodity involved. Typically, the Department of Agriculture contributes the foreign currencies and over-all direction; the cooperating group provides additional financial resources, personnel and equipment, and undertakes to complete the project. Because individual agricultural commodities are relatively homogeneous in nature, export promotion can be undertaken relatively easily by trade associations. In some instances, the cooperation of interested trade groups (usually the processors) in the foreign country is solicited. Generally, it is expected that the United States government will supply no more than one-half of the financial requirements. During fiscal year 1962, the Department of Agriculture contributed the equivalent of approximately $14 million for market development activities.

Projects of this nature are undertaken only if it appears that there is a reasonable chance of success, if they do not conflict with over-all United States foreign policy, and if the trade group (which may be either industry- or nation-wide) represents the United States commodity interests. For some commodities, such as cotton, wheat and other grains, promotional work is carried on in many areas of the world; for the more specialized items, including poultry, certain fruits and hides and skins, activities are limited to specific countries in which the possibility of finding a market seems most promising.

Some of the more important organizations engaged in overseas promotion include the Cotton Council International, the Great Plains Wheat Producers Association, the Soybean Council of America, among many others. Examples of the individual projects include surveys of potential agricultural markets, advertising campaigns, merchandising clinics, distribution of samples and the use of motion pictures and slides.[4]

The cooperative program has been employed in EEC countries to increase exports of such commodities as wheat, feed grains, poultry, tobacco, cotton, soybean products and raisins.

Other forms of government promotion. Other types of activities are undertaken by the United States Department of Agriculture to strengthen and expand markets for agricultural products in the EEC and other parts of the world. The Department participates regularly in international trade fair exhibits most of which have been held in Europe and Japan. Grants and contracts are awarded to foreign institutions to carry on research designed to lead to expanded markets. In general, extensive efforts are made to introduce new forms of processed food and raw material products, marketing procedures and packaging to foreign consumers. The techniques employed are unusually diverse in nature and reflect a considerable amount of imagination on the part of United States agricultural interests.

Another important function of the Department of Agriculture is that of making information available to United States processors and exporters concerning market conditions abroad. The Department publishes a considerable amount of material regarding import regulations, packaging requirements, marketing systems and other information valuable for an acquaintance with and deeper understanding of foreign marketing.[5]

Opportunities for United States firms. A major factor determining the extent to which the United States maintains markets for agricultural products will be the degree of protectiveness pursued by the EEC. Equally important, however, will be the alertness of United States exporters to Community developments and the ability to forecast new consumption patterns and trends.

America's greatest advantage in world trade has been in its ability to introduce new and better products. The rapid growth in per capita income in the EEC has given Community consumers an opportunity to experiment with new products and to turn to high quality foodstuffs. European buyers have tended to be conservative and resistant to change, but this is likely to be altered considerably with the spread of mass communications and with the increase in personal income. For example, one noticeable change accompanying the growth in per capita income has been the increased use of refrigerators. This will probably lead to an increase in the use of frozen foods as well as perishable commodities.

Changes are also taking place in the marketing and packaging of foodstuffs. The European food industry is characterized by many small stores, each of which sells a narrow range of products. However, there are an increasing number of self-service stores and supermarkets.[6] Accordingly, American processors and exporters can expect that there will be a continued trend toward processed and "convenience" foods—frozen, packaged and canned. Continued sales abroad require not only promotional work in foreign countries, but also efforts at home including product development, and appropriate packaging and labeling. There has been some criticism that United States shipments do not meet high quality standards.

A new market is developing in Europe with the expansion of per capita incomes and the growth of a middle-income group. Although much of the increased spending in the new consumer market will center on the durable goods, the consumption of most non-durables, particularly food, is likely to expand and to change in content.

NOTES

[1] The European Free Trade Association, which was created shortly after the establishment of the EEC, provides for a free internal movement of all goods and services *except* agricultural and fishery products.

[2] The Food and Agriculture Organization estimates that agricultural production has been increasing at an annual rate of 2.9 per cent; population, 1.8 per cent per year. See FAO. *The State of Food and Agriculture, 1962.* Rome: 1962, p. 15.

[3] The basic authorities for market promotion abroad include the Agricultural Act of 1954 and the Agricultural Trade Development and Assistance Act of 1954.

[4] For a current description of market promotion abroad, see *Semiannual Reports on Activities Carried on Under Public Law 480,* 83D Congress, Washington, U.S. GPO.

[5] A relatively comprehensive analysis of current conditions and opportunities in overseas agricultural markets is provided in the weekly publication of the United States Department of Agriculture, Foreign Agriculture Service, *Foreign Agriculture* Including Foreign Crops and Markets. Washington, U.S. GPO.

[6] See Gilbert, Robert A. *International Investment.* New York: Simmons-Boardman Publishing Corporation, 1963, p. 18.

Future Prospects of the Common Market and American Business

THE EEC GROWTH POTENTIAL — MOVEMENT OF PRICES IN THE EEC — BALANCE OF PAYMENTS PROSPECTS — IMPACT OF EEC FUTURE PROSPECTS ON AMERICAN BUSINESS

The first six years in the life of the European Economic Community have already seen some important changes in the economies of the member states. In terms of output, national income, wages, investment, internal and external trade, the progress made has been substantial. Industry has started to integrate and has displayed improved efficiency. The spirit of cooperation among the members has been heartening, and the drive to attain the objectives set forth in the Treaty of Rome has been well-sustained.

Although the trade of the Community with the United States has increased and American direct investments in the territory of the Common Market have grown, the impact of the EEC has obviously been greater upon its members than it has upon this country. The full effects of the institution upon American business lie in the years immediately ahead.

This chapter analyzes the potential impact of some Common Market developments upon American business: the growth of population and employment, the future movement of the EEC gross national product, price changes and the balances of payments during the 1960's. Other aspects of the effects of Common Market developments on American business have been discussed in previous chapters: the progress of economic integration, the ability of the EEC industries to supply its internal demands as well as those of its associated overseas countries and territories, the effectiveness of its tariff structure and the possible results of the Kennedy round of tariff negotiations under the Trade Expansion Act of 1962.

The EEC Growth Potential

The growth potential of the European Economic Community has occupied the attention of the officials of this institution for a number of years. A Working Party, directed by Pierre Uri and acting under instructions from the EEC Commission, has recently submitted a report presenting projections (not forecasts) of certain aspects of the growth potential of the Community—with the exception of Luxembourg—for the period 1960-1970.[1]

Population and employment. The population of the Community, with the exception of Luxembourg, was estimated at 171,104,000 in 1960 and is projected to attain 180,364,000 in 1970, increasing by about 9,260,000 for the ten-year period at an average rate of approximately .925 million a year. The employed population stood at an estimated 71,865,000 in 1960 and is expected to reach 76,861,000 in 1970, increasing by about 5 million, or 500,000 per year. The average rate of growth in employment is estimated at approximately 7 per cent a year for the Community as a whole, although there is a wide difference in the rates among the several members.[2]

Population is one of the basic factors determining the internal market potential of the EEC, and the number of employed people indicates the volume of workers on hand to sustain the Market's productivity. Although growth in the number of employed is substantial, it may not be sufficient to sustain a large spurt in industrial output unless it is more efficiently employed and utilized in conjunction with larger increments of capital.

Gross national product. The Uri Report estimates that the gross national product (GNP) of the EEC will increase by 4.75 per cent a year, moving from 100 per cent in 1960 to 159.1 per cent in 1970 at 1960 prices. The rate of growth is estimated to be the highest for Italy—5.85 per cent—and the lowest for Belgium —3.85 per cent. The projected increase is slightly greater from

1960 to 1965, when the GNP rises by 127 per cent of the base year, than from 1965 to 1970, when it grows by 125.3 per cent.[3] Evidently the rate of GNP increase slows as capacity and resources are more fully utilized. This projected growth is somewhat smaller than that which Walter Salant and his associates estimate for the United States GNP (1960-1968); 4.8 per cent a year, or from 100 per cent in 1960, to 145.7 per cent in 1968.[4]

The increase in the GNP of the Community is estimated to be slower for the decade 1960-1970 than it was for 1950-1960. The Common Market GNP grew to 173.9 per cent of the base year (1950) during the latter decade; 14.8 percentage points more than the estimated increase during the former.[5]

By contrast, the increase in the United States GNP is estimated as larger during 1960-1968 than during 1950-1960. During the latter period the rate of growth was 3.3 per cent and during the former it is estimated at 4.8 per cent a year.[6] In 1960, capacity and resources were being relatively less fully utilized in the United States than in the European Economic Community.

The shares of the EEC gross national product allocated to private consumption, public consumption, fixed capital and business investment are presented in Table 11.1.

Business investment is projected to increase at a faster rate, 1960-1970, than the other segments of GNP, apparently indicating that, in the opinion of the authors of the Uri Report, business in the Common Market plans either to expand, to improve or both.[7] The gross marginal efficiency of capital is estimated to develop at

TABLE 11.1

DIVISION OF COMMON MARKET GNP BETWEEN PRIVATE
AND PUBLIC CONSUMPTION, FIXED CAPITAL AND
BUSINESS INVESTMENT
1960-1970
(Average annual increase in per cent)

Private consumption	5.25
Public consumption	3.00
Fixed capital	5.35
Business investment	5.95

Source: Uri Report, pp. 70-75.

the rate of 3.3 per cent a year during the period.[8] The projected growth in private consumption is substantially larger than that for public consumption, which might indicate a drift away from socialistic or national enterprise.

The rate of increase in business investment is not even throughout 1960-1970. For 1960-1965, the rate is estimated at 6.75 per cent a year; for 1965-1970 at 5.2 per cent. The part of *directly productive investment* in the GNP is likely to increase, in the opinion of the authors of the Uri Report. In 1960, its share is estimated at 13.5 per cent; in 1965, it is expected to attain 14.7 per cent and by 1970, 15.1 per cent.[9] The division of the total Common Market GNP among the members in 1970 is presented in Table 11.2.

The increase in EEC gross national product is to be achieved by a growth in employment as well as by an increase in capital and output per man-hour. Although figures projecting the output per man-hour are not available for all of the members of the Community, it is apparently the opinion of the authors of the Uri Report that it will increase. For Germany, the output per man-hour is estimated at 4.87 DM in 1960 and 7.87 DM in 1970. In Italy, the output per man-hour is estimated to increase by 4 per cent annually during the decade.[10] Salant and his associates are of the opinion that an increase in the output per man-year averaging 3.7 per cent annually will be required to enable Western European countries to attain a GNP growth of 4.3 per cent a

TABLE 11.2

DIVISION OF TOTAL COMMON MARKET GNP
AMONG THE MEMBERS
1970
(Percentages of total)

Belgium	6.2
France	32.6
Germany	35.5
Italy	19.6
Netherlands	6.1

Source: Uri Report, English summary, p. 51.

year.[11] The increase in the EEC gross national product is likely to be accompanied by a rise in labor cost.

Labor's share of the gross national product has been smaller in the EEC countries in the past than in the United States. In 1960 its part of the GNP amounted to 55.2 per cent in Belgium; France, 60.7; Germany, 62.0 and the Netherlands, 56.9 per cent. In the United States it amounted to 68.9 per cent for the same year. By 1968, this share is estimated to increase for the EEC nations by approximately 3 per cent, from 61 to 64 per cent of the total GNP.[12]

Movement of Prices in the EEC

Many economists feel that capitalist societies generally thrive best during periods of slightly rising prices. This belief is partially based on the fact that accounting systems are established on the basis of *historical cost*. Where prices rise substantially between the time that the materials, goods or components have been purchased and the time the products are sold, accounting systems, based on historical cost, tend to exaggerate profits. This is due to the fact that these systems include the market price rise together with the business mark-up in the calculation of profits. Where prices fall markedly during the period of manufacture or stocking, these systems tend either to minimize the actual profits earned or to indicate a loss by subtracting the market price decline from the business mark-up.

This phenomenon does not characterize the calculation of profits in accounting systems based on *replacement costs* which eliminate market price movements from the calculation of profits. However, this principle introduces other complications and business firms generally eschew its use. Where profits, *as reflected in the accounts,* appear to be good, business is inclined to pursue expansionist policies. Where the reverse is true, they are likely to restrict their operations.[13]

Periods of price increases have characterized many of the capitalist economies, and some analysts feel that they have served to promote business expansion. Rising prices often result from monetary inflation, and two major types of inflation are generally recognized. One is termed "demand-pull" inflation which arises when demand is increased by reason of increased income in the hands of consumers. This increased income frequently stems from a failure of the government to balance the budget and the consequent monetization of the deficit. It is also occasioned by increased credit extended by banks and increased earnings.

Another type, "cost-push" inflation, results from increases in manufacturing and distribution costs, which usually take their roots in the increased cost of imported raw materials and higher wage rates. Sometimes these increased costs are parried by the use of more efficient manufacturing and distributing methods. At other times, they are absorbed by a reduction in profits. Where they are not successfully parried or absorbed, they may result in an increasing level of prices.

Early EEC price patterns. Table 11.3 presents the price movements of consumer goods in the Common Market countries and the United States, 1954, 1959-1963. With the exception of Belgium, these prices rose to higher levels in the EEC countries than in the United States. The EEC Directorate General for Financial and Economic Affairs characterizes the price increases, 1957-1960, as the cost-push type due largely to labor shortages. During the period 1960-1962, increasing demand stemming from exports and higher consumer incomes were held to be responsible for a demand-pull type of inflation. The pressure on prices for 1963-1970 will doubtless come, these authorities hold, from rising costs rather than from growing demand.

A similar situation prevailed for the wholesale prices of industrial goods as Table 11.4 indicates. The increase in these prices was especially great in France and Italy.

The prices of exported goods, an important factor in a nation's balance of payments position, rose more rapidly between 1953 and 1960 in the United States than in the Common Market countries. The increase in these prices during these years was estimated at 0.2 per cent a year for the EEC members and 1.1 per cent annually in the United States. The rise in the export unit prices of United States manufactures at that time, as compared with those of the EEC, was even more striking; in the

TABLE 11.3

GENERAL PRICE INDEXES OF CONSUMER GOODS
EEC COUNTRIES AND THE UNITED STATES
(1958 = 100)

	1954	1959	1960	1961	1962	1963[a]
Belgium	94	101	102	103	104	105
France	82	106	110	114	119	125
Germany	92	101	102	105	109	112
Italy	91	100	102	104	109	116
Luxembourg	95	100	101	101	102	106
Netherlands	90	102	103	105	108	112
United States	93	101	102	103	105	105

(a) 1963: U.S., March; Italy, Netherlands, April; Belgium, Germany, France, May; Luxembourg, June.
Source: EEC, *Bulletin Général de Statistiques*. No. 6 (June), 1963, p. 59.

TABLE 11.4

WHOLESALE PRICE INDEXES OF INDUSTRIAL GOODS,
EEC COUNTRIES AND THE UNITED STATES
(1958 = 100)

	1959	1960	1961	1962	1963[a]
France	107	111	114	115	118
Germany	100	101	101	100	99
Italy	99	100	100	101	105
Netherlands	100	100	100	101	101
United States	100	102	101	101	101

(a) 1963: U.S., March; Italy, Netherlands, April; Germany, France, May.
Source: EEC. *Bulletin Général de Statistiques*. No. 6 (June), 1963, p. 54.

former they rose by 2.4 per cent a year and in the latter by 0.3 per cent annually.[14]

The difference in the behavior of the prices of United States and Common Market exports, as compared with those of consumer and wholesale prices, is partially explained by the fact that the EEC nations were concentrating their improvements in industrial efficiency in the export lines, while the United States export industries lost some of their competitive drive.

Estimated future price movements in the EEC. The Salant

Study estimates that export prices of the EEC nations will increase at the rate of 1.5 per cent a year between 1961 and 1968.[15] These authors have estimated the GNP price increases for four European countries, 1961-1968, at about 2.75 per cent a year for a total of 26.7 per cent for the whole period.[16]

This substantial estimated rise in GNP prices is based on the assumption that labor's share in the EEC gross national product will increase and labor costs will rise by 3.2 per cent a year during 1961-1968. All of the increased labor costs will not be passed forward in the form of price increases. The difference between the increase in labor costs—3.2 per cent a year—and the rise in GNP prices—2.75 per annum—represents roughly the amount of these costs which business will absorb either through a reduction in profits or an increase in efficiency.[17]

These projections apparently assume that the average per unit of output costs of EEC industry will remain constant and will not decline, 1961-1968, as output increases. Contrary to some of the literature on the subject, the Salant Study apparently assumes that further economies of scale are limited for EEC producers and that increased output may lead to operations beyond the point of maximum plant efficiency.[18]

Although other information is not readily available to determine if the EEC industries will be operating under constant or decreasing average costs, much of the published opinion leans to the view that these firms are of the decreasing cost type and that they have not as yet reached the point of maximum efficiency. Indeed, it was the feeling of the architects of the Treaty of Rome —and it continues to be the view of the officials of the organization—that many of the firms remaining in the area would move down to lower points on their cost curves as their output increased.

The Common Market does not approach the size of that of the United States in terms of national income, and few of its industries yet equal the dimensions already attained by the larger American plants. It is the expectation of both the officials and businessmen of the Common Market that EEC industries will attain economies of scale similar to those enjoyed by American firms. They also expect that cartels will disappear, as they already have started to do, under the impact of competition and anti-trust measures. Although some of the larger United States enter-prises are already producing beyond the point of maximum efficiency, all of them are not. Some of those that are past this point are endeavoring, through automation and other cost-reduc-ing methods, to prolong the length of their decreasing cost curves so that the point of maximum efficiency will lie beyond their present outputs. In view of existing plant capacities and recent improvements in technology, it appears that many EEC indus-tries can increase their outputs before they attain the points of maximum efficiency.

Future price estimates for Common Market products should take account of the prospects for greater economies of scale. If this were done, the projected GNP price increases might not be as steep as the Salant Study projects and they will taper off as increasing output operates to reduce the impact of higher labor costs. Increasing labor costs will be counterbalanced by more efficient employment of workers, attained by the employment of larger amounts of capital, better technology and by greater sales.

GNP prices in the EEC countries are not likely to rise, through 1965 or 1966, by more than 1 to 2 per cent a year. They should then reach a plateau and tend to level off through 1969. The plateau is not assumed to be entirely flat; prices will prob-ably continue to rise but at a slower rate. After 1969, when com-petition in the Common Market will have increased the size and reduced the number of enterprises in each field, the markets will probably be dominated by firms which practice monopolistic competition. It is difficult to predict the movement of prices under such conditions. Much will depend upon the price policies of these enterprises and the success of EEC anti-trust policies and regulations.

Several assumptions underlie these projections. It is assumed in the first place that there will be no inflation arising from failure of the Common Market countries to balance their budgets and the consequent monetization of the resulting government debt.

In the second place, the monetary, credit and banking institutions and authorities are assumed to pursue conservative policies so that little inflation will be occasioned by the operations of financial institutions. Finally, increasing demand resulting from higher wages, larger incomes and greater exports is assumed to be counterbalanced by greater industrial efficiency and more important economies of scale.

Should any of these assumptions prove invalid, the projections could miss the mark. Given the dedication of the officials of the EEC and the member nations to the ideals of fiscal and monetary stability, these assumptions appear to be reasonable. As one indication of the determination of the EEC nations to maintain stable prices, France took drastic measures to curb price increases during the autumn of 1963. These included restrictions upon wages, prices, credit as well as steps to reduce government expenses and increase receipts.

Balance of Payments Prospects

The countries of Western Europe, including the EEC members, are generally held to be international reserve accumulating nations while many of the others tend to live from hand to mouth, spending their foreign exchange about as rapidly as it is earned. The former countries accumulate reserves in periods of balance of payments surplus to act as a cushion in times of deficit. The latter have such heavy needs for imports that they are either unwilling or unable to accumulate reserves. One result of these divergent practices is that the countries of Western Europe are somewhat less subject to the stresses and strains of their external economic relations than the others.

In spite of their reserve accumulations, the balance of payments surplus or deficit of the EEC nations is a matter of some concern to American businessmen who deal with these countries. If they should continue to run surpluses on their balances of payments, trade with the Common Market is likely to remain relatively free of controls. Should deficits appear, restrictive measures may be applied to their external economic relationships.

EEC balance of payments projections. Table 11.5 presents

the projected balances of payments surpluses of the EEC as a whole and of its members for the years 1960, 1965 and 1970. The estimated surplus shows a decline from $3,143 million in 1960 to $1,849 in 1965 and a rise to $1,953 in 1970. Compared with 1960, the whole period, 1960-1970, is expected to show a decline in the balance of payments surpluses of the EEC members.

The Uri Report apparently bases these projections largely on internal developments in the EEC and does not take into account all of the changes in the economic relations with outside nations which could alter the future external trade balance. The Salant Study sheds some light on this matter.

According to this Study, the United States is expected to attain a surplus, in 1968, on its *basic balance* of $2.71 billion, under the initial assumptions, and $0.24 billion under the alternative assumptions.[19] The basic balance, as defined in this study, includes the balance on the current account, including investment income, and that on aid and long-term capital flows. It is used in preference to the *total* or *over-all balance* to facilitate the international comparison of homogeneous magnitudes.[20] The surplus as defined in the Uri Report is presumably that of the total or over-all external balance on the balance of payments as a whole and appears to include, in addition to the items comprising the basic balance, short-term capital movements, gold and errors and omissions.

Although the Salant Study does not project the balances of

TABLE 11.5
BALANCE OF PAYMENTS SURPLUSES OF THE
EEC COUNTRIES, 1960, 1965, 1970
(In millions of dollars)

	1960	1965	1970
Belgium	162	117	142
France	632	598	565
Germany	1,918	839	1,031
Italy	126	128	—
Netherlands	305	167	215
EEC total	3,143	1,849	1,953

Source: Uri Report, pp. 70-75.

payments of countries other than the United States, it is clear that substantial improvement in this nation's 1968 basic balance would be obtained at the expense of its trading partners. Some of the balances of payments of these trading partners will doubtless show either smaller surpluses or even deficits in 1968 as a result of the improvement in the United States balance.

The basic balance of external transactions of the United States has been in deficit since 1947, and the deficits have been especially large since 1958. The EEC nations, on the other hand, have generally shown surpluses since 1958. The projections of the Salant Study envisage a reversal of some importance in these external trading positions. Although it is not likely that the EEC nations will run persistent deficits during the 1960's, their surpluses as projected in Table 11.5 may well be reduced to smaller proportions.

Among the factors operating to reduce the size of the Common Market external balance surpluses, the following are of special importance: the potential growth of the Community GNP and the concomitant rise in its imports; the greater attraction of the internal EEC market to third country outlets; the increasing competitiveness of United States business.

Impact of EEC Future Prospects on American Business

There is little doubt but that the Common Market faces an important growth potential in the years immediately ahead which presents opportunities and challenges to American business. Although the projections outlined in the previous sections of this chapter are based on the most reliable data available, they involve a number of assumptions which may not prove valid in the years ahead. In addition, they are general and there may be important differences in the way in which they materialize among the several members of the EEC. The alert businessman will watch these developments with care before making any definite trading or investment commitments.

Impact on American business of Common Market GNP developments. The growth in the Common Market GNP means that the output of goods and services of the institution will increase during the 1960's, that national income and purchasing power will rise. American importers are likely to find more goods available for import and American exporters may discover a larger demand for the goods which they sell on the markets of the institution. American direct investments in branches, subsidiaries and licensing arrangements will doubtless face a growing demand for their products on the EEC internal markets and stiffer competition from the other firms located in the area. Portfolio investors should find a considerably widened choice as a result of this growth. The opportunities afforded by the EEC, however, should be compared with those of other nations, especially the United States.

The projected growth rate of the EEC is slightly smaller than that of the United States; 4.75 as against 4.8 per cent a year. The gross national product of the United States is expected to increase from $518.7 billion in 1961 to $743.2 billion in 1968.[21] The GNP of the Common Market should increase from $181.2 billion in 1960 to $230.2 in 1965 and $288.4 in 1970.[22] From the point of view of the movement of the gross national product, it would appear that the United States offers slightly greater opportunities, and perhaps more thorny competitive problems, than the EEC.

Although the rate of growth of the GNP for the European Free Trade Association *as a unit* is not available, the Salant Study has given the following percentages representing the estimated annual rate of GNP increase, 1960-1968, for the member countries: Austria 4.5, Denmark 3.25, Norway 3.25, Portugal 4.5, Sweden 3.25, Switzerland 3.25, United Kingdom 3.3[23] The projected average rate of growth for EFTA, although larger than that which prevailed in 1955-1960, is probably lower than that for either the United States or the EEC. From the point of view of the GNP, EFTA appears to offer somewhat fewer business opportunities than either the United States or the Common Market.

The substantial increase in both private and public consumption which is expected to prevail in the Common Market, 1960-1970, augurs well for a rising demand for imports and for products made by branches, subsidiaries and licensees located in the area. The large projected growth in business investment indicates that Common Market business firms are likely to be more heavily capitalized during the 1960's than they were in the past. It also tends to sustain the contention that the industries of the Community will move more toward the decreasing cost and away from the constant cost type. These larger and more efficient enterprises may also pose more severe competition for American firms located in the area.

The extent to which the projected higher EEC labor costs will be reflected in increasing prices, taken out of business profits or be counterbalanced by a rise in productivity will vary from industry to industry. From the available evidence, it appears that increased wage rates will mean both lower profits and greater productivity as a general proposition. American firms which plan to go overseas in quest of lower wage rates and higher profits during the 1960's may find that their expectations will not be fully realized.

Impact of EEC price movements on American business. American imports from the Community should not be hampered by price movements, and American exporters should not count on inflationary price rises in the area to stimulate their sales. American branches, subsidiaries and licensees in the Common Market will face a price situation similar to that which prevails in the United States.

Projections of price movements for the European Free Trade Association are not available. Since the economic integration of the Association is less extensive than that which is projected for the EEC, the reduction in the number and the increase in the size of its industries may be expected to be somewhat less. The EFTA industries may, therefore, come to benefit less from the economies of scale and lower costs than those in the Community.

Impact of the EEC balance of payments on American business. By 1960, the comfortable international reserve situation of the EEC nations enabled them to abandon all controls over current account transactions and many of those restricting the international flow of capital. Their ability to continue liberal trading practices in the future will depend upon the further accumulation of international reserves as their foreign trade progresses,

No satisfactory definition of "adequate international reserves" has as yet been formulated and generally accepted.[24] As a rough measure, some nations utilize a fixed percentage of merchandise imports. Thus, if merchandise imports of a country amount to $10 billion a year, and the country likes to keep 20 per cent of these imports in reserves, it will endeavor to maintain reserves of $2 billion. Arbitrary quantitative measures of adequacy, however, do not take into account the effect of improvements in the international payments system. Under a poorly functioning system of international payments, a nation may feel that it needs to keep large reserves; if the payments system were improved and functioned more efficiently, a smaller magnitude might prove equally satisfactory.

The international payments system has been improved since 1960 and the need for large reserves has consequently become less pressing.[25] Present indications point toward further improvements in this mechanism and a decline in the amount of reserves required. This is a matter of some importance, because the amounts of available gold and dollars—the principal components of reserve holdings—may not increase greatly in the years ahead. The United States is the principal source of additional dollars and, to a lesser extent, gold. Other nations accumulate these reserve components when the United States runs deficits on its balances of payments and when they show surpluses.

The Salant Study estimates that the United States balance of payments will be improved by 1968 and will show a small surplus by that year.[26] If these projections prove valid, a smaller volume of reserves will be *available* to the EEC by that year. If the surpluses of the EEC nations decline relatively during the 1960's, they will hold proportionately smaller reserves relative to merchandise imports than they have been accustomed to have. They may find it necessary then to either take measures to improve their reserve positions or to alter their criteria of reserve adequacy.

Although it is difficult to predict the steps which the EEC members will take should their balance of payments positions deteriorate, it does not appear likely that they will erect any important barriers to international commerce unless this deterioration continues for a long period or becomes severe. The EEC governing institutions frown upon import, capital movement and exchange controls as do those of the General Agreement on Tariffs and Trade (GATT). Further, the re-application of controls is tantamount to a confession of weakness and would not be taken lightly.

It appears that the EEC probably will not erect any additional barriers to international commerce during the decade of the 1960's. Nevertheless, it is possible that the members may employ internal measures designed to improve their external positions by preventing inflation, rising prices and costs. Deteriorating balances of payments, however, could make the EEC less willing to grant tariff reductions under GATT negotiations than they would have been under other circumstances.

The members could also be somewhat reluctant to further reduce or eliminate the remaining barriers to capital outflows. On the other hand, they might be somewhat more receptive to the inflow of capital in the form of direct investment in their territories. American exporters to the EEC are not likely to face any additional trade barriers, and United States direct and portfolio investors as well as importers may well be encouraged.

No projections showing the future trend of the EFTA balance of payments surpluses and deficits are available. The findings of the Salant Study lead one to believe that they may show a deterioration similar to that estimated for the EEC. It does not appear likely that this deterioration will bring the member countries to employ important additional controls over their foreign economic transactions.

NOTES

[1] Communauté Economique Européenne (Commission), "Les Perspectives de Développement Economique dans la CEE de 1960 à 1970." (Mimeographed). Brussels: Services des Publications des Communautés Européennes, 1962. A summary in English of this Report has been prepared: European Economic Community (Commission), "Report by the Working Party on Problems of Economic Structure and Long-Term Development on Economic Development Prospects in EEC from 1960 to 1970." (Mimeographed). No place or date indicated. The original Report is hereinafter referred to as the Uri Report; the English summary as Uri Report, English summary.

[2] Uri Report, pp. 29-33.

[3] Uri Report, English summary, p. 22.

[4] Walter S. Salant, Emile Despres, Lawrence B. Krause, Alice M. Rivlin, William A. Salant and Lorie Tarshis. *The United States Balance of Payments in 1968.* (A report prepared at the request of the Council of Economic Advisers.) Washington: The Brookings Institution, 1963, p. 41. The Salant Study projects annual rates of growth (1960-1968) of five EEC members which are essentially similar to those of the Uri Report as the following table shows:

Annual Rates of Growth of the GNP as Presented in
the Uri and Salant Reports
(Percentages of annual increase)

	Uri Report 1960-1970	Salant Report 1960-1968
France	5.0	4.95
West Germany	4.1	4.2
Italy	5.6	5.85
Belgium	3.25	3.85
Netherlands	4.5	4.6

Source: Uri Report, English summary, p. 22; Salant Study, p. 43.

Although different methods, cyclical and other assumptions and data were utilized, the similarity of the results obtained in the two studies augurs well for the accuracy of the projections. The Uri Report used two sets of hypotheses in preparing its projections of GNP: "Variant B" presents the projected figures under favorable circumstances which the Uri Working Party believes will be attained; "Variant A" gives an estimate which might prevail if the circumstances were less favorable. Since the Working Party apparently prefers Variant B to A, the former is employed throughout this chapter.

[5] Uri Report, pp. 67-68.

[6] See also Organization for Economic Cooperation and Development. *Policies for Economic Growth.* Paris: OECD, 1962, p. 28.

[7] This is apparently also the opinion of Salant and his associates. See Salant Study, *op. cit.,* pp. 50-55.

[8] Uri Report, English summary, p. 67.

[9] Uri Report, pp. 63-74.

[10] Uri Report, English summary, pp. 10-17, 28, 39.

[11] Salant Study, *op. cit.*, p. 45. The United Kingdom, France, Germany and Italy are included in the estimate.

[12] *Ibid.*, pp. 48-49.

[13] Cf. Max J. Wasserman. "Inflation and Enterprise in France, 1919-26." *The Journal of Political Economy*, XLII, No. 2 (April 1934), pp. 202-236. During periods of severe inflation, business firms sometimes employ the principle of replacement costs in preference, or as a complement, to that of historical costs. See Max J. Wasserman. "Accounting Practice in France During the Period of Monetary Inflation (1919-1927)." *The Accounting Review*, VI, No. 1 (March 1931), pp. 1-32.

[14] Salant Study, *op. cit.*, p. 39. EEC (Commission), Directorate General for Economic and Fiscal Affairs, *The Economic Situation in the Community*, 4th Quarterly Survey, Dec. 1962, pp. 5-7.

[15] Salant Study, *op. cit.*, p. 83.

[16] *Ibid.*, p. 50. The four countries are: France, Italy, Germany and the United Kingdom.

[17] *Ibid.*, pp. 47-50.

[18] *Ibid.*, p. 101; especially footnote 4.

[19] *Ibid.*, p. 289.

[20] *Ibid.*, p. 5.

[21] *Ibid.*, p. 41.

[22] Computed from figures presented in the Uri Report, pp. 28, 67-68.

[23] Salant Study, *op. cit.*, p. 43.

[24] Cf. *International Reserves and Liquidity*. International Monetary Fund, Washington, 1958.

[25] See "U.S. Balance-of-Payments Deficits in Perspective." *Federal Reserve Bank of St. Louis Review*. Vol. 45, No. 7 (July 1963), pp. 5-16. Robert V. Roosa, "Reforming the International Monetary System." *Foreign Affairs*. Vol. 42, No. 1 (October 1963), pp. 107-122.

[26] See the projected U. S. basic balance of payments presented in the Salant Study, *op. cit.*, p. 289.

12

The Future of the Common Market Idea

THE EEC, EFTA, AND EUROPEAN COOPERATION — REGIONAL
ARRANGEMENTS IN LATIN AMERICA — REGIONALISM: AN
EXPANSIVE OR CONTRACTIVE FORCE

Although neither the EEC nor the EFTA will be fully implemented until the 1970's, both are firmly established and appear
to be viable institutions. Regionalism holds great promise for
these European countries in the nature of economic, political and
social benefits, yet the implications of such organizations are
world-wide in scope. In this concluding chapter, some of the more
important aspects of the future of the common market idea are
examined briefly: What is the relationship between various
regional organizations? Under what circumstances is the EEC
likely to be expanded? To what extent is the common market idea
being employed in non-European areas? Is regionalism likely to
have an expansive or a contractive effect on world trade?

Regional vs. world-wide approach. Policies pursued by
governments are of major concern to private traders and investors. The international economy during the 1930's was frequently
characterized by economic nationalism and self-seeking commercial policies; private trade and investment dwindled sharply
as a result of instability and uncertainty. In contrast, the post-
World War II period has been characterized by a high degree
of cooperation between governments. Private economic transactions have generally been at a high level since the war, following efforts by governments to provide a framework conducive
to trade and investment.

Two separate methods of solving mutual problems can be distinguished in the post-war period—the regional and the world-wide approach. The regional approach is represented by various organizations in Europe and Latin America, such as the EEC, EFTA, the Latin American Free Trade Area, and the Central American Common Market. The world-wide or international approach is reflected by the General Agreement on Tariffs and Trade and by four specialized United Nations institutions, the International Monetary Fund, the International Bank for Reconstruction and Development, the International Finance Corporation, and the International Development Association.

The various international institutions have attempted to promote stable exchange markets, to reduce or alleviate restrictive commercial practices, and in general, to promote a higher level of world trade, investment and income. The regional organizations have sought economic objectives of a narrower scope. Despite a diversity of objectives, there has been a minimum of disagreement among the regional organizations and between the regional and international organizations; generally the various goals have not been inconsistent. A major concern, however, is to ensure that as regional blocs come to be implemented, actions are not pursued by each which are detrimental to others and to broader world-wide interests.

The EEC, EFTA, and European Cooperation

Fear has been expressed that the establishment and implementation of the two European trading blocs—the EEC and the EFTA—will be an obstacle to European cooperation and that developments of this nature can lead to economic warfare.

Inter-bloc trade. There is a relatively large volume of trade between the EFTA and the EEC, hence it is desirable that satisfactory economic relations be maintained between the two. The EFTA countries have in recent years obtained from 25 to 30 per cent of the total value of their imports from the EEC countries. They ship about 25 per cent of their total exports to the EEC. From 15 to 20 per cent of the EEC's total imports have been from the EFTA, and 20 to 25 per cent of its total exports have been to the EFTA.

As an illustration of the absolute volume of trade, during fiscal year 1963, EFTA exports to the EEC amounted to the equivalent of $6,060 million (f.o.b.), and its imports from the EEC totaled $8,220 million (c.i.f.). Since mid-1959, the value of trade between the two groups has increased somewhat more than 5 per cent a year.[1]

An enlarged EEC membership. Cooperation among European countries will continue through various institutional arrangements. A merger of the two trading blocs, which at one time was considered likely, is not expected to occur in the near future, however.

Most of the countries of Western Europe cooperated successfully on economic matters through the OEEC, which was initiated in 1949 at the time of Marshall Plan assistance. In the mid-1950's, an effort at closer integration was proposed within the framework of an all-European free trade area. This proposal failed, partly because prospective members were unable to agree on the degree and type of economic and political integration necessary for a viable institution. The OEEC continued in existence, but the EEC was formally instituted in 1957 and the EFTA in 1960.

For a time, it was expected that European cooperation might be achieved by an expansion of membership in the EEC. Denmark, Ireland and Great Britain applied for membership under Article 237 of the Treaty of Rome in 1961, and Austria, Spain, Sweden and Switzerland requested negotiations leading to some form of association. Israel and Portugal have also given serious consideration to some type of commercial agreement with the EEC.

The Treaty of Rome makes provisions for the inclusion of additional members, and the present members have restated their willingness to consider applications. Article 237 specifies that any *European* state may apply for membership in the EEC. Conditions of membership are to be contained in an agreement between the applicant and member states which must be ratified by each member country. Countries becoming members under Article

237 will normally be expected to accede to most of the provisions of the Treaty of Rome.

The Community may also conclude an agreement under Article 238 to create an associate status for other countries. The agreement creating the association contains the reciprocal rights and obligations of the applicant state and the EEC. Presumably associate status is appropriate for countries which can not accept all of the principles of the Treaty of Rome because of political neutrality or because of a backward economy unable to compete directly with the EEC.

During the months following the British application there was hope that some type of arrangement might be designed whereby several of the European countries, including some EFTA members, might join the EEC either as full or as associate members. Three major issues were relevant to the British discussions: the nature of Britain's economic ties to the Commonwealth; a satisfactory method of including other EFTA members in the EEC; and an acceptable arrangement with respect to British agriculture. The inclusion of Great Britain was generally considered a prerequisite for Community membership on the part of other EFTA nations. Following several months of deliberation, these early hopes were destroyed in 1963 when EEC negotiations with Great Britain were terminated.

Despite Britain's inability to secure membership in the EEC, cooperation is to be maintained between the British and the EEC members on economic and political matters. The Western European Union, an advisory body with membership consisting of the six Common Market countries and Great Britain, is to constitute a forum for discussions which are to be held on a quarterly basis. A major objective will be to maintain close economic relations between the EEC and Great Britain.

Association of Greece. British failure to become a participant should not be interpreted as meaning that in practice the EEC is unwilling to increase its membership. In fact, a treaty was signed in 1962 whereby Greece became attached to the organization as an associate member under Article 238. The creation of a mutually-acceptable association proved to be an arduous task because the Greek economy, which is largely agricultural and relatively undeveloped, is quite different from that of the EEC countries. A second factor was that this was the earliest effort to interpret and apply Article 238. The association represents the first direct link between the Common Market and a European country.

The treaty envisages full membership for Greece following an extended period (twenty-two years) during which Greece is required to make appropriate changes and adjustments. A customs union and the free movement of workers between Greece and the EEC are to be established gradually within a twelve-year period beginning in 1962; other special efforts are to be made to develop the Greek economy and to integrate it with the EEC by the end of the twenty-two year period. Attention is to be directed toward increasing the output of energy, aiding the development of small- and medium-sized firms, and improving the economic infrastructure and the agricultural sector. Although it will be allowed to take advantage of opportunities offered by the Common Market, precautions are to be taken to protect Greece's economy from competition from firms in the more advanced member countries.

The EEC countries have already lowered their tariffs on imports from Greece to the level previously reached in the reduction of the Community's internal tariffs; internal tariff reductions scheduled for the future will also apply to Greek goods. Greece, in turn, is required to reciprocate and to comply with the Community's timetable of trade barrier liberalization; exceptions are made for certain commodities (items representing about one-third of Greece's imports from the EEC) in an effort to establish industry in Greece. Financial aid is to be made available from the European Investment Bank to institute investment projects and to develop infant industries.

Greece's association with the Community is important in at least two respects; it indicates the difficulties and problems involved in increasing the number of EEC participants; it is also some evidence that the EEC does not feel it necessary to remain a relatively small, self-centered group indifferent to broader world problems.

Association of Turkey. Turkey is a second country which is in the process of becoming associated with the EEC under Article 238. An agreement was signed in mid-1963 and is expected to be ratified with only a minimum delay. An Association Council—a joint body composed of representatives of the Turkish government, the EEC, and individual EEC states—will supervise and implement the agreement.

The agreement provides for an adjustment period divided into three distinct and successive stages. During the first or *preparatory* phase, which is expected to last five years, an effort will be made to put the Turkish economy on a sound footing. Efforts will be implemented by the Community, particularly through financial assistance provided by the European Investment Bank. During the second or *transitional* phase (within a twelve-year period) a customs union will be gradually introduced between Turkey and the EEC. Other provisions of the Treaty of Rome, including those relating to the free movement of workers, the right of establishment, transport policy and anti-trust rules, will be accepted by Turkey during this second stage.

During the last or *definitive* phase, a supplementary protocol will be applied and the economies of these countries will be closely coordinated. Ultimately Turkey will be in a position to apply for full membership in the EEC if this appears desirable.

The EEC as a political entity. The EEC is usually considered to be primarily an *economic* institution. However, the EEC is also a *political* arrangement, principally because many economic changes which are being made involve political issues. In general, members of the EEC must surrender a degree of national sovereignty to certain EEC institutions; the Council of Ministers, for example, makes many decisions on the basis of a majority vote, thus avoiding the possibility of a national veto. In many cases the Community's executives can act without prior approval of governments of member states; they are responsible not to national states but to the European Parliament. Decisions of the Community are binding in the territory of member states and do not have to be embodied in the national legislation to be effective.

The EEC is not just an international arrangement; it has blended elements of supranationalism with traditional inter-governmental cooperation and negotiation. Some of the early founders had hoped that the EEC, along with the European Coal and Steel Community and Euratom, would provide a basis for political federation.

The six EEC countries, following several months of negotia-tions in mid-1961, indicated their intention to achieve the degree of political integration implicit in the Treaty of Rome. Continued cooperation and negotiation are required for the establishment of political institutions; progress has been made in this direction, but complete agreement has yet to be reached. France has not supported supranationalism and has indicated a preference for a political union taking the form of an association of sovereign states in which decisions would be subject to the veto of individ-ual governments. The Netherlands and Belgium, on the one hand, desire a more closely integrated type of political union.

One effort to strengthen the political institutions of the EEC was the resolution adopted in June 1963 by the European Parlia-ment that the latter's powers be broadened. The Parliament's role has been largely consultative, but it has been an influential body. However, there is a belief on the part of many Europeans, par-ticularly since the breakdown of negotiations with Great Britain, that its role needs to be broadened and the Community institu-tions in general strengthened to promote political unity. The Parliament consists of 142 members appointed by and from the national parliaments of the Six. Members of Parliament sit by party, rather than by country, and accordingly are bound by common political rather than national views.

An increasing amount of attention is expected to be directed toward developments in the political sphere in the future. Many observers feel that extensive economic integration, as would be embodied in a common currency and a common tax policy, will entail additional political ties. Close political association has been the ultimate objective of many Europeans who envisage a "United States of Europe."

The ability of the EEC to act as a political entity will

strengthen its position and give it considerably greater bargaining power in world economic and political affairs. Close political integration of the EEC will also very likely make it more difficult for additional countries to participate in the EEC, particularly as full members.

The extent to which the EEC will be expanded to include other members is difficult to estimate. Many unpredictable political and economic factors will have an influence on the course of events. Present EEC members have indicated a willingness to consider prospective European membership applications, and the EEC remains open for European countries willing and able to join. At the same time the Six have indicated a reluctance to dilute the Treaty of Rome simply to increase the size of the organization. The EEC recognizes that membership is impossible for some countries but that a close relationship should be maintained with them.

The Organization for Economic Cooperation and Development. It is likely that the most important organization for maintaining close economic relations among the Western European countries in their transactions with North America will be the Organization for Economic Cooperation and Development (OECD). The OECD, which began its formal existence in 1961, is the successor organization to the Organization for European Economic Cooperation and includes the members of the EEC, the EFTA, Canada and the United States.[2] The objectives of the OECD are to harmonize the trade and aid policies of the member countries and to maintain close cooperation on economic affairs. Consultation and cooperation on the part of individual members are expected to promote the economic welfare of the entire group. For example, efforts have been made to coordinate domestic and monetary policies of member countries. The OECD's Working Party on Better Payments Equilibrium has attempted to promote understanding and to coordinate monetary and balance of payments problems.

The OECD's activities depend upon the voluntary response of member countries. Actions taken by the group require a unanimous vote; however, on any particular measure, a member unwilling to participate yet not wanting to veto the measure is permitted to abstain. The OECD is not a tightly-knit organization; nevertheless it does provide a valuable framework within which countries of the Atlantic community seek to resolve mutual problems. It is probably the most important economic body representing an Atlantic partnership. It is a significant grouping because the membership includes most of the major industrial and trading nations of the free world.

Other cooperative efforts. The ability and tendency of the more important Western nations to cooperate is also represented by an agreement between ten major industrial countries and the International Monetary Fund (IMF) in 1962. Under this agreement, the former stand ready to lend their currencies to the IMF in instances where additional international reserves are needed to forestall or cope with an impairment of the international monetary system. The countries involved in this agreement include Belgium, Canada, France, Germany, Italy, Japan, Netherlands, Sweden, United Kingdom and the United States.

These same countries, in 1963, considered the feasibility of the creation of a new unit of international currency in an effort to improve the world monetary system and to lessen the burden on the dollar as the key reserve currency.

Summary. Cooperation has been maintained among the European countries in part because they, along with non-European countries, participate in several international economic organizations. The most important of these are the General Agreement on Tariffs and Trade (GATT), the International Monetary Fund, and the Organization for Economic Cooperation and Development. The General Agreement, which was examined in chapter 3, sponsors multilateral negotiations among member countries in an effort to lower trade barriers. The International Monetary Fund, an institution consisting of over 100 countries, promotes cooperation and action on balance of payments problems.

The existence and active operation of the OECD, the GATT, and a number of international arrangements suggests that there are interests and objectives which transcend those of the more

narrow regional organizations. Disagreement on economic matters has arisen and will continue to arise among the major trading nations and blocs; it appears likely, however, that most
differences will be resolved through existing organizations.

Regional Arrangements in Latin America

Economic integration has become a popular concept in
other areas of the world, notably in Latin America. Several
regional arrangements have been considered and even initiated
in Central and South America, but only in recent years has
there been any notable success in the execution of plans. An
increasing awareness of the potential benefits to be derived from
economic integration has led to the establishment of the Central American Common Market and the Latin American Free
Trade Association.[3]

The Central American Common Market. The first major
step was taken toward the creation of the Central American
Common Market (CACM) in 1958. This Market includes El
Salvador, Guatemala, Honduras, Nicaragua, and Costa Rica.
By mid-1963, Costa Rica had signed, but not ratified the group's
basic treaty, the General Treaty of Economic Integration. A
sixth country, Panama, is expected to continue as an associate
member for a time.

Annual per capita incomes for the area amount to the equivalent of about $200, with the highest incomes in Costa Rica,
the lowest in Guatemala. Aggregate population is about 11
million, but the rate of population growth is much higher than
the world average. It ranges from 2 to 3 per cent a year for
individual countries. The region is highly specialized with three
products—bananas, cotton and coffee—representing about 75
per cent of the value of its exports. Deteriorating terms of trade
have proved to be a problem since the early 1950's.

In an effort to reduce over-dependence upon a small number
of commodities, the member countries have agreed that most
internal trade barriers will be eliminated and a common external
tariff will be established within a relatively short transitional period of five years. Most tariff changes are to be completed by the

end of 1966. Several industries are to be integrated as the Treaty is implemented, in the hope that each country will be able to produce certain items more economically than others. An integrated industry is accorded special treatment within the market area. The result of these efforts is that individual nations will specialize, but the region will become more diversified. Other efforts are being made to develop close cooperation and coordination on political, social and economic matters. For example, a development bank has been established to encourage the development of new industrial units.

Latin American Free Trade Area. The most important regional organization in Latin America is the Latin American Free Trade Association (LAFTA). Its membership includes Argentina, Brazil, Chile, Colombia, Ecuador, Mexico, Paraguay, Peru and Uruguay. Argentina, Brazil and Mexico are the most industrialized of the group; Paraguay and Ecuador are the most underdeveloped. The member countries have an aggregate population of about 180 million and an annual per capita income of about $300. LAFTA represents over three-fourths of the population and income in Latin America. The LAFTA members are major suppliers of a variety of primary commodities including coffee, tin, copper, and wheat. In 1961, the export trade of member countries accounted for almost 4 per cent of world trade. About 90 per cent of their trade is with non-member countries.

LAFTA was established by the Treaty of Montevideo in 1960. It provides for the gradual elimination by 1973 of most internal trade restrictions; progress has been made in this direction, but it has not yet involved major readjustment on the part of member countries. Restrictions have generally been removed on the "easy" items, and no major sacrifices have been required. Efforts are being made to promote and finance new regional industries in countries where economic production seems most likely. Through cooperative action, regional diversification is to be promoted, especially in the nature of industrial development.

Rationale for economic unification in Latin America. Several factors have accelerated the movement toward economic integration in Latin America. The fundamental reason, however, is that many of the countries are underdeveloped and believe that regional integration could provide a framework within which economic advancement might be promoted. Integration in Latin America is likely to provide a pattern for other developing nations.

European integration undoubtedly served as a model for Latin America although the conditions and problems of the two areas are extremely different. One notable feature is that there is a minimum amount of trade among the Latin American economies. About 10 per cent of the volume of its trade is internal; most of the rest is with the United States and Western Europe. Internal trade has been hampered because of poor transportation and communication facilities, trade barriers and lack of economic complementarity. Despite a lack of complementarity, it is anticipated that integration will provide a basis for the reorientation of internal production and trade; complementary activities are to be coordinated and thus provide an opportunity for economic growth.

The Latin American economies are determined to reduce their dependence upon raw material production and exports. In recent years, prices of primary commodities have deteriorated relative to prices of finished goods and services. During the ten-year period 1953-1962, for example, prices of manufactured goods *increased* by almost 10 per cent while prices of primary commodities *decreased* by almost 10 per cent. Deterioration in the terms of trade for primary producing countries reflects a long-term trend; the demand for many primary commodities is believed to be income inelastic and consumption of such items does not increase as rapidly as does world income.

Prices of raw materials are also notoriously unstable; wide and frequent price fluctuations have had an adverse impact on the balance of payments and economies of these countries. Such problems are intensified for many Latin American countries because of their dependence upon one or two commodities such as bananas, coffee, wool, meat, sugar, tin or copper as a major source of foreign exchange earnings.

In order to diversify and to industrialize their economies, and permit the initiation of new enterprises, the Latin American countries seek the broad, protected markets which would be afforded by regionalism. It is expected that resources can be allocated more efficiently within a regional market than within the confines of a narrower national market. Firms will be able to sell products in a market larger than the national ones; frequently national populations and incomes are too small to support the more complex industries. Many industries might be classified "infant industries"; initially they may be unable to compete in world markets, but they can operate profitably within a regional market.

A number of Latin American governments are concerned that they will lose European markets as a result of the preferential tariff treatment which the EEC has afforded to the associated African states. These states are also important producers of bananas, coffee, copper and tin. It is argued that economic unification will enhance the bargaining power of the Latin American countries in order that they may retain their overseas markets in raw materials.

Obstacles. Perhaps the most important obstacle to economic integration in Latin America is political instability on the part of some member governments. Political instability creates an unfavorable atmosphere for close cooperation between governments. It leads to capital flights, discourages domestic and foreign investment and thus makes it more difficult to maintain a satisfactory rate of economic growth.

Latin American integration is also hampered by high and unequal rates of inflation in different economies. The price increases which characterize some Latin American countries are detrimental because they contribute to balance of payments disequilibrium among member countries as well as with the rest of the world. Inflation also discourages productive domestic and foreign investment.

Impact of Latin American integration on United States trade. United States commodity trade with Latin America has increased significantly in recent years. By 1962, commodity exports to the

Latin American republics amounted to $3,222 million (approximately 17 per cent of total United States exports). Imports from Latin America amounted to $3,386 million (about 20 per cent of total imports). Major United States exports to Latin America include industrial and electrical machinery, automobiles and parts, and chemical products. Major imports from Latin America include petroleum, nonferrous metals and ferroalloys, coffee, cane sugar and other foodstuffs.[4]

The Central American Common Market and the Latin American Free Trade Association are likely to have a far smaller impact on American business than their European counterparts, the EEC and the EFTA. For one thing, the Central and South American economies are considerably less important in terms of output and income and are relatively less industrialized. Their potential for growth, except for population, also appears less important. They produce a relatively narrower range of commodities and products than do the economies of Europe. The dependence upon relatively few kinds of exports and the lack of diversification causes instability in their domestic and external transactions.

Taken alone and without the assistance of other factors making for growth and development, these two institutions apparently do not hold great promise of effectuating substantial changes in their member economies. The Central and South American economies suffer from inherited impediments to meet the growing wants of their people, limited resources, lack of skills and education of the labor force, shortages of qualified management personnel and insufficient capital resources. Although a common market and free trade association will surely prove to be of help, much more will be required for future economic development.

The arrangements are likely to have the greatest impact on United States exports and imports insofar as regionalism becomes a successful device for promoting industrialization and economic growth. If regionalism succeeds as a method for the promotion of internal growth and higher per capita incomes in Latin America, it will indirectly serve to stimulate that area's demand for United States goods and services. United States sales have been limited in the relatively poorer countries because of a lack of purchasing power. Regionalism is likely to affect the composition of trade with Latin America and to increase the total volume of such trade.

Although the over-all impact on American business in general may be small, specific business firms trading with, and investing in, these regions may feel the effects of the changes engendered by these institutions. These organizations are likely to bring about a greater degree of specialization in both industry and agriculture; the size of certain industries may increase and new industries develop.

American importers can conceivably find a somewhat wider range of goods which will prove saleable on the United States markets, and perhaps some improvement in the quality of the goods already in manufacture. For those American importers who are willing to assist financially in the development of promising sources of supply, the CACM and the LAFTA may provide new opportunities.

If new industries do spring up and old ones grow in size and integrate, American exporters can conceivably find an increased demand for industrial equipment, semi-finished goods and components. A substantial increase in demand for general imports must await the growth of the national incomes of the area and larger earnings of dollar exchange from exports. There will probably be little change in the external tariffs of the LAFTA which result from the new institution, while the external tariff of the CACM may bring about some changes in the country destination of United States exports to the region.

The growth of these institutions should serve to improve the *business* climate for American direct investors, but not necessarily the government or *political* climate with the frequent occurrence of nationalization and expropriation. The decline in the internal tariffs of the two institutions will provide wider markets and substantially improve the distribution of goods within the areas. The prospects for licensing, with its minimum investment of capital, appear favorable for those lines for which

Central and South American manufacturers possess the requisite technical capacities.

Other proposed unions. Other areas of the world, including Africa and Asia, reflect evidence of an interest in economic integration, generally on the premise that such organizations will enhance opportunities for economic growth. For example, Portugal and its overseas territories, already merged in a monetary zone known as the Escudo Area, have proposed a closer integration of the economies within the zone. Internal trade barriers would be gradually removed and a development program would be initiated to raise the levels of living.

Another proposal for integration involves the four territories which have formed the new state of Malaysia. The Agreement which established Malaysia calls for the elimination of internal trade barriers, the establishment of a common external tariff and a unification of the separate economic and commercial policies. Although many serious problems are envisaged during the transitional period, it is believed that complete economic integration is needed if Malaysia is to remain a viable political entity.

Many of the African states are becoming increasingly interested in the establishment of economic communities. These are not likely to be of immediate interest to the American businessman, since the total volume of United States export trade to all the African states accounts for only about 5 per cent of United States export trade.

Regionalism: An Expansive or Contractive Force

The impact which regionalism may have on international trade and investment has become a major consideration following the development of the EEC, the EFTA, the two Latin American trading blocs, and other proposals for regional groupings in Asia and Africa. The existing and proposed trade blocs may either encourage or discourage, advance or retard, efforts toward the liberalization of international commerce.

Regionalism is certain to provide a better use of resources within such an area; whether or not this comes at the expense of world-wide specialization and exchange remains to be seen.

Regionalism and GATT. Member countries of regional arrangements impose discriminatory trade restrictions against non-member countries—this is the essential nature of customs unions and free trade areas. Generally, trade discrimination has been opposed in world councils; that is, one country is not expected to offer another country or group of countries preferential tariff treatment. This concept, for example, is embodied in unconditional most-favored-nation treatment.

An exception to the non-discrimination rule has been applied in the case of free trade areas and customs unions which are permitted to discriminate against non-members. The GATT, the agency concerned with commercial practices, condones discrimination under such circumstances. However, regional groupings cannot impose more restrictive external barriers if their operations are to be sanctioned by GATT. Thus, as an illustration, the EEC's common external tariff can be no more restrictive than were the original national barriers of participating countries.

Actually it is through the GATT that there is a hope that the regional organizations can be induced to lower external barriers with respect to the rest of the world. For example, during its early years of operations, the EEC offered to reduce its common external tariff by 20 per cent on a reciprocal basis. A session of GATT tariff negotiations is scheduled for 1964 in Geneva. This session could lead to a substantial reduction in tariffs on the part of the EEC, EFTA, the United States and other contracting parties.

Regionalism as a contractive force. It is not altogether certain that regionalism will be a positive force for liberal trade; there are in fact several reasons why the regional trading blocs may become "inward-looking" and thus retard world-wide organization and cooperation. The regional import barriers which are established may become permanent obstacles, and though intra-regional trade will expand, inter-regional (international) exchange may suffer.

A major reason why regionalism could fail to be expansive in nature is that it may not be politically expedient for national governments to pursue trade liberalization on a world-wide basis. Firms and industries may become firmly entrenched behind regional trade barriers and offer strong resistance to increased external competition stemming from lower barriers. Under such circumstances, regional barriers provide at least a partial substitute for national restrictions. Agricultural interests in the EEC provide an example of successful opposition to liberal trade. Whether governments can counter such resistance remains to be seen; an encouraging sign is the trend on the part of governments to offer alternatives in the form of adjustment assistance to those domestic firms and industries adversely affected by lower trade barriers.

A desire for regional self-sufficiency may be another factor which may strengthen contractive tendencies. Some blocs may feel that this is desirable for political and military security. For the regional blocs which comprise the less developed countries, economic independence may be the sequel to political independence. The Latin American groups, for example, maintain that economic diversification is essential, and they plan to provide adequate protection to make certain that new domestic industries have an opportunity to become firmly established.

Finally, it is certain that regional objectives will take precedence over international objectives insofar as conflicting goals arise. It is likely that regional trade barriers will be used in the belief that they contribute to internal employment, that they provide protection from cheap foreign labor, or that they are needed for some other domestic objective.

Regionalism as an expansive force. The basic factor which is likely to lead to future trade liberalization is that all of the major trading areas—the EEC, the EFTA, the United States and Latin America—are either foreign trade oriented or heavily dependent upon the rest of the world for items which cannot be readily obtained internally. The European blocs need raw materials; the United States needs both strategic and non-strategic minerals and many types of foodstuffs; Latin America needs capital equipment and other items for development. Not one of these trading areas is sufficiently large or adequately diversified to supply member countries with essential resources and product markets.

Regionalism will also be a stimulant to world trade insofar as such arrangements promote increased productivity, a higher level of national and world income, and increased demand for consumer and capital goods. European families, for example, are becoming increasingly able to afford many consumer durables and luxury goods which were previously limited to high income families. The underdeveloped countries are securing an increasing volume of capital goods and equipment with which to implement their programs of economic development. In general, there is a trend toward a higher level of world trade and commerce, a trend which is likely to be fostered by regional arrangements.

The existence and development of common markets and free trade areas suggest that the world may be moving toward cooperative economic efforts on a regional rather than a world-wide basis. There is little evidence, however, that regional efforts have conflicted with those undertaken on a broader scale. Some students of the problem are convinced that regionalism may be a desirable end in itself. Still others expect that the regional organizations are but intermediate steps toward more extensive cooperation on a world-wide basis.

The degree of success attained at the GATT tariff conference in Geneva in 1964 will be one of the first concrete indications of the nature of international commercial policies likely to be practiced for at least the next several years. Most GATT members have expressed a willingness to cooperate in the relaxation of all types of restrictions for all classes of commodities in an effort to promote the liberalization of world trade. A resolution adopted by the Ministers at the GATT Ministerial Conference in May 1963 suggests the attitude which has generally prevailed:

"That a significant liberalization of world trade is desirable, and that, for this purpose, comprehensive trade negotiations, to be conducted on a most-favored-nation basis and on the principle of reciprocity, shall begin at Geneva . . .

"That the trade negotiations shall cover all classes of products, industrial and nonindustrial, including agricultural and primary products.

"That the trade negotiations shall deal not only with tariffs but also with nontariff barriers."

Perhaps the most important factors influencing the commercial policy of these countries will be the success of their respective economies in the attainment of an adequate growth rate, price stability, and a low level of unemployment. Nations have been more willing to pursue liberal trade policies when domestic prosperity prevails. When a substantial share of national resources comes to be unemployed, actions are frequently taken which conflict with a liberal international commercial policy.

NOTES

[1] Statistics have been derived from EFTA. *EFTA Bulletin.* December 1961, p. 15; and November 1963, p. 15.

[2] Japan has been invited to become a member of the OECD. Present members also include Greece, Iceland, Ireland, Spain and Turkey.

[3] The two regional arrangements include all major countries in Latin America except Venezuela and Bolivia. These two countries may eventually become part of LAFTA.

[4] See Bureau of the Census. *Statistical Abstract of the United States, 1963.* U. S. Department of Commerce. Washington: U. S. GPO, 1963, pp. 876-877.

SELECTED BIBLIOGRAPHY

A. Books and Other Publications

Adler, John H., Schlesinger, Eugene R. and van Westerborg, Evelyn. *The Pattern of United States Import Trade Since 1923: Some New Index Series and Their Application.* New York: Federal Reserve Bank of New York, 1952.

Balassa, Bela. *The Theory of Economic Integration.* Homewood, Illinois: Richard D. Irwin, Inc., 1961.

Beever, R. Colin. *European Unity and the Trade Union Movements.* Netherlands: A. W. Sythoff, 1960.

Benoit, Emile. *Europe at Sixes and Sevens: The Common Market, The Free Trade Association, and the United States.* New York: Columbia University Press, 1961.

Campbell, Alan and Thompson, Dennis. *Common Market Law.* South Hackensack, N. J.: Fred B. Rothman & Co., 1962. There is a 1963 supplement available.

Clark, Colin. *British Trade in the Common Market.* London: Stevens & Sons, Ltd., 1962.

The Common Market. United States Department of Commerce. Washington, D. C.: GPO, n.d. Reprints from *Foreign Commerce Weekly* and *International Commerce,* containing: Buchdahl, Walter, "Exporters Await Impact of EEC's Tariff Adjustment"; Herter, Christian A., "International Trade Vital to World Peace"; Heck, Harold J., "Study of 181 Items Exported to EEC Reveals Little Ground for U. S. Complacency"; Hammond, Charles, Jr., "EEC's Growth Peaks, Wages Climb in First Half of '62"; Drumm, Thomas E., Jr., "Europe — A Mass Market"; Anonymous, "EEC Represents Great Market in Highly Industrialized Area"; Buchdahl, Walter, "Rapid Growth of Common Market Spurs Import Demand"; Buchdahl, Walter, "European Economic Community Moves Toward the Customs Union"; Buchdahl, Walter, "The European Economic Community as a Market for Imports."

Comparative Tariffs and Trade: The United States and the European Common Market. (Present and projected U. S. and European Common Market tariff rates on the complete Brussels Tariff Nomenclature; and in the same classification, imports of the U. S. and the European Common Market.) Supplementary Paper No. 14. 2 vols. New York: Committee for Economic Development, 1963.

Dowd, Lawrence O. (ed.). *The European Economic Community: Implications for Michigan Business.* Michigan Business Reports No. 36, International Series. Ann Arbor, Michigan: Bureau of Business Research, School of Business Administration, University of Michigan, 1961.

Employment, Growth and Price Levels. Joint Economic Committee, Congress of the United States, 86th Congress, 1st Session, June 29, 30, July 1 and 2, 1959, S. Con. Res. 13, Part V, International Influences on the American Economy. See especially the testimony and exhibits of: Ball, George W., pp. 991-1017; Depres, Emile, pp. 1018-1037; Scitovsky, Tibor, pp. 1037-1051.

The European Common Market and Its Meaning to the United States. New York: Committee for Economic Development, 1959.

Factors Affecting the United States Balance of Payments. Joint Economic Committee, Congress of the United States. Compilation of Studies Prepared for the Subcommittee on International Exchange and Payments, 87th Congress, 2nd Session, Joint Committee Print. Washington, D. C.: GPO, 1962, pp. 87-173. This collection of studies includes in Part 2, The Common Market: New Challenges to U. S. Exports, papers by: Kravis, Irving B., "The U. S. Trade Position and the Common Market"; Krause, Lawrence B., "The European Economic Community and American Agriculture"; Markham, Jesse W., "Competition in the European Common Market"; Kindleberger, Charles P., "Protected Markets and Economic Growth."

Fayerweather, John. *Facts and Fallacies of International Business.* New York: Holt, Rinehart and Winston, 1962.

Frank, Isaiah. *The European Common Market: An Analysis of Commercial Policy.* New York: Frederick A. Praeger, 1961.

General Agreements on Tariffs and Trade: Analysis of United States Negotiations. (Vol. IV. Unofficial English translation of the Common External Tariff of the European Economic Community, showing originally established rates of duty and revisions resulting from concessions granted in the 1960-61 tariff negotiations.) United States Department of State. Washington, D. C.: GPO, 1963.

Humphrey, Don D. *The United States and the Common Market: A Background Study.* New York: Frederick A. Praeger, 1962.

Mangan, Robert E. (ed.). *American Business Looks Abroad.* Proceedings of the 19th Annual Stanford Business Conference, September 1960. Stanford, California: Graduate School of Business, Stanford University, 1961.

Market Europe. New York: Morgan Guaranty Trust Company of New York, 1961.

Meeting Foreign Competition at Home and Abroad. Proceedings of the First 1961 Economic Institute, February 15, 1961, containing addresses by Gottfried Haberler, Tino Perutz, Norman T. Ness, Ralph E. Smiley, Jackson E. Spears, George Donat, William Blackie and moderator Erwin D. Canham. Washington: Chamber of Commerce of the United States, 1961.

Nystrom, J. Warren and Malof, Peter. *The Common Market: European Community in Action.* Princeton: D. Van Nostrand Co., Inc., 1962.

Pincus, Joseph. *The Central American Common Market.* Washington: Regional Office for Central America and Panama Affairs. U. S. Department of State, Agency for International Development, 1962.

Piquet, Howard S. *Aid, Trade and the Tariff.* New York: Thomas Y. Crowell Co., 1953.

Report, Part I, Special Study Mission to Europe and Report, Part II, A Study of European Economic Regionalism: A New Era in Free World Economic Politics. House of Representatives, Committee on Foreign Affairs, 86th Congress, 2nd Session, House Report No. 1226, Union Calendar 523, pursuant to H. Res. 113. Washington, D. C.: GPO, 1960.

Robinson, Richard D. *Cases in International Business.* New York: Holt, Rinehart and Winston, 1962.

Salant, Walter S., Despres, Emile, Krause, Lawrence B., Rivlin, Alice M., Salant, William A., Tarshis, Lorie. *The United States Balance of Payments in 1968.* Washington: The Brookings Institution, 1963.

Sannwald, Rolf and Stohler, Jacques. *Economic Integration.* Princeton, New Jersy: Princeton University Press, 1959.

Scott, John. *The New Europe: Can Six and Seven Make One?* A report to the publisher of *Time.* New York: Time Inc., 1961.

Shanks, Michael and Lambert, John. *The Common Market Today—and Tomorrow.* New York: Frederick A. Praeger, 1962.

Statistics on the European Economic Community. United States Department of Agriculture, Economic Research Service, Development and Trade Analysis Division. Washington, 1962.

Stein, Eric and Nicholson, Thomas L. (eds.). *American Enterprise in the European Common Market: A Legal Profile.* 2 vols. Ann Arbor, Michigan: The University of Michigan Press, 1960.

Strauss, E. *Common Sense About the Common Market.* New York: Rinehart and Co., Inc., 1958.

Streeten, Paul. *Economic Integration.* Netherlands: A. W. Sythoff, 1961.

B. Other Bibliographical Sources

Business International publishes a number of periodicals, reports and studies of interest to businessmen who are engaged in international operations and transactions. Some of its services are described in its *Business International Executive Services*, 1963. Its weekly periodical, *Business International*, contains articles and news items of interest to those doing business in the EEC and the EFTA areas. Among the other publications of this firm see especially: *Investing and Licensing Conditions in 44 Countries; Europe's Mass Markets: A Guide to EEC and EFTA; Profit Performance of U. S. Corporations Abroad; Business International European Roundtable* (Brussels, October 9-15, 1960); *Europe's Rules of Competition; Charting Paths Through Europe's Transition to a Common Market.* Correspondence relative to subscriptions to the publications and services of this firm should be addressed to: Business International, 757 Third Avenue, New York 17, N. Y.

The Chase Manhattan Bank publishes a periodical, *Report on Western Europe*, containing articles, news items and statistics on the EEC and the EFTA. Copies may be obtained from: The Chase Manhattan Bank, New York 15, N. Y.

The Chemical Bank New York Trust Company publishes a periodical, *International Notes*, which contains from time to time articles dealing with the EEC and EFTA. Copies may be obtained from: The Chemical Bank New York Trust Company, International Division, 20 Pine Street, New York 15, N. Y.

The European Economic Community issues a large number of publications including statistical and other periodicals, pamphlets, studies, reports and books. The organization issues annually a list of publications currently available which may be obtained from: The European Community, Information Office, 808 Farragut Building, Washington 6, D. C.

The European Free Trade Association issues a number of publications including statistical and other periodicals, pamphlets and studies. A list of its currently available publications may be obtained from: The European Free Trade Association, Information Office, 711 14th Street N.W., Washington, D. C.

Morgan Guaranty Trust Company of New York issues a monthly periodical, *The Morgan Guaranty Survey*, which contains articles on

the EEC and EFTA from time to time. Copies may be obtained from: The Morgan Guaranty Trust Company, 23 Wall Street, New York 15, N. Y.

Price Waterhouse and Company, with offices and correspondents throughout the world, publishes a series of booklets of interest to those engaged in international transactions and operations. One series, *Information Guide for Those Doing Business Outside the United States of America,* includes a number of studies of business conditions in specified foreign countries which usually contain information on business formation and operation, exchange regulations, taxation, labor legislation. The *Key Investment Factors in 56 Countries* presents, in tabular form, information on exchange controls, foreign business ownership, investment guarantees and local capital available. *Current Foreign Exchange Information* gives essential facts concerning exchange regulations in a number of countries. Information concerning United States taxes of interest to international businessmen is given in: *Reporting on Foreign Corporations and Trusts; Tax Accounting Problems in International Operations and Tax Guide for U. S. Corporations Doing Business Abroad.* For information concerning the acquisition of these publications, contact either the New York or any local United States office of Price Waterhouse and Company.

The United States Department of Commerce publishes a large amount of material of interest to those who do business with the Common Market. The principal publications are given in Appendix C, Selected Sources of Business Information on the EEC and EFTA countries.

Appendix A

Leading Commodities in the United States Import Trade with the EEC, 1956-1960

Foodstuffs
  Meat Products
  Cheese
  Vegetables and preparations
  Cocoa and chocolate
  Beverages
    Wines
    Brandy
Animals and products, inedible
  Leather
  Leather manufactures
    Boots, shoes and other
      footwear
  Furs and manufactures
Vegetable products, inedible
  Rubber manufactures
    Automobile, motorcycle, truck
      and bus tires
  Vegetable oils and vegetable
    waxes
  Bulbs, roots or corms
Textile fibers and manufactures
  Textile fibers
    Wool, unmanufactured
  Textile semimanufactures
    Wool semimanufactures
    Man-made fibers
      Filaments not over 30 inches
  Textile manufactures
    Cotton manufactures
      Cloth
      Wearing apparel
    Jute manufactures
    Flax, hemp and ramie manu-
      factures

Wool manufactures
  Worsteds and woolen fab-
    rics,
  Wearing apparel
  Carpets, rugs and other
    floor coverings
  Silk manufactures
Wood and paper
  Wood manufactures
  Paper and manufactures
Nonmetallic minerals
  Stone, lime, gypsum and
    products
  Glass and glass products
    Cylinder, crown and sheet
      glass
  Clay and clay products
  Precious and semiprecious
    stones
    Diamonds
Metals and manufactures
  Steel-mill products, excluding
    pig iron and scrap
    Steel bars
    Wire rods
    Plates and sheets
    Structural shapes
    Tubular products and fittings
    Wire and manufactures
    Nails
  Iron and steel advanced
    manufactures
  Ferro-alloys, ores and metals
  Nonferrous ores and metals
    Aluminum and manufactures

Copper and manufactures
Brass and bronze
    manufactures
Tin
Zinc and manufactures
Precious metals, jewelry and
    plated ware
Machinery and vehicles
  Machinery
    Electrical machinery
      Radio apparatus and parts
    Industrial, office and printing
      machinery
      Metalworking machinery
        and parts
      Textile and sewing
        machinery and parts
      Office appliances
      Typewriters
Vehicles and parts
  Automobiles and parts

Automobiles, new
Bicycles and parts
Aircraft and parts
Chemicals and related products
  Coal-tar products
  Industrial chemicals
  Fertilizers and fertilizer
    materials
Miscellaneous
  Photographic goods
  Scientific and professional
    instruments, apparatus and
    supplies
  Musical instruments, parts and
    accessories
  Books, maps, pictures and
    other printed matter
  Clocks, watches, clockwork
    mechanisms and parts
  Art works and antiques

Source: United States Department of Commerce, *Trade of the United States with the European Economic Community and the United Kingdom, 1956-60.* WTIS, Part 3, No. 62-8, March 1962, pp. 5-6.

Appendix B

Leading Commodities in the United States Export Trade with the EEC, 1956-1960

Foodstuffs
  Meat and meat products
  Grains and preparations
    Barley
    Corn, except seed
    Grain sorghums
    Oats
    Rye
    Wheat
    Wheat flour
  Fodders and feeds
    Oilcake and oil-cake meal
  Vegetables and preparations
  Fruits and preparations
    Fresh fruits
    Dried and evaporated fruits
    Canned fruits
Animals and products, inedible
  Hides and skins, raw,
    except furs
  Leather
  Furs and manufactures
  Tallow, inedible
Vegetable products, inedible
  Synthetic rubbers
  Naval stores, gums and resins
  Soybeans, except canned
  Flaxseed
  Vegetable oils, fats, and
    waxes, crude
    Linseed oil
    Cottonseed oil
    Soybean oil

Tobacco, unmanufactured
  Cigarettes
Textile fibers and manufactures
  Raw cotton, except linters
  Man-made fibers and yarns
  Other textile materials,
    including rags and waste
  Textile fabrics, apparel, and
    related manufactures
  Fabrics
  Wearing apparel
Wood and paper
  Lumber and sawmill products
  Woodpulp
    Special alpha and dissolving
      grade
  Paper, related products, and
    manufactures
Nonmetallic minerals
  Anthracite coal
  Bituminous coal
  Petroleum and products
    Crude petroleum
    Gasoline, blending agents,
      and jet fuels
    Gas oil and fuel oil
    Lubricating oils
  Sulfur, crude
Metals and manufactures
  Iron and steel scrap
  Iron and steel-mill products
    Plates and sheets
    Tinplate

Metal manufactures
Nonferrous ores and metals
  Aluminum ores, scrap and
  metal
  Copper ore and concentrates
  Refined copper
  Copper scrap and copper-base
  alloy scrap
  Nickel and nickel alloy scrap,
  bars, rods, etc.
  Molybdenum ore and
  concentrates
  Vanadium ores, wastes,
  pentoxide, etc.
Machinery and vehicles
Machinery
  Electrical machinery and
  apparatus
    Radio, television and other
    electronic equipment
  Industrial machinery
    Power generating
    machinery
    Construction, excavating
    and mining machinery
    Metalworking machinery
    and machine tools
    Textile, sewing and shoe
    machinery
    Manufacturing, service-in-
    dustry and miscellanous
    industrial machinery
  Office, accounting and
  computing machines
  Agricultural machines and
  tractors
Automobiles, parts, and
accessories

Motortrucks, buses, and
  chassis, nonmilitary, new
Passenger cars and chassis,
  new, nonmilitary
Aircraft, parts, and
  accessories
  Passenger transports, new,
  30,000 pounds and over
Chemicals and related products
Coal-tar products
  Crude coal-tar and other
  cyclic products
  Coal-tar and other cyclic
  intermediates
Medicinal and pharmaceutical
  preparations
Chemical specialties
  Plastics and resin materials
Industrial chemicals
  Acids and anhydrides,
  organic and inorganic
  Alcohols
  Synthetic collecting reagents
  and other organic
  chemicals
Pigments, paints and varnishes
  Carbon black
Fertilizers and materials
Miscellaneous
  Photographic and projection
  goods
  Scientific and professional in-
  struments, apparatus and
  supplies
  Phonographs, records, blanks,
  and parts
  Commodities for relief or
  charity
  Food

Source: United States Department of Commerce, *Trade of the United States with the European Economic Community and the United Kingdom, 1956-60.* WTIS, Part 3, No. 62-8, March 1962, pp. 3-4.

Appendix C

Selected Sources
of Business Information
on the EEC and EFTA Countries

The objective of this book is to supply information of a general background character to enable readers to assess the impact of the economic aspects of the Common Market on their business operations. Many of the works listed in the bibliography provide additional and more detailed background information on specific topics treated in this volume.

It is impossible to conduct a successful business solely on the basis of general background information—specific facts are needed to arrive at rational decisions. This appendix presents a selection of sources available to businessmen which can supply the information needed for specific business situations, decisions and policies.

1. The United States Department of Commerce. The United States Department of Commerce is probably the most important single source of international business information in the world. Two of its bureaus, the Bureau of International Commerce, which gathers and furnishes information concerning the business and economic life of foreign nations, and the Business and Defense Services Administration, which is a repository of data on commodities and industries abroad, are of particular interest to American business.

The data which the Department of Commerce gathers are obtained from the foreign missions of the United States abroad, its embassies, legations and consulates. The most important of these posts overseas are staffed with commercial and economic officers whose functions, among others, are to report periodically on business and economic conditions in foreign countries. In addition to the regularly scheduled periodic reports which these officers are required to file, they prepare "voluntary," or non-scheduled reports on new developments in their respective areas and ordinarily will supply special reports, not covered by the foregoing, when requested to do so.

These reports are read and filed by the country and functional desk officers of the Department of Commerce in Washington. Some of these reports are "classified," since they contain information which might reflect unfavorably on foreign governments and firms or to protect sources of intelligence, but many of them are not. The unclassified information is made available to American businessmen in a variety of ways.

Visits, telephone calls, telegrams and letters to the Department of Commerce will usually elicit answers to many questions concerning specific import, export and investment questions. The Department of Commerce maintains thirty-nine regional Field Offices located in the principal commercial cities of the United States and all of the information and services which it provides is promptly available from them. A list of these offices, their addresses and telephone numbers, is given regularly in the Department's weekly publication, *International Commerce*.

International Commerce makes much foreign business information available through its news items and articles. In addition, it regularly carries sections devoted to import, export, business representation, and investment (including licensing) opportunities abroad; United States and foreign government as well as international agency actions and programs of interest to international traders; the worldwide business outlook; special articles on important economic developments abroad; lists of visiting buyers and officials; lists of construction projects planned by foreign governments; lists and decriptions of trade fairs and centers overseas; reports prepared by American Trade Missions, which have returned from tours abroad, presenting facts, gathered on the spot, concerning business opportunities and developments in a number of foreign countries.

The Department of Commerce publishes a series of pamphlets or manuals dealing with investment in specific countries which furnish information required by businessmen who contemplate establishing branches, subsidiaries or licensing arrangements overseas. The *Statistical Reports* of the Department give data on foreign trade with, and market information on, various countries and regions together with analyses of their characteristics and trends. The *Overseas Business Reports* present statistics and information on the trade, production and consumption of other nations and foreign industries. The Department's *Trade Lists* are rosters of firms abroad engaged in various lines of business. These lists are useful to firms which seek representation overseas or to represent foreign firms in the United States, sources of supplies for imports as well as export outlets. The *World Trade Directory Reports* of the Department provide financial and credit information on certain foreign firms.

2. Banks and Financial Institutions. Many of the commercial banks and financial institutions located in the principal commercial centers of the United States maintain branches and correspondent relations with banks abroad. Through these branches and correspondents they gather considerable information on business abroad, individual firms, foreign business laws, practices and taxation. Some of the larger institutions have research, country and commodity departments.

These banks are able to provide a variety of business intelligence services especially as concerns the credit standing of foreign firms. Since many of these institutions have had considerable experience in the financing of foreign ventures, they are in a position to supply useful advice on the feasibility of international transactions as well as on foreign business procedures.

Many of these large metropolitan banks maintain correspondent relations with the smaller inland banks of the United States, and the information and services which they provide can frequently be obtained from a visit to one of their local bank correspondents. In addition to the materials which they have on hand, they are often equipped to service requests for specialized information through the use of their foreign facilities.

3. *Consulting and Business Service Firms.* A growing number of consulting and service firms are in the business of providing information, advice and a variety of services to companies which desire to trade or invest abroad. Some of them undertake specific investigations for their clients. These firms tend to specialize in specific countries, products, types of investment or licensing, market surveys, credit risks as well as other specific international operations. A few of them maintain a business information service available on a subscription basis.

4. *Public Accountants and Lawyers.* Certain public accounting and legal firms have branch offices or correspondents abroad or foreign practitioners attached to their United States staffs, and are in a position to supply consulting services on legal matters, incorporation laws and procedures, taxation and business practices. Some of them publish information brochures and manuals on specific phases of business in the Common Market.

5. *Advertising Agencies and Market Research Firms.* Some American firms engaged in advertising and market research have established branch offices abroad, and others maintain correspondent relations with foreign companies in these fields. They are usually able to provide data on foreign markets, market analyses and surveys for specific products, advice on selling and merchandising abroad.

6. *Foreign Firms and Business Services.* There are many companies in the fields of business information and consulting services, as well as accounting and legal firms, advertising agencies and mar-

ket research houses located in the EEC and EFTA areas which perform services similar to those found in the United States. Since some of these companies are highly experienced and possess specialized information in both their fields and countries, they may frequently be consulted with profit by Americans who propose to do business in the areas of these institutions. Banks and the ministries of commerce in the EEC and EFTA ordinarily do not supply foreign businessmen with the detailed information that their American counterparts do.

7. *Foreign Embassies, Consulates, Trade and Investment Offices.* Almost all foreign countries maintain embassies or legations in Washington, D. C., and many of the larger nations have consulates located in various cities in the United States. In addition to diplomatic representation and the usual consular services, these foreign missions frequently are in a position to furnish American businessmen with facts concerning the business and economic organization of their countries and to provide advice on specific business proposals.

A number of EEC and EFTA nations maintain trade and investment offices, usually located in New York, which specialize in fostering the development of trade and investment relations with the United States. Both these offices and the embassies in Washington generally maintain reference libraries which can be consulted by American businessmen.

8. *The Information Office of the EEC.* The European Economic Community maintains an information office and library in Washington, D.C., where all of the many publications of this organization may be freely consulted. The library includes a number of works dealing with the Community and is staffed by competent information specialists familiar with the sources of facts about the institution and its member countries.

Author Index

(n Footnote; b Bibliography)

Subject Index